TALES FROM THE CYMBAL BAG

Historical and Hysterical Memoirs of Lennie DiMuzio

Jump Back Baby Productions

BY LENNIE DIMUZIO

with Jim Coffin

TALES FROM THE CYMBAL BAG

HISTORICAL AND HYSTERICAL MEMOIRS OF LENNIE DIMUZIO

BY LENNIE DIMUZIO
WITH JIM COFFIN

Published by Jump Back Baby Productions LLC

ISBN 978 0615399485

Designed and Produced by Ed Uribe for Dancing Planet MediaWorks

Edited by Thèrése DiMuzio and Ed Uribe

Photos Lissa Wales, Craigie Zildjian/Zildjian Cymbal Co., Rick Malkim, Dave Yost, Rob Cook, Dale's Drum Shop, Thèrése DiMuzio, Cecilia DiMuzio, Freddie Sargent, Francine Bellson, Peter Lanzaroni, Sabian Cymbal Company, Cathy Rich, Ed Sargent

Cover Photo Kevin Monaghan

Photos Note: Countless artists and individuals have provided Lennie and Jim with photos over the years. Sadly, many of these folks are no longer with us. The authors gratefully acknowledge all those who have contributed and assisted with photos.

A special note of acknowledgment and gratitude goes to Craigie Zildjian, president of the Zildjian Cymbal Company, for her assistance and contribution to the compilation of historied Zildjian Photography.

Visit Lennie online at www.lennied.com

Tales From the Cymbal Bag is dedicated to the memory of Lissa Wales (July 27, 1957–October 1, 2005) who, with her camera, was the chronicler of the drumming world and especially the JEWOPs.

After a Herculean battle, Lissa finally succumbed to leukemia. She was always in the right place at the right time to get the photos that appeared in all the major percussion publications. The percussion world will miss her lovely smile. We will always remember her through her beautiful photographs.

Bon appétit. Enjoy the book! (1962)

Contents

Foreword 6
About Lennie 7
About Jim 8
Special Events in the Music and Drum Business 9
Acknowledgments 11
Introduction 13
Chapter 1: Jump Back, Baby 15
Chapter 2: Got Drums, Will Play 19
Chapter 3: Hup Two, Three, Four 27
Chapter 4: Ring-A-Ding, Splang 35
Chapter 5: Papa Jo Jones and the "Red Devils" 45
Chapter 6: Oldies But Goodies 49
Chapter 7: So, You Want a Cymbal Endorsement? 53
Chapter 8: Cozy and Philly Joe: A Pair to Draw From 57
Chapter 9: Gene Krupa: Got the Drums Out in Front 61
Chapter 10: Hair Today, Gone Tomorrow 67
Chapter 11: Buddy Rich: Drumming Legend 71
Chapter 12: Barrett Deems: He Made Coffee Nervous 81
Chapter 13: Clinics to Die For—and We Almost Did 85
Chapter 14: Little Big Horn and a UFO 89
Chapter 15: Rack of Lamb for Two for One 93
Chapter 16: Kenny Clare: A Swirling Dervish 99
Chapter 17: Love Those Ks 103
Chapter 18: From the Sublime to the Ridiculous 109
Chapter 19: Irv Cottler: Bootin' Ol' Blue Eyes 115
Chapter 20: Louie Bellson: A Double Kicker 119
Chapter 21: Lennie D. and Armand Z.: Joined at the Hip 127
Chapter 22: A Potpourri of Cobham, Rich, Mr. A. Z., W. Newton, and Joey Lead Boots 133
Chapter 23: Some Short Cameos 137
Chapter 24: Gabriel, Blow Your Horn, and a German General 143
Chapter 25: A Couple of Dozing Off Stories and a Big Surprise 151
Chapter 26: More Tales, With Some That Defy Description 155
Chapter 27: Tommy Thompson, Crotales, and the Tokyo Symphony 159
Chapter 28: A Bunch of Thumpers 163
Chapter 29: Get Me Outta Here, Can't Stop, and a Bald Professor 167
Chapter 30: Steve Smith and Some Bats? 171
Chapter 31: From Hush to Rush: Neil Peart 177
Chapter 32: Frankfurt, Dobermans, a Fiat—Oh My 181
Chapter 33: Things That Go Crash in the Night 185
Chapter 34: The Cream of the Crop, and Two Big E's 189
Chapter 35: Tales and Snippets: #1 199
Chapter 36: An Apple for the Teacher—Plus a Cymbal 209
Chapter 37: Tales and Snippets: #2 221
Chapter 38: Special Cymbals for the Cymbalists 231
Chapter 39: Memories of Armand Z 237
Chapter 40: Tales and Snippets: #3 241
Chapter 41: Have You Heard This One? 255
Chapter 42: It's Not Over Yet, Baby 265
Chapter 43: A Tribute to Bob Zildjian 281
Chapter 44: Finally, the Finale 285
Chapter 45: Suggested Reading 287

Foreword

Clangin', Bangin', and Hangin'...

Is it possible that one person could know, have worked with, and contributed to the sound of practically every major drumming figure in the world for the past half century? The answer is yes, and Lennie DiMuzio is that person. From his first notes on the drums at the age of seven, he has spent his life in the percussion world, and worked in the percussion industry for more than sixty years. His forty-two years of product development and artist relations work for the Zildjian Cymbal Company is legendary, and he continues his work today with the Sabian Cymbal Company. Seventy years after those first notes on the drums he's still clanging cymbals, banging the drums, hanging out with the best, and meeting and nurturing today's rising young stars.

Lennie and Ed working on Tales *at Ed's studio in 2006*

Many have said, figuratively speaking, that Lennie could *write the book* on who's who in drumming, the drumming business, and artist relations in the music industry. The fact is they are literally correct, and here you have that book: *Tales From the Cymbal Bag*. Lennie always dreamt of writing a book about his life in the drumming world, and the subtitle of this book, *Historical and Hysterical Memoirs...*, aptly describes both Lennie's approach to the book and his many adventures. Lennie's journey through his years in the business, and his association with so many great musicians, artists, and industry figures is historical, and their doings often hysterical. But these stories also portray a passion and love for drumming, the drumming world, and especially the multitude of people he has met and with whom he has worked. That Lennie remains a close friend to these many individuals bespeaks his big heart, the value he places on loyalty and friendship, and his love of life and the drumming world, of which he is such an integral part. In the cut-throat music industry where one can frequently encounter the phrase, "It ain't personal, it's just business," Lennie is just the opposite. For him *all* business is *completely* personal and all about the individual. He has been an inspiration for many and has helped many get started, and continue, in the often-difficult music business.

Still today Lennie continues to seek out new talent and anyone else who needs a helping hand in *the biz*. He does this with the same fervor and enthusiasm of his younger days and, as a result, many more will benefit from his goodwill and his contributions to the percussion community and his friends all over the world.

Hanging out with Lennie over the course of working on this book has been a tremendous pleasure. I have known Lennie for some 30 years and I too am one of the many who have both enjoyed and benefited from Lennie's friendship, goodwill, and kindness. It is an honor to have been asked to write a few words of prologue for *Tales*. This book began its journey many years ago, and it is long overdue. We had to overcome what at times seemed like insurmountable obstacles to bring it to print, but we persevered and this life-long dream of Lennie's is now a reality.

It is with heartfelt happiness that I extend to you, our reader, a warm welcome to the historical and hysterical world of Lennie DiMuzio.

—Ed Uribe

About Lennie

Lennie grew up in Cambridge, Massachusetts, and was born into a very large family. Although his immediate family consisted of one brother and one sister, his grandparents had thirteen children and thus a huge extended family. He started playing drums at the age of seven, and by the age of twelve he was playing local gigs on his home-made drumset, made out of a washboard with some pots and pans. He also travelled with minstrel and vaudeville shows in and around New England, and enjoyed singing with the barbershop quartets of these shows. Lennie continued playing throughout his high school years in his and his saxophonist brother Eddie's band. This lasted until he was drafted into the Army during the Korean War. Fortunately Lennie was sent to Germany to join the occupational troops in Wurstburg, Germany. Playing on military bases and in clubs, and entering various talent contests in Europe, eventually led him to be transferred to the first division infantry regiment band for his final year of service.

Upon his release from active duty, Lennie returned home and enrolled in the New England Conservatory of Music under the GI bill. He studied performance and music education for two years, then left the Conservatory. He wanted to exclusively pursue a playing career, rather than teach. He enrolled in the Schillinger House in Boston, which is now Berklee College of Music. While studying at the Schillinger House, Lennie also took private lessons from one of Boston's finest drum teachers, Charlie Alden. During this time Lennie was also starting a family with his wife Peggy. While raising his new family and playing in Boston, Lennie met the president of the world's largest cymbal company, Armand Zildjian. Armand and Lennie became great friends, and he joined the company in 1961 as a cymbal tester. Lennie worked directly under the supervision of Avedis Zildjian and his two sons Armand and Robert. Lennie grew with the job very quickly. He soon became manager of sales, artist relations, and special cymbal selection. Lennie was also involved with many other aspects of the company, including advertising, marketing, and product development.

He was soon promoted to director of artist relations and later in his tenure also served as director of both the orchestral and the educational departments.

Lennie's work in the music world has led him to enjoy many achievements and receive many accolades. He's written articles for the Percussive Arts Society and the Encyclopedia of Percussion, and performed countless clinics and educational presentations, all while meeting and befriending the greatest drummers of all time. Lennie's longtime association with the Percussive Arts Society earned him the Presidents Industry Award in 1997, celebrated with a special banquet sponsored by the Zildjian Company. Lennie's sixty years of experience in the drum and cymbal world has been influential in shaping the careers of many of today's leading drummers and percussionists. He is considered an icon in the percussion world.

Zildjian Announces Promotion

DiMuzio

DiMuzio is one of the longest-serving members of Zildjian, originally joining as a cymbal tester in 1961. His reputation in the industry as an authority on cymbals is pre-eminent. "It has been Lennie's knowledge and perception of the drum world that has led to the overwhelming strength and success of Zildjian's artist endorsement program," noted Armand Zildjian.

Musical Merchandise Review
November, 1987

About Jim

Jim Coffin has had a varied music career, from performer to clinician, educator to business executive. He received his BA and MA from the University of Northern Iowa, where later, as a professor, he started both the percussion and jazz programs. He also taught in three Iowa high schools. Prior to his tenure at UNI, he was a professional musician in California.

For more than twenty years Jim was employed in the percussion industry, overseeing marketing, sales, educational, and artists' activities, as well as product development for two drum companies: First with the Selmer Company when it was the distributor of Premier Percussion, followed by the Yamaha Corporation and Yamaha Percussion. He served on the Board of Directors of the Percussive Arts Society, and was secretary for the PAS Executive Board. In 1999 he received the PAS President's Industry Award, and in 2005 he received the PAS Outstanding Supporter Award.

Jim is the author of ***The Performing Percussionist, Volumes I & II***, and ***Solo Album*** (Barnhouse Publications). As a clinician, soloist, conductor, and adjudicator, he has appeared in more than forty states and five Canadian provinces. Since retiring in 1993, he has been a marketing consultant, an educational services consultant for NAMM, a presenter of music business seminars to college and university music business majors, and a percussion clinician for World Projects Tours.

He is an active editor and writer, a published fiction author, a contributor to ***Drum Business*** and ***Stick It*** magazines, and for ten years he was the associate editor of the drumset column in ***Percussive Notes***, as well as a column writer.

Listed among Jim's many speaking engagements are appearances at the Iowa Bandmasters Convention, Music Educators National Conference, Percussive Arts Society International Conference, and the American School Band Director's Association. Included in his many honors is being noted as an outstanding jazz educator in Duke Ellington's autobiography, ***Jazz Is My Mistress***, and being inducted into the Iowa Jazz Educator's Hall of Fame as part of the Iowa High School jazz contests. The Woodward-Granger School honored Jim by naming an event the Jim Coffin "Foundations in Jazz" Festival, and in 2006 the Iowa Bandmasters made him an Honorary Lifetime Member.

Special Events in the Music & Drum Business

IAJE—International Association of Jazz Education. This now defunct organization held an international conference each year in addition to state activities. It was very significant for both jazz educators and the industry, as well as students and up-and-coming musicians.

MENC—Music Educators National Conference; National Association for Music Educators. Headquarters in Reston, Virginia. MENC holds national and regional conferences.

NAMM—National Association for Music Merchants; International Music Products Association. Headquarters and museum in Carlsbad, California. NAMM has two international conventions for members only each year in January and July.

PAS—Percussive Arts Society. An international organization with headquarters and a museum in Indianapolis, Indiana.

PASIC—Percussive Arts Society International Conference. This is a yearly event in addition to state PAS chapter meetings.

PMC—Percussion Marketing Council. Hosts programs to bring increased public awareness to drumming.

DCI—Drum Corps International. This organization regulates all drum corps activities and contests.

Mid-West Band Clinic—This is held each year in December in Chicago, Illinois, for band directors and band students.

Lennie, Jim, and Lloyd McCausland at the Percussive Arts Society Convention circa 1985. This trio is also known in the industry as the famous JEWOPs (Junior Executives Without Power).

Rick Malkim, drummer and photographer, contributed many of the pictures for this book.

*"Saint Leonardo" and his bronze halo, Miami, Jan. 11, 1992.
Lennie and David Yost, photographer and drummer, contributor of many of the photos of Gene Krupa, Buddy Rich, and many of the other drummers appearing on these pages.*

Acknowledgments

Lennie and I extend our thanks to the following individuals who helped in the early stages of this book: Ray Brych, David Hakim, Michael Finkelstein, and Jim Peterczak, and to Colin Schofield and Roy Burns, who assisted us with various dates, names, and information regarding certain events.

A special thanks to all the many drummers who so kindly contributed pictures from their personal collections, and, finally, a very special thanks to Ed Uribe, our close friend, without whose assistance and expertise this book would not exist.

From Lennie:

My life has been touched and filled with so many fantastic stories about all types of people, especially the drummers, all beautiful people, full of fun and friendship. I believe that I was blessed by the almighty drum god. My sincere thanks and gratitude to all for being such a big part of my life.

I have learned that we should not underestimate drummers' talent and creative abilities. Drummers can be found in all walks of life. They are doctors, lawyers, businessmen, artists, and professors. They have excelled in all of their endeavors and will continue to shape the world of music. If I missed out on meeting one of you, believe me, you are a friend I haven't met yet. So, jump back, baby, and sleep fast.

Most of all, I thank my wife Peg, my children Thèrése, Cecilia, Lucy, and Lennie Jr, my grandchildren, brother Eddie and sister Margie, my uncles and aunts—wherever you may be—and especially my aunt Lucy (aka Sister Madelyn Francis). Thank you all for teaching me respect and caring for other people. A special thanks to my son-in-law Darin Colucci.

To my daughter Thèrése ("Tootie"), a special note of gratitude for her tireless energy and constant support, as well as for her expertise and help in completing this book.

A special thanks to Ed Uribe's wife Robin for her help and contributions in many aspects of bringing this book to print.

To all of my hometown buddies at the Liver Alley Burn Club, the Duxbury American Legion, the McNulty Village gang, the Green Harbor Yacht Club, and Jack and Joyce Grandy: Thank you for being patient and listening to all of my stories, and for your helpful advise and assistance with the book.

I would also like to acknowledge, especially for the younger generation now coming up in the industry, some of my special friends. They were very inspirational, shaped the foundation of the early percussion industry, and helped make it what it is today. To many, these will just be names, but they were all leaders in their respective fields and should, and will, never be forgotten. Early drum shop owners, players, and inventors: Roy Hart and Remo Belli, Roy Knapp, Chuck Molinari, Bob Yeager, Danny Bergour, Al Wolf, Henry Adler, Frank Ippolito, Al Duffy, Micky DiPersa, Jack Adams, Bill Crowden, Charlie Donelli, Maury Lishon, Marvin Dahlgren, Babe Fabrizi, Ellis Tolan, Bobby Grasso, Clarence Walberg, Emil Richards, Takashi "Hagi" Hagiwara of Yamaha, Chuck Bernstein, Ben Strauss of Rogers Drum Company, Clary Vater, Ron and Isabel Spagnardi of *Modern Drummer* magazine, and Bill Ludwig II. (Sadly some of these individuals have passed away, but the contributions they made to the industry will never leave us.)

I thank all of my friends at the Zildjian Company along with dear friends and colleagues, Remo Belli and Lloyd McCausland; Joe Testa; Vic, Kelly, and Tracy Firth.; Alan and Ronnie Vater; Bill Morgan; Joe, Carol, and Cathy Calato of Regal Tip; Jimmy Catalano of

Ludwig; Don Lombardi of DW Drums; Roy Burns of Aquarian Drumheads; Herb Brockstein of ProMark; Frank DeVito of Danmar; Joe Hibbs of Tama Drums; Dan Del Florentino of the NAMM Association; Ian Croft of *Drummer* magazine; and Jonathan Mover of *Drumhead* magazine.

Also thanks to my dear friends Frank Epstein of the Boston Symphony Orchestra; Sam Denov (retired) of the Chicago Symphony Orchestra; Tony Cirone (retired) of the San Francisco Symphony Orchestra; and Neil Grover, Freddie Buda, Dean Anderson, Pat Hollenbeck, and Richard Flanagan of the Boston Pops Orchestra. To my friends at Berklee College of Music, the Percussive Arts Society, National Association of Jazz Educators, Drum Corp International, and Marching Bands of America. To Bob Morrison (Executive Vice-President of Music for All), to my friends at the New England Conservatory of Music (where I had all my formal music education), to all my colleagues at the National Association of Music Merchants, and the Music Educators National Conference.

My very special thanks to Bob Zildjian, his wife Margaret, their children Billy, Andy, and Sally, to Nort Hargrove and John Teague, and the entire staff at the Sabian Cymbal Company.

Also a special thanks to the makers of *Crown Royal* Canadian whiskey for its liquid support in helping me steady my nerves and maintain my cool in the evenings.

Last, but not least, my heartfelt thanks to my good buddy Jim. Without his ceaseless encouragement and dedication this book would not exist. As he often said, "Lennie, please. We need to finish this book before we both croak." Go in peace, brother. You're the man.

From Jim:

Thank you, Lennie, for those kind words. But without your escapades and years in the drumming biz, there wouldn't have been any stories to write. I am so glad we became friends, which allowed me to be part of your entourage as we went from one bizarre episode to another. Those were the days.

After leaving academia, I worked for the Selmer Company in Elkhart, Indiana, when they were distributing Premier Drums. When I joined Selmer, I didn't have a clue what my job was. What saved me was they didn't have a clue what my job was. There were several fellow employees who showed me the way, and the best was Rollie Bunn. Thank you, Rollie. Also, thanks to Jim Catalano, who assisted me and became a good friend. He went on to head Ludwig Drums and is a top guy in the drumming world.

There are many people to thank at Yamaha, especially the ones who were with me the first five years when the drum marketing group was located in Grand Rapids, Michigan. Thanks to Ken Kramer, Jay Wanamaker, and Jerry Andreas, and a special thank-you to my secretary Susan Wienczkowski, who kept us all in line. Thanks to my outside consultants—Jim Sewrey, Jim Petercszak, Ed Soph—and my crazy but effective advertising guys from New York—Steven Ross and Robbie Clyne. What a great time we had.

I thank Billie and my children Kim, Marc, and Cris, who, later in their lives, understood that my business career necessitated that I be away from home a lot. Maybe after they read this book, they will understand even more.

Last, a huge thank-you to my wife Kathy, who, after she realized that my writing this book was more than a weekend hobby, recognized that when I was typing at the computer, spewing an occasional expletive, she should leave me alone while the muse was in force. Her understanding, support, and love have carried me through this exciting journey with Lennie.

Introduction by Jim Coffin

Just as every tune has an intro followed by some choruses, so does this book. After all, it's all about the music business, musicians, and our world of great drummers. The main thrust of the book is to cover more than four decades of Lennie's experience in the cymbal and drumming industry.

It all began with Lennie playing drums at the early age of seven and continued through his teen years playing in minstrel and vaudeville shows, and playing with different bands throughout New England. He later joined the Army and toured with the first infantry band while stationed in Germany, eventually joined the world-famous Avedis Zildjian Cymbal Company in 1961. You will read about his travels with Armand Zildjian and all the great drummers and other people associated with the wonderful world of drums and percussion. We write about the older generations of drummers right through to the top artists of today. We hope this book will pique your interest enough that you will further explore the early drummers and how they shaped and contributed so much to our art form and our history, and, of course, explore the drummers and music of today.

You will also learn about cymbals—how they are made, what or who determines sizes and thickness, and the drummer's choice of cymbals, all told in Lennie's own inimitable style. You will laugh, sometimes so hard tears will come to your eyes. Lennie was, is, and always will be a character. One definition of *character* is "an eccentric and amusing person." The eccentric part I agree with, but I must change the *amusing* to *hilarious*. Lennie is a fun-loving, expressive guy who loves drumming, drummers, the music business, and all musicians. There is an old saying among those who know Lennie: "Look up the word ***character*** in the dictionary and you will see a picture of Lennie." Throughout the book he is constantly saying, "we became very good friends" when referring to the many folks he writes about. Friendship has always been very special to Lennie and is one of his top priorities in life. Countless people consider Lennie a dear friend, and he truly is one-of-a-kind.

I feel the need to explain that Lennie's life has not been one big party. Being an artist relations manager for a major company might seem very glamorous on the surface, and to some degree it is. But it also requires that you get up and go to the office on every one of those mornings following the late nights spent entertaining the artists. The job also requires countless days of travel away from home and family. It is great fun, but it can also be very stressful and tiring. All the artists, educators, and industry folk who attend educational conventions want to be taken out to dinner and be entertained. When music dealers come to the big NAMM conventions, they like to be taken out and entertained as well. It is known as being "wined and dined" and this is an important part of doing business in all industries. But being an artist relations manager is what we truly loved to do, and, regardless of whatever difficulties presented themselves, we had a ball. Dealing with artists has changed. It used to be that all of the business was handled directly with the artist by an artist relations manager like Lennie, or me (when I was an artist relations manager for Premier or Yamaha drums). Everything was very personal. Then it changed to dealing with a roadie or manager. Now, in some instances, it is with an agent or attorney. The old handshake agreement for many has gone the way of contracts and legal representation. But it is still a wonderful, fun, and albeit demanding job. It takes incredible "people skills," hanging-out chops, and the ability to get by and do your work on a few hours of sleep.

We hope you will enjoy our efforts. Sit back, fasten your seat belt, and get ready to learn and be entertained.

BOSTON EVENING

AMERICAN

WEATHER

Clearing,
Cooler Tonight
Details on Page 2

CAMBRIDGE
SOMERVILLE

Vol. 52—No. 182 72 Pages Friday, October 21, 1958 Price 5 Cents

Four Generations—Observing their 60th wedding anniversary tomorrow, Mr. and Mrs. Leonard Portanova of Andrew st., Cambridge, prepare to celebrate at a giant family party with 13 children, 42 grandchildren and 30 great-grandchildren in attendance. Aiding them in the preparation are their daughter, Mrs. Rose DiMuzio (right), grandson, Leonard, and (lending moral support) great-grandson, Leonard, Jr.

American Photo by Ollie Noonan

Four generations: Observing their 60th wedding anniversary tomorrow, Mr. and Mrs. Leonardo Portanova celebrate with their 13 children, 42 grandchildren, and 30 great-grandchildren in attendance. Aiding them in the preparation are their daughter, Mrs. Rose DiMuzio (right), their grandson Lennie (sitting on left), and (lending moral support) great-grandson Leonard, Jr.

Chapter 1

Jump Back, Baby

Regardless of the weather on May 4, 1933, in Cambridge, Massachusetts, the sun shone on the DiMuzio family and the drumming world when Lennie sprung forth. Although difficult to substantiate, many believe that after the doctors cut the cord, cleaned him up, and slapped him on his little behind, Lennie did not cry, but loudly exclaimed, "Jump back, baby!" And it has been that way ever since.

Lennie (center) with classmates

Lennie recalls, "The Depression was still being felt in 1933, not much money to be had, but at my grandparents' reconstructed home, the door was always open. Our huge home had been made into a sort of duplex by a wall down the middle, thereby splitting it in half, ending up with five large rooms on either side. Upstairs were the bedrooms, where everyone would double or triple up in a bed. My grandparents had a very large family, 12 siblings, so both sides were filled with aunts, uncles, lots of cousins, my mother Rose, and my older brother, Eddie. Imagine what it must have been like with such a huge family all living under one roof. As unlikely as it sounds today, in those days it was quite common.

"We grew up with a lot of people around, and although in those days there was not much money, we never went hungry. The food wasn't gourmet, but we always had a lot of pasta with meatballs, bread pudding, chicken necks, soups, vegetables, and grandfather's homemade wine. Now, that wine would sometimes almost choke you to death because he didn't get the best grapes, and after fermenting and aging, it was like drinking straight vinegar.

Grandpa Portanova, Sister Madelyn Francis Portanova, Grandma Portanova

"Grandpa lived to age 92, a tough guy who worked as a roofer most of his life. On his 90th birthday, he arm-wrestled all of his kids and he

Lennie's uncles

Lennie's aunts and uncles

Uncle Mike and cousin Christine Portanova, Brother Eddie

The Ozark Trio

took them all down. Grandpa loved everyone, and everyone loved him. We all loved those wonderful years with all the family and friends."

Lennie came to his musical talent naturally because there was a lot of music around his house. His mother sang and played the ukulele while many of his uncles played instruments: Tony, saxophone; Joe, guitar and banjo; Mike, clarinet; and Johnny, a little drums and he also tap danced. When the uncles played, Lennie would start banging on everything in sight, so something had to be done.

The Ozark Band

"My uncle Johnny got me started on drums," Lennie recalls. "He made my first drumsticks by whittling and then shaving them out of a couple of the rungs from a broken chair. My first drumset was homemade and consisted of a washboard with a couple of wooden braces at the bottom, two cookie pans on the side, pie plates as slam cymbals, along with a couple of bicycle horns—sort of a Spike Jones drumset. Man, I could wail on that set."

Minstrel show with Brother Eddie, Lennie, Eddie Riley, Billie McKinnon

As Lennie recalls, his brother Eddie would drool every time he looked at his uncle's sax and he quickly managed to get his own horn. Now the two brothers were ready to form their own group and hit the music scene.

"Like most kids in those days, we were part of a gang, and so from our gang we recruited Phil

Brother Eddie, Aunt Sister Madelyn Francis, Mother Rose, Lennie

Natile, who was studying the clarinet with my uncle Mike, and the three of us, Eddie, Phil, and me, formed the Ozark Trio. Don't ask me why three Italian kids would call themselves the Ozark Trio. Anyway, our church, the Church of the Blessed Sacrament, put on minstrel shows to raise some money, and these shows got to be real popular, and after we got a little better, we became regular performers. We added another guy and formed the Andrew Street barbershop quartet, and for the first part of the minstrel show we put on blackface and sang all the great "moldy oldies."

Father Tierney Stages His 26th Minstrel Show

—o—

Blessed Sacrament Minstrels In School Hall

—o—

The Blessed Sacrament Parish Minstrel society will stage its 26th annual minstrel show at the parish school hall, Lake street, between Pearl and Magazine, tonight and tomorrow night.

Esther M. Dolan, who has directed all of Father Thomas Tierney's 25 preceding shows, will direct this one also. Bert Ryan will be in his familiar post as interlocultor.

The show will feature such eminent end men as Bill Linskey, Jim Hannon, Bill O'Brien, Ed Desjardin, Nick Saccardo, Bill Kane, Joe Hennessey, and Harry Bean.

The pretty front line girls who will present their colorful routines are Connie Marcellino, Mary Puntonio, Mary Parrow, Lorraine St. Hilaire, Marion Buckley, Peggy Dempsey, Peggy Murphy, Catherine Murphy, Mary King, Marguerite Kelly, Mary T. Kelly, Pat Shea, Mary B. Kelly, and Mary Gallagher.

Other entertainers include: Doris Baker Johnson, Mary E. Hanley, Joe Hanley, Nick Sacardo, Mary Cavenaugh, Jack Rogers, Al Dirie, and the famous Barber Shop quartet with Ed Portanova, Phil Natle, Len Portanova, and Bill McKannoh. Andy Caroselli is pianist.

A chorus of 125 boys and girls of the parish will help make the show, which is produced by Dave Avery, a big success. Dancing will follow.

Newspaper article announcing minstrel show

"After intermission, black face off, we would come out as a trio, plus a big fat kid playing a washtub that had a pole stuck in a hole in the center and on it was a string. He would bend the pole and pluck the string and get a pretty good sound. So we would rip it up, play all the old crazy tunes, and our last tune was a real show-stopper. We'd play 'When the

Lennie, Mother Rose, Brother Eddie

Saints Go Marching In' and I would lift my homemade drum kit over my head, scrubbing on the washboard like crazy with thimbles, while rolling on the floor. Eddie would then join me rolling on the floor, and the place went crazy. We should have had a video. All of that along with practicing after school became part of growing up."

Some of us who know Lennie intimately might find it hard to imagine that he was involved with the church, but the church played a big part in his young musical life, as well as with a brief flirtation with the boxing world. (That story will come later in this narrative.) Lennie loved the drums so much that one might wonder if he was like a modern-day Moses, found in a drum case drifting down the Charles River.

Grandma and Grandpa Portanova's 65th wedding anniversary

Lennie continues, "My parents divorced when I was two years old, and my mother, who worked all the time as a waitress, had never pressed my father for any money. After seeing that I was starting to get pretty good even on that homemade drumset, she decided my father should help me get a real drumset. My father was a pretty good drummer, playing around Boston, mostly in Chinese restaurants where the mobs hung out, and were known for good entertainment. My dad had changed his last name from DiMuzio to Cooper since most of the booking agents in Boston were Jewish, and in order to get work, many of the Italian musicians changed their names. When I was 15, my mother sent me to Boston to meet Ed Cooper, the Big Kahuna, and get my first kit. This was the first time I spent time with my dad since my parents had gotten divorced.

"My dad told me to meet him at Henry Savage's music store. It was really a hock shop, but they called them music stores because they had a lot of used instruments. I waited in front of the store, and I saw my dad pull up in a beautiful convertible, looking very cool. He had on a beautiful suit, a sharp tie with a stickpin, big cuff links, mafia-style hat with a wide brim, high crown, a camel-hair overcoat, and white spats. Can you dig it—white spats. All that jive shit. Anyway, I met Mr. Savage, a really nice guy, and while he and my dad were talking, I was looking around the shop and spotted this Gene Krupa marble-colored Slingerland set. I told Mr. Savage I liked that set, and he pulled it down. It had a one-headed 12-inch rack tom, a one-headed floor tom, a Radio King snare, a good bass drum, and a cymbal arm. It wasn't top-of-the-line, but a decent set around $150. I was tickled pink, wetting my pants, in hog heaven."

Can't you just picture a young Lennie D. going crazy over his first real drumset? All drummers have been there. Now comes the capper on this story.

"Mr. Savage asks my dad, 'Mr. Cooper, how do you plan on paying for this?' My dad looks down at me and asks me how much money I had on me. I'd been working after school and had saved a few bucks, although I would give most of what I'd made to my mother. I had five dollars, so I told Dad I had five bucks, and he told me to give it to Mr. Savage. Now, Mr. Savage had been tearing up some paper and

Uncle Johnny Portanova on trumpet

Lennie, Brother Eddie, Cousin Johnny Portanova

was making a little payment book. In it he wrote: One drum set $150—down payment $5. Mr. Savage asked, 'How much can you pay weekly?' I was making about $6 a week so I said probably $3, so he wrote down $3 per week and gives the book to my dad. My dad gives me the book, telling me I had to pay Mr. Savage $3 every week, and I told him okay, I'm working and I can do that.

"I got the payment book and we loaded the drums into the convertible and drove to the underground train where my dad informed me that this train would get me to Cambridge, where I could phone my mother to come and pick me up. Then he drove off."

Lennie gives a little laugh and says, "Can you believe it? That son-of-a-bitch is dumping me at the train station and I'm saying, 'Yeah, Dad, wonderful, you're a beautiful dude, thanks so much.' I lugged those damn drums down the stairs onto the train, the four pieces and the hardware—I didn't care how heavy they were, strapped around my neck, hanging down to my balls—but when I got to Cambridge, I was stuck. Called my mom and she said to take a cab home and we'll pay for it. Man, when I got home and told my mom what had happened, she went ballistic, called my dad every name in the book, and said 'that cheap bastard wouldn't even drive me home and didn't pay a freakin' dime toward the drumset."

In spite of the somewhat off-the-wall father-son experience, Lennie had his drums. Let the good times roll.

Chapter 2

Got Drums, Will Play

Frank DiMare on guitar, Lennie on drums, Eddie on sax, Sonny Cataldo on accordion

Lennie had his drumset, Eddie had his horn, and they started their little jazz band. Depending on what jobs they were trying to get, they would use the name the Eddie Cooper or the Lennie Cooper Band. They added John, a cousin who played piano, so the band consisted of a sax, clarinet, piano, and drums. Back in those days a bass wasn't that critical, and as Lennie said, "We didn't know what the hell we were doing anyway." Eventually, they added a trumpet player to the band, and after a lot of practicing and rehearsing, they began playing high school dances, weddings, functions around town, Christmas parties, and the famous church minstrel shows.

Before they got good enough to perform, a decision was made to rehearse at their cousin John's house in Arlington Heights, not far from Cambridge. The idea made sense because that is where the piano was and they could leave the drumset there until they got a job.

"Eddie and I packed up my drums and went to

Eddie on the sax with Lennie on the bongos

the bus that would take us close to the Arlington Center, where we would have to run across the street to catch the trolley to John's house. The bus stopped at the top of a hill, and we didn't know what the roads were like, where we were going, because this was the first time we'd done this. I got off the bus first, set the bass drum on the ground, and went back for my trap case. Well, the goddamn bass drum starts rollin' down the hill, bangin' and thumpin', I'm chasing it for about 75 to 100 feet, the people on the bus are laughing, Eddie is breaking up. By the time I caught it, it had some broken lugs and I had to lug it back up the hill. We got the rest of the stuff, got on the trolley, and went to John's house. What we went through just to play."

As time went on, they got better, and when Lennie was around 17, they decided to track down their dad, Ed Cooper, and check out his band and get to know some of the musicians. By this time, the incident of buying the first drumset was forgotten, and to have a dad who was a musician was considered pretty cool, and, according to Lennie, "He wasn't a bad dude, just cheap." So off the two brothers went to Boston and tracked down the band. The quartet was made up of a sax, keyboard, bass, and drums, and for those days they were considered to be "big time." The bass player was Sonny D., one of the best bass players in Boston and a bebopper with a lot of connections. Lennie picks up the story:

"Eddie and I were doing some functions in the church, and they were going to have a big fundraiser. After brainstorming, we came up with an idea that we thought was a stroke of genius: Call Sonny D. and ask him if he could get a big jazz artist to come to Cambridge and perform at the Blessed Sacrament church. We called and Sonny said he would get Stan Getz. Can you imagine, Jim, how excited we got—man, the great Stan Getz playing at our church? We went through all kinds-a hell to get posters and publicity out through the area and the school. Here we were, the Eddie and Lennie Cooper Band presents the great jazz artist—Stan Getz. The greatest thing since sliced bread and we did a hell of a job selling tickets and putting posters up all over town. Now the plan was that Eddie would stay at the church and I would meet Sonny D. and the band at Central Square at seven o'clock, drive down Pearl Street to the church, show them around, and maybe have a sound check—wasn't that nuts? We didn't know anything about a sound check—just show up and blow, that was the bag. The excitement continued to build for a couple of weeks. Stan Getz was coming to the Blessed Sacrament church.

"Well, the big night comes and we're all prepared, psyched up, looking forward to a hell of an evening. Eddie is at the church and I get up to Central Square around 6:30. 7:00, 7:30, 8:00, 8:30—no band. What's going on? We'll get killed if we don't get a band. [Lennie is getting excited just reliving the story,

The Lennie Cooper Band with Lennie D. on drums

Lennie on drums, NEC student on bass, Lennie's brother Eddie on sax, a young Phil Wilson (current Berklee College Professor) on the piano.

getting louder and louder.] I called Eddie and said what do we do? He said to call everybody. Now, I had told Sonny D. where the church was, you know, a couple of miles down Pearl Street on the right-hand side. I called around—nothing—no band. I called Eddie again and he said that I'd better get my ass down there because we were going to have to play. They must have got caught in traffic.

"I hurry to the church and we set up and are playing, and then at 10:00 in walks Sonny D., Stan Getz, a groovy chick on piano—I think maybe she was Mary Lou Williams—and a real happening cat on drums—it might have been Louis Hayes from New York, I can't remember. We did our hellos and thank-yous, a lot of apologies, and the band goes backstage to cool down a little, have a pop, and meanwhile the kids are screaming and banging because they want to hear Stan Getz play. About 10:30 they come out and start playing some out-of-sight stuff—some avant-garde bebop. They played steady for about a half an hour, and the kids didn't have a clue as to what they were playing. Finally the kids start stomping, banging, and yelling, 'We want Eddie and Lennie, we want Eddie and Lennie; we want "Flying Home" and "Walls of Jericho," and the blues.' Stan didn't know who in hell Eddie and Lennie were—maybe a comedy team. It was bizarre. Eddie finally says that he's going to go out there and blow, and I said that he couldn't do that—play next to Stan Getz. C'mon! Eddie says he's going and walks out next to Stan, who is in the middle of a tune, smoking a cool bebop tune, and Eddie begins blowing all these bad notes, burping, farting, and fuming in his horn. Stan wants to know who in hell is this asshole and finally walks off the stage, and Eddie is still out there blowin' away. I can't describe it.

"So, I push out my drums, John comes out and sits at the piano, and there we were, playing dumb tunes while the great jazz players were standing in the back of the stage, pissed off and insulted. They finally walk out, and as they left, the kids were booing them. Unbelievable. The audience was 15 to 17 years old and they didn't understand what Stan and the guys were doing musically. We ended up playing and finally got the kids dancing. What a night that was, plus a horror show when we had to come up with the bread for the band."

Eddie and Lennie's band started playing a lot of jobs for the school and became quite well known in the area. Occasionally, Lennie and Eddie would skip school on Mondays and go to downtown Boston where, at the RKO State Theatre, big bands played in the afternoon. Next to where they lived in Cambridge was a variety store run by a friend of theirs, a frustrated musician who finally went into the booking business, and he gave the brothers free tickets to bands such as Buddy Rich and Woody Herman.

"On the other side of Cambridge was St. Mary's church, and they had a big audito-

Stan Getz and Lennie, circa 1965

Priest Still Eyes Graziano

LaMotta Avoids Foes in Title Go Here

By SAM COHEN

Johnny Buckley tossed a snea r at the Goodwin A. C. and its announcement of yesterday that the wi ner of the Joe Blackwood-Red Priest 10-round bout at the Boston Garden, on Friday, will meet Tommy Sullivan.

Buckley, who manages Priest, said yesterday that he is waiting to see if Rocky Graziano and Tony Zale officially sign for a fight in Chicago or Cleveland this summer, and if nothe will offer Graziano $25,000 to fight Priest in Boston. Should the fight between Zale and Graziano come off, then he intends to repeat the offer to the winner.

"Sullivan had his chance against Priest and couldn't beat him with a 15-pound pull in weights, now the redhead is going to stay in the middleweight devision where there is plenty of opportunity for him to draw big gates here with Graziano or Zale or even Jake LaMotta," Buckley went on to say.

FIGHTING BETTER

"Red is fighting better than ever right now and Blackwood will find it out Friday. We took this match with Blackwood to help out Rip Valenti who was in a hole when Sullivan took sick and had to cancel his fight with Blackwood. Other than this fight Friday, it's going to be Graziano, Zalee or LaMotta for Priest. And until they come along Red will keep fighting middleweights, not heavyweights, for that is what Sullivan practically is now," Buckley concluded.

Jake LaMotta, who has long been recognized as the uncrowned king of the middleweights could

Sure Looks Fit

Red Priest, N. E. middleweight champ, looks in great shape for his battle with Joe Blackwood at Garden as he steps into ring to train at new Garden gym with his trainer, Ferddy Trozzi, looking on.

Al "Red" Priest in training

rium," Lennie remembers. "When I was about 16, I got a free ticket to see Buddy Rich's band play there. I had never seen anyone play like Buddy—so fast and with so many drums. Incredible! I was blown away with Buddy's playing, but I was also taken aback that the crowd seemed to get upset. The kids wanted to dance and hear the big band hits of the day (such as by Count Basie and Harry James) and they weren't connecting with Buddy's music. Buddy was featuring his musicians and there were a lot of solos and, of course, drum solos, but the crowd didn't seem to get it. Some of them walked out. Can you imagine that? Walking out on Buddy Rich? But it happened. Even I didn't really understand his genius at that time."

I'm going to move away from music for a bit to relate the pugilistic career of Lennie Balboa: The Cambridge Stallion—the Massachusetts version of Rocky Balboa. Remember the big house that was divided by the wall, with the Portanova family on one side and the Priest family on the other? One of Lennie's cousins, Al "Red" Priest, was the middleweight champion of New England. Unfortunately, he fought so many years in the amateurs that by the time he turned professional and could fight for the middleweight title of the world, it was too late, as his juice and strength had run out. (Red did get a shot at Kid Gavilan, pictured below fighting Sugar Ray Robinson, but unfortunately lost and never got to fight Sugar Ray.) Having a cousin in the fight game was an incentive for Eddie and Lennie to join their church's Catholic Youth Organization boxing team.

"Eddie and I did pretty good on the boxing team, and it helped us when our gang had to fight another gang in town. Eddie went a little further in the fight game than I did because of my drumming, and I wanted to save my nose. I was pretty fast but finally met a guy who ripped me up pretty good; that ended my boxing career. After Cousin Red quit the ring, he opened a little barroom in Central Square, and of course he wanted the Eddie and Lennie Cooper Band on the weekends. We probably made about seven or eight dollars a night, which was pretty good money back then."

In the end, Lennie left the boxing ring and went back to the bandstand, although at times

Kid Gavilan, Ray Robinson

there was a connection between the two, as you will see in the upcoming narratives.

"We were playing at the church dance and a cute little girl came up and was winking at me, making googly eyes, and I was checking her out. Come to find out that there was a rival gang there from east Cambridge, and I guess one of their guys was trying to scoop her up, and all the time she had eyes for me. While we were playing, this rough-looking dude comes up and stands in front of the band, pointing at me and making a fist, like he was going to get me. During intermission, I told my brother he had better walk with me across the dance floor, which he did. Eddie was tough. It looked like the east Cambridge gang was geared up to have a little skirmish right there on the dance

Lennie shows his stuff

floor, so we told Mr. Avery, who was running the dance. He called the cops and they came down at the end of the dance and parked outside. Having the cops there avoided a big mess because we had rounded up all of our dudes and were ready to rumble, but it never materialized.

"I must admit we played some weird jobs—like the time we played for a Gypsy wedding in Cambridge. It was a low-budget wedding and it ended up with both sides of the family on the dance floor getting pissed off with one another. Words were passed back and forth and soon a fight broke out between the relatives, and this was before the wedding even started. One of the mothers tried to break it up, she got slugged in the jaw, and then her nose got broke. It was a mess, went into a riot outside the raunchy hall, then turned into a shoot-out and someone got their brains blown out. The cops showed up with a paddy wagon and carted them off to jail. What a scene.

"As a young kid, I used to work out at the local YMCA lifting weights. While there I met a guy named Bill Woods, who was instrumental in getting me a job in Alaska. Bill was a big guy, about 6 foot 2, was Mr. Texas as a top body builder, and was very nice. He convinced my mom that the job in Alaska was legitimate and that I'd make lots of money and that it would be a great life experience for me.

"Five of us—Bill, three other students, and I—drove to Alaska in an old Buick, through the Dakotas, across Canada, and finally on the Alaskan highway. What an experience. It took us about 12 or 13 days because the Alaskan highway in those days was dirt and we had to fight mud slides, trucks turned over, potholes, washouts, and the road was only about one and a half lanes. We finally reached Fairbanks, where we lived in a Quonset hut. Additions to the crew were a couple of Indians, Eskimos, and old-timers who had been gold miners. It was something else, the old frontier—guns were legal, cowboy duds, it was turning back the pages, and there were a lot of crazy things that happened. There were millions of bugs at night, so you had to stay in-

Bill Woods, Mr. Texas USA

Working on the Alaska Railroad

doors after 5:30 in the evening. We were chased by a brown bear, and the boss shot it. The Indians skinned it, and they ate the bear meat along with deer meat they had. No doubt we had plenty of food, but it was definitely not food we had ever eaten before.

Lennie working out with the steel rails

"After that first summer, I returned home to Boston. I used the money I had made in Alaska to purchase an old beat-up Kaiser sedan. The next summer my brother Eddie and I, plus three friends of ours from Cambridge, drove the Kaiser back to Alaska. Unfortunately all of our buddies got fired almost immediately because they didn't know what hard work really was. So after a month, we decided to throw in the towel and drive back home."

Eddie and Lennie continued playing together as well as with other musicians. Just as their nice reputation began to spread, Eddie was drafted and sent to Korea, ending up on the front lines with a troop in charge of radio communications. Lennie remembers that his brother was afraid because a couple of their friends had already been killed in Korea.

The boss skinning the bear he shot

"I was playing quite a lot making a few bucks to help out the family. As we were still living with my grandparents, any job that came along I would take. I have to tell you about one particular gig I was playing. I played every Saturday and Sunday afternoon on a small cruise ship with an organist and his wife, who played accordion and sang. The ship cruised from Boston to Provincetown, MA and would dock for two or three hours and then head back to Boston. That gig was friggin' torture, especially when they would eat on the deck and the ocean got rough, everyone would be puking their brains out and running to the shit house, which was right in back of the stage where I was sitting. Phew! The boat smelled like a pig pen. (No accordion jokes here fellas. They were very popular in the 50s and 60s and many bands were centered around one.) Speaking of Provincetown, it was three years later that I went back with a five-piece rhythm and blues band for the summer and I took my wife and kids with me.

"Provincetown, MA, is a neat place, a beautiful Portuguese fishing village full of talented artists, writers, and musicians. The streets were filled with galleries, open café restaurants, and a great place to hang out in the summer. But little did we know that it also had a very large gay population of both guys and gals. In fact, I used to get hit on every night, and the free drinks were endless, plus there were a couple of waitresses who were drooling over my wife Peg (ha, ha). However, they were all beautiful people and I always remembered the old saying, 'Different strokes for different folks, and everybody in their own bag.'

"Sunday afternoon the club I played in had jam sessions, and the place was always packed. I happened to be late one Sunday afternoon for the gig and didn't make the session in time. In the meantime a young redheaded kid strolled into the club who just came off the tour boat from Boston for the afternoon. He said he was a drummer and was on his way to hook up and join the Benny

Goodman band and wanted to sit in. The cats in the band thought he was jivin' a little bit but let him play. When I got to the club, the boys in the band told me that they finally heard a real drummer and that I should go out and get a legitimate day job (ha, ha). No wonder, that dude happened to be the great Roy Burns! Of course Roy was spectacular, and the boys said that he tore the house down. I sat down and spoke to Roy. I was thrilled to meet him. It was just a chance of fate that I would meet him about five years later and sign him up as an endorser for the Zildjian Company. And so it was. Five years later, after working with the Zildjian Company, Armand Zildjian said to me that there was a young hot drummer with the Benny Goodman Band coming out to the factory to check out some new "pies" (cymbals). Roy walked in, we looked at one another, and both said, 'I know you!' And bingo we both said in unison, 'Provincetown and the jam sessions, what a coincidence, yeah!' Armand and I set Roy up with a set of cymbals, went to lunch, hung out, and had a ball."

The Benny Goodman Band with Roy Burns on drums

Lennie, Roy Burns, and Armand Zildjian selecting new cymbals for Roy Burns in the vault of the old Zildjian factory in Quincy, MA in 1962

Roy Burns with the Benny Goodman Band, 1957

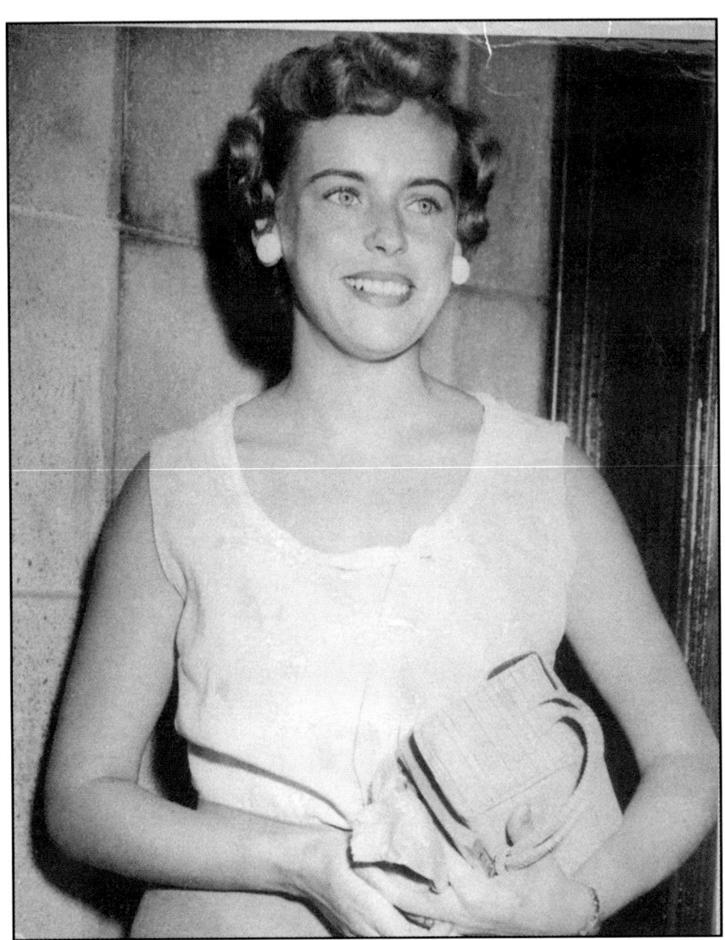

Margaret "Peggy" DiMuzio

Lennie and Peggy on their wedding day

Chapter 3

Hup Two, Three, Four

TALENTED: Army Pvt. Leonard DiMuzio, 20, holds a plaque awarded for winning first place in a recent Northern Area Command talent contest in Germany. The son of Mrs. Rose DiMuzio, 29 Andrew st., he is a drumming instructor with Company B of the 1st Infantry Division's 16th Regiment. Private DiMuzio, whose wife, Margaret, lives at 128 Hamilton st., was a musician with the Jack Sherman Trio, Boston, before entering the Army a year ago. He has been in Germany since last November. (U. S. Army Photo).

Lennie in talent contest

The year was 1952 and Lennie was 19, playing and working as much as he could when the Army came knocking and he suddenly found himself in uniform. He attempted to get into the Army band, and believe it or not, Alan Dawson, one of our drumming legends, who was stationed at the same camp in charge of the percussion department where Lennie was sent for his boot training, was waiting to be discharged. Alan auditioned Lennie, and tried to pull some strings to get Lennie into the band. Unfortunately there was an Army rule that you were trained and sent overseas with the same company you trained with during war time. As a result, Alan couldn't make it happen. Alan was one of Charlie Alden's top students and Lennie had taken a few lessons with Charlie before he was drafted. (Charlie was a well-known Boston drum teacher.) This was a great connection for Lennie, but in spite of Alan's request, Lennie was stuck in the infantry.

"I took a drum with me to boot camp and would play any chance I got in order to try to get someone to notice that I was a drummer. It didn't work. A lot of guys did crazy things to get out of the Army, especially during the war, and sometimes they worked—like a buddy of mine from Boston who went into the Army with me and played the 'I'm nuts' game, faked all kinds of shit, came to be known as Crazy Joe, and eventually got out on a Section Eight. Fact is, no one really wanted to go to Korea."

"In May of 1953, while at home on leave from boot camp, I married my high school sweetheart, Margaret "Peggy" McNeill. Peg had lived about four or five blocks from me and went to

Margaret, high school picture

Lennie and Margaret's wedding day

Cambridge Latin High School, which was right next door to Rindge Technical School where I was a student. The two of us had walked to school down the same streets. We had never spoken, but I had certainly noticed her. At that time our band was playing for the school's dances, so Peg was aware of who I was. While I was out driving with a buddy of mine in my four-door Kaiser, we noticed two girls—one tall, the other short—walking down the street, minding their own business but looking mighty fine.

"I beeped the horn like a wise guy, and they waved, so I pulled the car over to the curb. It was Margaret and her girlfriend, and I had seen them around but wasn't sure who they were. But because they knew of me, they got into the car.

"As we were driving the girls home, Margaret remarked that I didn't know who she was or where she lived. On one occasion, when she was coming out of church, I had said to my brother Eddie to check out that cute little blonde. Remembering that moment, I asked Margaret if she went to Blessed Sacrament church and she said yes. I then asked if she had a brown knit dress; again she said yes."

Lennie in an Army dance band rehearsal

And then that suave and debonair Lennie nailed it by saying, "You're that little cutie I see coming out of church after the 10:00 mass.' It was love at first sight, and from that day we started dating.

"Margaret's parents were quite strict with her and her seven sisters. She was very attractive and her mom and dad watched her like hawks.

"Margaret went with me to some joint where I played, and it was kinda late when we left to go home, around 1:00. I had a pop or two at the gig and when I made the turn to her street, I took it a little too wide, the car jumped the curb up onto the sidewalk and crashed into her fence. Her father was standing there and I almost killed him. He grabbed a flashlight from someplace, was cussing me out, I jumped out of the car and ran for my life. That was the first time I met her dad.

"Margaret and I went together for six or seven months and then I got drafted. While in boot camp I figured that if I wanted to see Margaret again when I got home, I'd better marry her. We had a small wedding at our grandparents' house. There was no time for a honeymoon, no money, and I had to hitchhike back to camp.

"The Korean War was still raging, and I figured that was where I would be sent. But they had a rule that no two members of the same family would be in Korea at the same time. Because Eddie was already there, I was sent to

Lennie's early Army days

Lennie Jr., Margaret, Lennie Sr.

Würzberg, Germany. After about six months in the First Army Division, called the Big Red, and living with a lot of mud and crabs with a bunch of hillbillies, I met up with a couple of guys. One was John Leonard, a physical trainer and a champion body builder. The other guy was a sax and clarinet player from Long Island, Bernie Lee, who like me was stuck in the infantry, wanting to get into a band. I entered some contests held in the Enlisted Men's Clubs and won some of them. Bernie and I formed a trio with a groovy German piano player, Gunter Schmidt.

"After I hooked up with Bernie and Gunther we started entering more contests as a trio. The Army had many talent contests and we entered as many as we could. Believe it or not, we started winning a bunch of the contests and finally made it to the finals.

"After my two-year hitch was up, I went back home to Cambridge and started looking for any kind of work playing. I got a job in downtown Boston with a country western band called Trenton Hall and the Hay Shakers. We played in an upholstered toilet, a club in the combat zone. I had to play seven nights a week plus Saturday and Sunday afternoons and wear a cowboy outfit for a lousy 45 bucks a week. What a dump! The place was full of derelicts, and the paddy wagon was parked outside the club every night to haul all the stiffs off to jail. It was really tough duty, but I needed the dough.

"A rock-and-roll band was playing upstairs, and I got to know all the cats in the band. One night, when the drummer failed to show up, the sax player, named Ernie Sola, told me that the drummer had been messing around with the wrong chick and got worked over by the mob. He asked me to join the band, and this began my rock-and-roll career. After about a year playing all the rock-and-roll toilets in town, I decided to go back to school and take advantage of the GI bill, and enrolled at the New England Conservatory of Music.

"I went to the conservatory for a couple of years—it was a good deal—and I met some groovy cats, including Phil Wilson. While there I studied with Charlie Smith, one of the Boston Symphony percussionists. Then I met Lloyd McCausland, who became a longtime friend, and I took lessons from him for a few months. At the first lesson he said let's play some rudiments on the snare drum. Man, I wasted him. He couldn't keep up with some of the stuff I was laying down. It was hysterical. Soon he decided I should take some marimba lessons. To this day we laugh about those times. I finally realized that I wanted to be a player, not a teacher, so I transferred to what was then known as the Schillinger Institute, which later became the Berklee College of Music, took some lessons, and played in a student big band led by Peter Cutler, a marvelous piano player.

"Through Peter I met Kenny Drinan, who was the bass player and singer in Peter's professional big band. I ended up playing in this big band, as well as with a small combo he had.

"Peter was such a terrible driver. When he drove to the Cape for gigs, he disobeyed pretty much

The newlyweds at the beach

every rule in the book—running red lights, passing on both sides of the road, and once even under the influence. It was a horror show, and Kenny and I were always asking Peter to cool out with his driving. Finally after about six months of white-knuckle trips, Kenny and I gave up and said "no more rides with Peter." Unfortunately, five or six years later Peter drove off the road, ran smack-dab into a tree, and killed himself. Poor soul.

"While attending the Schillinger Institute, I met Jake Hanna who was playing in the first string big band led by Herb Pomeroy. Jake grew up in Boston and played his butt off. I met a lot of other great players while I continued studying and did a little teaching. During this time, I started taking some private lessons from Charlie Alden, a teacher and drum shop owner in Boston. He had a great reputation and taught the late great Alan Dawson for many years. I met a lot of cats in Boston through Charlie, and he really helped me develop my reading chops. He got me to play some Broadway shows in the theater and a lot of floor shows in the clubs around Boston.

"I first met Armand Zildjian while I was studying with Charlie Alden. One day Armand came in to see Charlie and brought along drummer Barrett Deems. Barrett was with Louis Armstrong at the time and was a real funny dude. He always had a cigarette dangling from his mouth and two or three extra packs in his jacket. He was always puffing up a storm, and whistling and laughing out loud, and banging on everything in site. What a character. Once you met Barrett you would never forget him. They gave Charlie a gift. It was a poster that said, "Barrett Deems - The world's fastest drummer." I was just standing there watching and Charlie introduced me to Armand and Barrett. I was a young student and I thought it was very cool to be around these great and important people. All the while there was a gent sitting there

Red One Enters Four Contestants In Talent Finals

STUTTGART (Div Special)—Thirty-eight acts, including three from the 1st Div, played to standing crowds for two nights at the Crossroads Theater here in the USAREUR finals of the All-Army Talent Contest.

A panel of one civilian, one officer and one enlisted man chose M Sgt Charles Maluzzo, harmonica virtuoso, to represent the troops in Europe at the All-Army finals to be held in New York in June. Malluzzo, assigned to Hq 7th Army, appeared last on the first night's program, and dazzled both the judges and local fans with his rendition of Liszt's Hungarian Rhapsody.

Earlier in the show, Pfc Walter Whipple of the 1st Med Bn, and Pfc Charles Balian, Hq 1st Div Arty, won long ovations for their contributions. Whipple sang "Without a Song" and "Stranger in Paradise," and Balian, a pianist-composer, played his original composition, "Solitude." Both repeated the performances with which they placed second and third, respectively, in the Wuerzburg Area finals held at Leighton Lighthouse last month.

Pvts Bernard Lee and Leonard DiMuzio, winners of the Wuerzburg contest, went on second in the next night's show and had the packed house moving avidly to the rhythms of "Dark Eyes" and "Deep Purple." Lee is a saxaphone-clarinetist and DiMuzio plays drums. The length of the program kept the pair from going through their entire routine but despite the abrupt closing of their second number, the instrumentalists were warmly applauded by the enthusiastic audience.

In addition to the winner, special

(Continued on Page 7)

Left: 1953 Newspaper Article
Below: Lennie receives an award, 1953

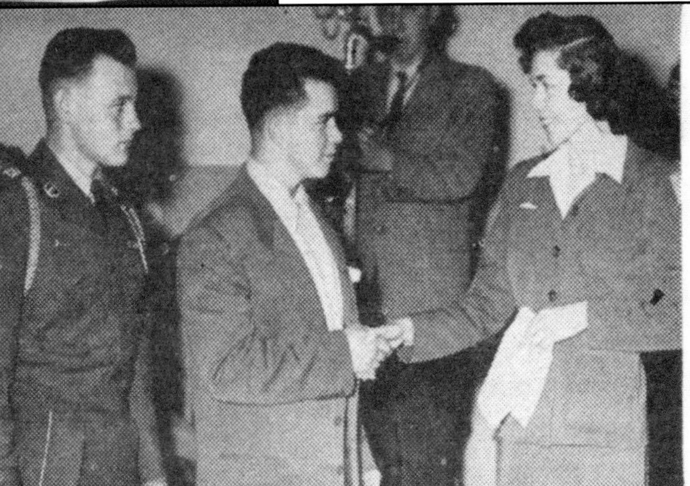

Pfc Lennie DiMuzio, RHQ Co, receives congratulations from Miss Joyce Seeman of the Ledward Bks Sp Sv Club for taking top honors in the 16th Inf Regt'l talent contest finals held last week. Looking on is the second place winner, Pfc Don Gaddis, Co B. (Spina, 16th)

Lennie on drums, Bernie Lee on sax, 1953

16th Drummer Wins Contest, Trip to Paris

Drumming his way to top honors in the 16th Inf Regt'l talent finals held last week at the Ledward Bks Service Club, Pfc Lennie DiMuzio won a three-day, expense paid pass to Paris.

Vieing for first place, DiMuzio beat representatives of the four Ranger battalions. The Ranger drummer incited the enthusiastic audience to wild cries of "go man, go" during his solo on the traps, bass, cymbals and cowbell.

Prior to entering the service, DiMuzio played in Boston night clubs with the Jack Sherman Trio.

Copping the second place five dollar prize in the finals, was Pfc Don Gaddis, Co B, with his electric guitar renditions of "Hucklebuck Boogie" and "St Louis Blues."

Tony Clementi on drums, Brother Eddie on sax, Charlie Menz on piano, Kenny Drinan bass

with his son waiting for his son who had the next lesson spot with Charlie.

INCIDENTALLY

By Paul J. Reale

Ken Drinan And Daughter, Nancy (Richard Green Photo)

Sticks You Can't Beat

DRUMSTICKS you can't beat...

That's the business of the D.S. Bunken Co. of Weymouth.

But don't let the title fool you.

There's no such person as D.S. Bunken.

D.S. stands for Drum Sticks, and Bunken is an amalgamation of nicknames of the company's founders, Ken Drinan of Quincy and his wife, Bunny.

Theirs is a relatively new and different operation for the area, and for New England, for that matter.

Ken, a widely known bass player and vocalist, says the firm is manufacturing drumsticks considered superior to anything available elsewhere in the country, by reason of a secret process he's developed.

Bunken sticks won't warp.

Warping has been a major problem with other drumsticks... the pores of the wood either give off or take in moisture, so that the sticks warp.

LONG AWARE of this shortcoming in sticks, for having spent nearly a lifetime in the rhythm section of various groups, Ken resolved four years ago to do something about it, applying his musical knowhow, a strong interest in woodwork, and what he calls "a fair mechanical background."

So he's come up with a technique for driving every bit of air from his sticks, while impregnating them with a plastic in such a way that neither air nor moisture can ever again be troublesome.

The procedure renders the sticks both dimensionally stable and much stronger.

Prominent drummers using the sticks include Joe Vespe of the Louis Prima Band, and Max Roach, and Jimmy Falzone

Kenny Drinan making the famous Bunken drumsticks with his daughter Nancy, 1965

"As Armand and Barrett were leaving, I mentioned to Armand that I was playing downtown at the Stage Bar Club and to please drop in some night and check out the band. When they walked out, the man who was waiting with his son asked me if there was some device or machine that measured how fast a drummer played. He said he was an engineer and wanted to know how fast Barrett could actually play since he too had seen the poster of Barrett. I told him there was no such device I knew of and that the poster was really publicity hype. I said Buddy Rich was known as 'the greatest,' and Gene Krupa was known as 'the most popular,' so Barrett had to use 'the fastest.' So he listened to my story and got a kick out of it.

"As I had mentioned to Armand, I had a steady gig playing downtown at the Stage Bar Club doing three shows a night. There were always three or four dancing girls, a singer, and a comedian. The laws of those days did not allow nude dancing in Boston, so the girls were called exotic dancers, and the joint was run by the mob. I can't actually talk about all the things I witnessed there, but, back to the point, one night Armand Zildjian came in with some of his golfing buddies after dinner to say hello. I was thrilled to see him and went right over. I began to tell him not to invite any of the girls over to the table for drinks, but before I could finish saying it, they moved in. It happened so fast. Anyway they sat down at their table and started ordering champagne. Well the girls had a slick deal going with the club. When they ordered champagne the waitress would bring it over in a bucket of ice and put it on the floor next to the girls. Then the girls would distract the guys for a few minutes and one girl would reach down and pour the bottle of champagne into the bucket emptying the bottle and then they would call the waitress over to immediately order another bottle of champagne. What a scam! At 30 bucks a pop (a lot of money in those days), they could rack up a hell of a bill in a short period. I had to go back for my next set and I could see this all happening from the bandstand, and you had to pay the tab or else, badda bing, badda bang, you'd be in serious trouble with the management. And you couldn't call the cops either. That was life in the combat zone and the way of life in the sixties.

"This story is a real thriller, and made headline news. One night one of the exotic dancers, Terry, asked me to drive her home. Her car had died and she lived in Cambridge, which was on

Kenny Drinan and Lennie just hanging out

USAREUR
TALENT CONTEST

CERTIFICATE OF ACCOMPLISHMENT

is awarded to

PVT LEONARD A. DIMUZIO US51 241 850 16 th Inf Regt

for winning

HONORABLE MENTION

in the Finals of the 1954 USAREUR Talent Contest, Sponsored by the Chief of Special Services, Special Activities Division, Headquarters USAREUR.

COLONEL, ARTILLERY
CHIEF OF SPECIAL SERVICES

my way home. I said, 'no problem, Terry.' I dropped her off and she asked me if I wanted to have a cup of coffee. I said okay and went into the house with her. While we were sitting in the kitchen and she was making the coffee, I noticed a shadow in one of the side rooms and heard some footsteps. I could swear someone else was in the house with us and walking around. Then all of a sudden, out of the dark room a man walked into the kitchen, stripped to the waist wearing a shoulder holster and holding a .45 handgun pointed at me. I immediately went into shock and kept yelling to Terry, 'Please tell him I'm the drummer in the band and I'm your friend and I just drove you home because your car broke down.' She moved in quickly and said, 'Frank everything is okay. Lennie is my friend. He's the drummer at the club. He just gave me a ride home because my car died.' I nearly passed out sweating my ass off, and I told Terry I had to leave immediately or else I was going to have a heart attack. She made some coffee for the dude called Frank, calmed him down, and I took off like a bat out of hell. The next night I went to the gig, and the dancer Terry never showed up for work. They said she called in sick, but in the evening *Record American* newspaper headlines read: 'Frank so and so, an escapee fugitive hit man from Walpole State Prison, was shot dead in a Cambridge apartment last night. Also held on harboring a criminal was Terry so and so, a Boston exotic dancer from the Stage Bar.' Jump way back, baby!

"Go figure that one out, I nearly got my balls shot off over a cup of coffee.

"During this time, I became close friends with Kenny Drinan. He was a very loyal person with a lot of character. We had both happy and sad times together, played a lot of gigs, and shared a lot of laughs. One day Kenny asked me about drumsticks—were there any good sticks on the market and why did they break. Kenny did a lot of research, which finally led him into the drumstick business. He started the Bunken drumstick and became as smart as any 'wood terminologist' in the business. Although he had a very successful production career, Kenny didn't have the opportunity to expand quickly and lacked financial skills. This led to his being taken advantage of by dealers and others, and eventually he went bankrupt. Kenny was married with five kids and worked very hard for his family. He died at the end of 1995. We all lost a dear friend."

After telling this story, Lennie said to me, "Jim, if any of Kenny's kids or family happen to read our book, I want them to know that I think of him a lot and he'll always be a part of me."

"One other time, I went to the Hi Hat club to see Buddy Rich and a small combo, and Buddy was tearing the place up. He took an up tune like "How High the Moon" or "Sweet Georgia Brown" and set a breakneck tempo. After awhile, I could see that Buddy was getting aggravated with the piano player because he couldn't keep up, and suddenly in the middle of the tune Buddy yelled, 'CUT—piano player, you take it.' Everyone in the band stopped playing and the piano player had to take chorus after chorus. He was sweating and looking at Buddy for a cue to bring the band back in, but Buddy made him keep playing. Finally Buddy stopped the guy and said, 'Hey, you, next time don't fall asleep on the goddamn stage.'

"Well, I'd been playing around Boston for quite a few years, still studying with Charlie Alden and playing at a club where Armand Zildjian would come bebopping in every now and then with his friends from the golf course, have dinner, check out the drummers, and see what was happening. I became friendly with

Lennie's Army buddy John Leonard

Charlie Alden, one of Boston's finest drum instructors and Alan Dawson's first drum teacher

Armand, told him I was studying with Charlie, who he knew because Charlie would go to the factory and buy a few cymbals. Once I asked if there was any work out at Zildjian and that I would love to go out to the factory and meet his father. Armand told me to come on out, so I took him up on the invitation, took a ride out, and there I was, a little bebop drummer from Boston at the famous Zildjian factory in North Quincy. I was totally thrilled and blown away. I met Mr. Zildjian, such a nice man, and he told me he was glad to meet me, and I also met Armand's brother Bob, and we all seemed to strike it off really well. Maybe because I was a working drummer, going to Berklee, and could swing the band, I don't know, but they gave me a job. It was 1961, I had just turned 28, and I had a job at Zildjian."

Bernie Lee on sax, Gunter Schmidt on piano, and Lennie on drums

Charlie Perry, Lennie, Charlie's son, Avedis Zildjian, Charlie's wife in front of the Avedis Zildjian Cymbal Company, Quincy, MA, (1965)

Ray Nelson, Okie Nelson (Zildjian employees), Avedis Zildjian, Lester Ramsey (Zildjian employee), at the Zildjian Cymbal Company in Quincy, MA circa 1970

Chapter 4

Ring-A-Ding, Splang

Fayette Street in Quincy, Massachusetts, the Avedis Zildjian cymbal factory, and 28-year-old Lennie beginning a career that would last 42 years. According to Lennie, Avedis Zildjian thought Lennie was a real cat because he was a good drummer, sported a goatee and long hair, and was real cool and "in the groove." The company at that time was small, with only 35 to 40 people working in the factory and six people in the office: Mr. Zildjian, the brothers Armand and Robert, two secretaries, and an accountant.

"The factory, testing and shipping, was downstairs, and the offices were upstairs. I really had nothing to do with the office at that time because I was a cymbal tester and worked downstairs. Along with me, there were two guys in the shipping room, one by the name of Bobby Goldstone, who helped me test cymbals and also pack the bundles. It was almost a year later when Leon Chiappini was sent over by Charlie Alden, to work in the testing room with Bobby and me. In the morning, Armand and Bob would work in the melting room. At around 12:00 or 1:00 Bob would go upstairs to his office and do the paperwork and work on sales, plus marketing and advertising. When Bob went upstairs, Armand would come into the testing area and work with me, testing cymbals for some of the drummers. Of course,

Early Zildjian employee, Leon Chiappini, Lennie, Bobby Goldstone, Jim Hall (1965)

the output wasn't much in those days, maybe 75 to 80 cymbals a day, but the number began to grow every year.

Zildjian cymbal specialist Bobby Goldstone and Lennie testing cymbals in the vault of the old factory in North Quincy, MA (1962)

"Unlike today, there weren't many different models or sizes. Zildjian offered only a few weights in those days—thin, medium, medium-heavy—and we would stamp them using a little rubber stamp. Everything was pretty much done by hand, and the cymbals that were made that day, or the previous day, would be brought into the shipping room on a little push cart. We would pick up each individual cymbal, feel the weight, the flexibility of the metal, how it would bend, and then hit it to see how it responded. We had a sound criteria that we went by, and we would separate

Barrett Deems (1965)

them into three piles—thin, medium, and medium-heavy. As we were testing, if one would jump out at us with a great sound and stiffness, an all-around gem, we would put it aside in our goody pile for one of our heavy-hitter artists or for the special dealers.

"The cymbals were placed on their respective racks in a vault. The smaller cymbals, the 13s through 16s, were placed on a special rack because they were usually thin. Another rack held the 17s and 18s divided into thin and medium-thin because they were primarily used as crash or crash rides. The 20s were mostly used as ride cymbals, along with the 22s. The 22s were not too popular at that time, but some of the players liked them.

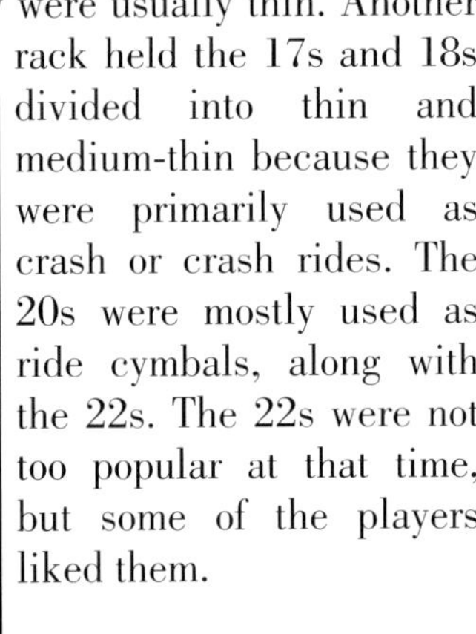

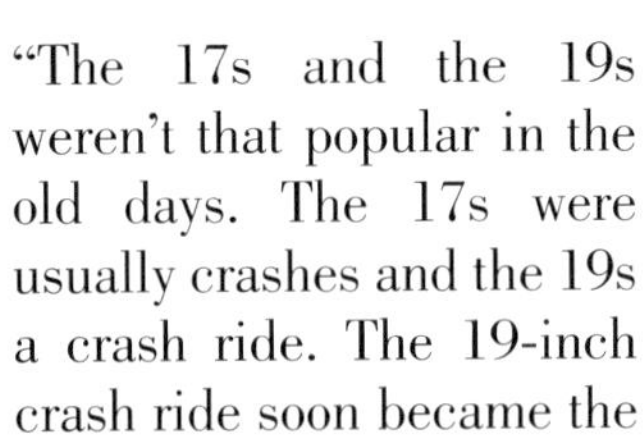
Kenny Clare, (1969)

"The 17s and the 19s weren't that popular in the old days. The 17s were usually crashes and the 19s a crash ride. The 19-inch crash ride soon became the signature ride cymbal for Joe Morello. Although we made 24s through 30s, they weren't very popular except with the Stan Kenton band. He wanted his drummers to have large cymbals for big rolls and a big sound at the end of an arrangement.

"The hi-hats were usually 13s or 14s, with occasional 15s, with the 14s being the most popular. All the hats were matched individually by hand by me and Armand. We put them on a hi-hat stand, played 'em, and tried 'em to make sure they had a great backbeat or a nice 'sock.' In fact, the hi-hats were often called 'sock' cymbals back then.

George Wettling (1964)

"At that time Zildjian had a very unique distribution channel. They sold directly to dealers and also distributors. That was pretty much unheard of in those days, but because Zildjian really had the only cymbals available, Zildjian could do pretty much what he wanted and could sell any way he felt was profitable. Because they were the best cymbals in the world, he could set up his own credit terms and sell to just about anybody.

Sam Woodyard (1962)

Cozy Cole testing cymbals in the Vault (1963)

Armand Zildjian, Max Roach, Lennie (1969)

"Although distributors generally bought in bulk," Lennie continues, "the dealers would buy cymbals in sets, a pair of hi-hats, and we would put in a thin crash and a medium or heavy ride. A few years after I joined, we started to stamp 'ride' on certain cymbals. We also had seconds, cymbals that were slightly damaged, which we would sell to a couple of drum shops only in Boston (Jack Adams and Rayburn's) that were friends of Armand. But after about ten years, we had to stop that practice because they were becoming too popular and other stores started wanting them and Mr. Z didn't want to deal with selling seconds to the market at large.

Tommy Thompson, Joe Morello, Lennie (1965)

"Mr. Zildjian was a unique man, spoke two or three languages, and handled all the credit and books with his own rather old-fashioned method of bookkeeping. Every dealer and distributor was listed in three little books, along with his special credit terms, and he knew everyone's credit limitations. Mr. Z wouldn't hesitate to get on the phone and ask a distributor or dealer for payment, telling them, 'It's been three months and you haven't sent a check. If you don't send a check, then I can't buy copper or tin to make cymbals, and if I can't make cymbals, I can't sell them to you. I need your check right away.'

"I used to hear him do that all the time," recalls Lennie. "He had such control over the finances that Armand and Bob couldn't sign a check for over $100 unless he okayed it. Unbelievable. Even though he was tight with business, he was the first guy to put his hand into his pocket if it was entertainment or dinners. He always carried a big wad of dough in his pocket, probably a couple thousand dollars, and he loved to pay cash for everything.

"He used to dress to the hilt—always with designer suits, shirts, pants, always looked fabulous, neat as a pin. And he always would keep his dignity. He would be in the factory early, maybe 7:00 to 7:30 a.m, since he lived only about four or five miles from the factory. First he would check the books and then walk around the factory, talk to everyone, and like a gentleman say hello and shake hands with all the guys, look at the manufacturing, check out all aspects of the cymbal making, and then go back upstairs. After some more work at his desk, he would go out to lunch; he would always go out for lunch and then come back around 2:00 and spend the next three hours at his desk, leaving for home around 5:00 or 5:30. He was remarkable and was the cat who built the dynasty. He had horse sense, keen judgment, and was an incredible businessman."

Jack Adams had the biggest drum shop in Boston, Jack's Drum Shop, and he would go to the factory because he liked to pick out his own cymbals. Mr. Zildjian, Armand, Lennie, and Jack would go out to lunch and talk about what was happening in town and discuss the drummers. Jack's was the exclusive Gretsch dealer in Boston and was the most popular place for drummers to hang out.

"Jack loved to pick out his own ride cymbals, although he let me choose the crashes and hats. He was very fussy and would drive to the factory in Quincy, park out in front, and come to the shipping room. It took me four or five visits to figure him out, and he was always busting my chops: 'This one's not high enough,' 'Too much shimmer,' 'This ride's not stiff enough.' When I knew he was coming out, I would get prepared. Between the shipping room and the vault area was a swinging door, and behind that door Armand and I would stash our goodies, those cymbals we picked out to be the absolute best. Jack usually would buy about ten ride cymbals, and you can imagine what it would be like to pick out ten cymbals out of a whole batch, rejecting and accepting some. So, I would pick out ten ride

Armand Zildjian, Jack Adams, Papa Jo Jones (1962)

cymbals from our very special goodies pile and have them in the vault room, and I would go in and out of this little room with the swinging door and bring out the cymbals one by one. He would try it and say, 'You know, Lennie, I'm not sure. Do you have any more?' I'd say sure and go back and get another one.

"I would go through the same ten cymbals, and after awhile he would get totally confused thinking he was hearing 15 to 20 different ride cymbals. Jack would end up buying those same ten cymbals that he had been hearing over and over again. I knew this would happen because after awhile it is very difficult to distinguish one from another. He fell for the game completely, and that stopped me from running around like a chicken with its head cut off.

"Jack was a wonderful guy and pretty much dealt with the cats, and he got burned a lot. He gave a lot of stuff out for nothing, put it out on loan, extended credit, and wouldn't press for the dough, and when it got out of hand, he would have to shut off a few guys. Down the road, when Jack got sick and had some family trouble, he finally lost the drum shop."

As more and more drummers began to come to the factory to check out cymbals, Armand and Lennie began to add to their "goodies stash." In the shipping office where they kept the goodies there was a little vault Lennie called the "treasure chest." In that vault were special cymbals for the top drummers, the heavy hitters. Some of those drummers were Barrett Deems, Kenny Clare, Papa Jo Jones, Philly Joe Jones, Ray McKinley, Cliff Leaman, "Big" Sid Catlett, and of course Gene Krupa and Buddy Rich. Other musicians were Wayne Newton, Mel Torme, Stan Getz, Dizzy Gillespie, Stan Kenton, and Maynard Ferguson.

Ray McKinley (1961)

One side note: Lennie had been working at Zildjian for about a year when he got a call from his friend Phil Wilson, the great jazz

Big Sid Catlett (circa 1950)

Armand Zildjian, John Pagnotti, Leon Chiappini, Buddy Rich, Jimmy Wesson, Lennie (1970)

trombonist who was in Woody Herman's orchestra. Woody was looking for a drummer, and Phil wanted Lennie to audition for the chair. But after a lot of consideration, being married and having kids, Lennie decided it might be best to hang in there with the Zildjian Company.

Zutty Singleton, circa 1940

Lennie was moving along happily in his formative years at Zildjian. You might recall he had some previous experience with bears in Alaska, and was about to have even more crazy encounters with bears on his first trip to Canada for some new business travels for Zildjian.

"The bearcat story took place in the mid-1960s, when Zildjian decided to put a second line of cymbals on the market. Because it was a new venture for the company, I was sent to Canada to check out a new small factory that had been put in place by Zildjian. This was the place where Zildjian was going to manufacture this second line and Bob Zildjian was overseeing this process.

"Now, Bob loved to hunt and fish, and over the years he got hooked up with a guy named Willard Way. Willard was from Canada, a big dude. He was the picture of a typical backwoodsman. He ran a beautiful hunting lodge near a picturesque lake called Charlie Lake. It was near a small town named Meductic. (Meductic is now where the Sabian Cymbal Company is located.) Bob had spent a lot of time fishing with Willard at Charlie Lake during the summer months and really knew and loved the area. When the company decided that a second line of cymbals was needed, Bob convinced his father and brother that Meductic provided the ideal location to manufacture this new line. They agreed, and that was the beginning of the Zilco line of cymbals. Now, as I mentioned earlier, this was supposed to be a second lower level and lower priced line than Zildjian. However, they sounded really good and a lot of the players couldn't tell the difference. Eventually, Mr. Zildjian took them off the market because they were just too good and

Armand Zildjian, Joe Morello, Lennie, 1966

Wayne Newton's drummer Harvey Lang, Lennie, Jimmy Wesson, John Pagnotti, Wayne Newton, Armand Zildjian, Leon Chiapinni, Zildjian employee, Jerry Doneghan (1972)

too close in quality to some of the main Zildjian line. Mr. Z always said, 'You can't make money selling steak at hamburger prices.' It was so true.

"While all of this was going on, there was one particular time when Bob wanted me to go up to Canada with him and Zildjian general manager, Bill Richards. We would fly up with his friend Stan, who owned his own plane and had a small flying school located on the South Shore of Boston. Now, this was to be my first trip in a single-engine plane and I was a little worried. The plane was a little cabbage cutter. Turns out Stan was a wild man in the air, and he and Bob knew they had a little lollipop city slicker on-board to scare the shit out of on the flight, and I was the one. After I nearly wet myself about five times, we made it to Meductic and the games began.

Louis Bellson testing cymbals in the vault circa 1967

"One evening after checking out the factory and doing the daily chores, everyone gathered at the main lodge for a big dinner with Willard and his wife Muriel, who was an incredible cook. In fact, she did almost all of the cooking for the people who rented the cabins. They had about ten cabins and also provided guides. Along with Bob, Willard, and his small crew of Nort Hargrove, John Monder, and Willard's son Mark that worked at the Canadian cymbal plant, we were going to pig out on moose steaks, salmon, deer meat, whatever. There were probably seven or eight of us at the dinner, and afterward we sat by the fireplace, had a few pops, and Willard started telling some great stories about the woods and the wildlife. Oh, boy! After we all started getting really toasted, he started on his bear stories and told me to be careful of the bearcats, as they could swim and bite as well. That's all I had to hear. He scared me shitless, and I was afraid to go back to my cabin. I was staying with Bill Richards in one of the small cabins on Charlie Lake, about 100 feet from the water.

"Bill and I finally decided to go back to our cabin and go to bed. We did, and when we got there, I crawled up onto the top bunk and tried to go to sleep. Bill put out the lights and all that there, when all of a sudden all hell broke loose. Pots and pans and dishes started to rattle and fly off the shelves, and something or

Renowned drummer, educator, and author, Billy Gladstone (circa 1950)

someone was banging and thumping on the walls of the cabin—it was like an earthquake. Bill started yelling and screaming, and I was there wondering what the hell was going on. I jumped up and almost whacked my head on the ceiling. Bill was saying that there was a bear outside trying to get into the cabin. I was flipping out. I jumped out of bed in my skivvies, and Bill said, 'Lennie, you know, we've got to get out of here and run for our lives.' We ran outside, and the only place to go was into the lake. Bill was yelling to head for the lake and jump in—we would be safe in the lake. Well, I ran like a son-of-a-bitch, jumped in, and started swimming. Bill wasn't in the water, and everybody was yelling to keep swimming and make some noise to scare off the bear. What the hell did I know about bears? After about ten minutes in the water, I was totally exhausted, up to my neck in the water, and seeing flashlights flickering on the shore.

"I suddenly realized I was the only one in the water, the rest of the guys were laughing, and then started yelling that I could come out of the water—the bear was gone. So I swam to shore and came out of the water, had nothing on but my shorts, everyone was laughing and jiving, falling apart, and then I realized that they were busting my aggies. There really wasn't any bear. They had set me up, rigged the cabin before dinner, and attached all of the pots and pans to wires and strings. When I went to bed, they waited until Bill put out the lights and then they pulled on the strings, beat on the cabin walls, and all hell broke loose. I had fallen for the bearcat story hook, line, and sinker. I was pretty gullible in those days."

In those early days, Bob Zildjian was involved mostly with international sales and advertising while Armand was involved with the manufacturing of cymbals, new product development, and artist relations. As one might imagine, there were occasional differences of opinion between the brothers over the marketing and advertising approach, so Mr. Zildjian always looked over all the ads and made the final decisions. He always wanted to see Zildjian on the back cover of *DownBeat* magazine. He eventually got his wish and Zildjian ads in *DownBeat* became one of the company's biggest advertising campaigns. This lasted for many years and was very successful.

"As I was getting more involved with the company, they wanted me to take over the sales department," Lenny remembers. "I started to travel a lot and go to trade shows, and at an early NAMM show in Chicago, I met up with Lloyd McCausland again. He had just started with Remo and had come off the road from playing the Ice Capades. Also, Jim, this is when I first met you. Bob Z. used to do all the clinics, and one day in the mid-'60s he told me that I was to take over for him on a clinic appearance because he was too busy to handle it. It was in Iowa; I think the Iowa Bandmasters. Now, I'd never done a clinic prior to that and wasn't used to speaking in

Lennie, John Burson, Mel Lewis, John Pagnotti, Billy Zildjian, Kim Dunning, Kenny Hadley (1975)

front of a lot of people. I basically didn't have a clue. However, Bob Zildjian gave me a lot of notes and instructions and said, 'Do what you do best—demonstrate and play cymbals, and you will be fine.'

"Just before the clinic started in a big ballroom, I looked in and there must have been 300-400 people. I said to myself, oh my god, what the hell am I doing here? I'd filled up the stage with all kinds of cymbals and had written a little history of the Zildjian Company. When I got introduced, sweat started running down my back and I realized then that I was in over my head. I went out, started reading, and after a few pages I noticed people were starting to fall asleep. Just about then, you raised your hand, Jim, stood up, and asked if I would demonstrate some of the cymbals. You were teaching at the University of Northern Iowa at the time. I said sure, so you came up on stage and helped me with the cymbals, and once I started demonstrating the cymbals everything changed. The presentation started flowing more smoothly. You saved the show that day."

Along with his sales activities, Lennie continued to work with the many drummers who were coming to the factory to choose cymbals, and Zildjian needed to expand its line using the information gleaned from the artists. Lennie was key in getting this essential information and providing it to Armand so they could develop the product that the drummers needed because their musical styles were demanding and changing often.

"I would tell Armand that we needed this or that to fill in the gaps because what we were making didn't always fit the young drummers' needs. For example, Joe Morello felt that our 20-inch ride was a little too big and the 18-inch ride or crash ride was too small. So, based upon Joe's needs, we began to make a 19-inch ride, and during Joe's heyday, that's what he played and that put the 19-inch ride cymbals on the rack along with the 20s.

"Now, Buddy Rich always wanted 12-inch or 13-inch hi-hats, but most players were using 14-inch or 15-inch hats that were on the thin to medium-thin weight. Buddy started using nothing but 13-inch hats, which made them quite popular for many years.

"Max Roach was another cat that in order to get the sound he wanted had a 14-inch on the top hat and a 15-inch on the bottom. He liked that set-up because it gave him a stronger 'chick,' and the extra inch on the bottom let him cuff it with his stick and get a different sound. Although it suited Max, not many drummers used that idea.

"Swish cymbals from China were popular back in the '20s and '30s, and many drummers really loved the sound. Dave Tough always played a swish; Gene Krupa too, and then later Mel Lewis got into that sound as well.

"Mel was a swish cymbal freak," Lennie recalls. "He always used a 20-inch swish ride to the right of his drumset and used it on the out chorus to really boot the band. He would come out to the factory and start checking out 22s, and if he found one he liked but it was a little too heavy, I would take it out and have one of the guys in the factory lathe it down to the weight that Mel wanted. He had precisely 20 rivets in his cymbal. In perfecting Mel's swish cymbals, we started with six to eight rivets and kept putting in rivets until we got the

John Pagnotti, Fred Sargent, Kenny Hadley, Lennie, Leon Chapinni, Dan Barker (1978)

sound he wanted. We used steel rivets in our regular swish cymbals and they got a decent sound, but we didn't really know about the different rivets that were available. Mel went out and researched a variety of rivets and came up with copper ones that we would insert in the holes that were drilled near the edge of the cymbal. These copper rivets had two prongs that we would bend and separate and press them flat to the cymbal. That cymbal, with the edges turned up and a special cup and the copper rivets, had a great, crunchy sound that Mel loved. We did an ad with Mel holding his swish cymbal in his lap, and we called it the 22

Early promotional picture of Mel Lewis (circa 1977)

Swish Knocker. Later on we did the copper rivet thing with 18s and 20s in addition to the 22, which gave us a popular swish ride and swish crash. Eventually Buddy Rich began to dig the sound, and played the hell out of it at the end of a song. Gene Krupa also loved the swish sound, and Dizzy Gillespie loved his own personal swish that he made all his drummers use.

"With all of the drummers coming to the factory wanting different sizes and weights, the cymbal line began to grow. As a result, I began to experiment with mixing weights in the hi-hats.

"Most big-band drummers felt that the small hi-hats weren't heavy enough. They wanted a bigger sound to cut through the band, so I got involved with matching up different combinations. At that time we were also making marching band cymbals, sizes 14, 16, and 18 inches. So I took a 14 heavy band cymbal for the bottom hat, put a nice medium-thin on the top, and when some of the drummers came by, I would lay that combination on them, and they dug 'em because they had a nice, strong 'chick.' I spoke with Armand and the advertising guys and we coined the name 'New Beat' hi-hats. We did a special ad, sent some to the drum shops, the drummers started to use them, and then the New Beats started going out the door like crazy. The New Beats hi-hats quickly became the standard of the industry.

"About this time, the mid-'70s, rock 'n' roll became very popular and Zildjian needed more rock cymbals to meet the growing market of this new style. That's when we came up with the Rock 21 and began advertising it.

"I told Armand we needed something new for the rock market—that it should be strong and cut through the guitars, and maybe be an odd size—and he told me to go for it. We developed a 'bomb tosser.' We made a 21-inch that was on the heavy side, with a large bell, but it still had a nice, clear ping tone and had some crash qualities. That 21 Rock Ride became very popular and became the perfect cymbal for rock 'n' roll.

"Because of that popularity, I began putting together more rock set-ups. Along with the 21 Rock Ride, I combined some heavier crash cymbals and added some rock hi-hats, using a medium-heavy on top and a heavy on the bottom. Those mothers really gave a powerful 'chick' sound, and the rock line became a very popular addition for the dealers' racks.

"As the music changed so did the style of drumming, so we developed new lines and expanded our cymbal offerings. Armand was a big help during this time of growth, but he had a lot of other manufacturing commitments and interests, so dealing with the artists, selecting cymbals, and some of the cymbal line decisions fell on my shoulders."

Lennie, Cliff Leeman, Jo Jones, Armand Zildjian

Fred Sanford, Armand Zildjian, Rab Zildjian, Vic Firth, Remo Belli, music shop dealer, Steve Gadd, Ed Thigpen, Lennie D., Jim Coffin (NAMM 1977)

Chapter 5

Papa Jo Jones and the "Red Devils"

Papa Jo Jones (circa 1950)

One of the great musical influences and great swingers of all time was Papa Jo Jones, born in Chicago on October 7, 1911. Known as Mr. Hi-Hat, Papa Jo joined the Count Basie Band in 1936 and, along with the Count, Freddie Green on guitar, and bassist Walter Page, created one of the great big-band rhythm sections. A native of Alabama, Papa Jo began his playing career with Walter Page's Blue Devils, followed by stints in Nebraska and Kansas City, when he joined the Basie Band. Over the years, Papa Jo recorded with several jazz greats, including Illinois Jacquet, Billie Holiday, Art Tatum, and Duke Ellington.

Lennie remembers the first time he saw Papa Jo: "There was a jazz club in town called the Hi Hat Club, and Symphony Sid was the big-time jazz disc jockey in Boston, and he was the main man who would broadcast some of the club's shows. I went over there one night to see Papa Jo Jones, and Jo was incredible. After the show was over, I hung outside the club till at least 2:00 a.m. because I wanted Jo's autograph. It was pitch-dark out. Finally, Jo comes out with one of the dudes from the band, Jo gives me his autograph and we're talking, and finally Jo calls a cab. The cab comes up and Jo says, 'Do you want to talk some more, son?' I say sure, and he says to jump in the cab, so I did, and can you believe it, the cab took us over to the Franklin Park Zoo, not far out of Boston. We're driving around that zoo, you can't see anything, and Jo is saying there's the elephants and I'm going, 'Yeah, how about that.' Then he says there are the tigers and the other animals, and to be polite, I'm nodding my head and going, 'Uh huh, that's right, man.' After about an hour, the cab driver drove back to Boston, dropped me off, and I got in my car and went home. That was my first encounter with the great

Papa Jo Jones (circa 1970)

Papa Jo Jones

Papa Jo Jones. Man, wasn't that out? Later on, when I got to be good friends with him, I came to recognize all of his idiosyncrasies, his unique personality, his humor, and I came to realize that he was special and a great talent, and that traveling constantly can be lonely, and I think he just wanted someone to talk to and hang out with that night."

Most of the drummers who came to the factory to pick out some cymbals all had their special manner of selection, but Papa Jo's method was really unique. While telling this story, Lennie couldn't help but chuckle a lot.

"One time, Papa Jo came out to the factory without calling ahead, walked in the front door unannounced, and everyone started going crazy. One of the gals gave me a call and told me that a famous drummer named Jo Jones was at the front. I thought that has to be Papa Jo and ran up to the front, and there he was.

"'I want to see Mr. Zildjian,' Jo said.

"Yes, Papa, of course," I replied. "By all means. I would be very happy to find him." Now Mr. Z happened to be there at the time and he came over to the door and shook Jo's hand. Jo immediately said, 'I want a job, Mr. Zildjian.'

"Now, Mr. Z was totally flabbergasted, shocked. He didn't know what Jo was talking

Papa Jo Jones, Armand Zildjian, Lennie

about. Jo repeated that he wanted a job, Mr. Z asked him what he wanted to do, and Jo replied that he would do anything, sweep the floors, clean the men's room, whatever it would take. He went on and said that he wanted to work at Zildjian to be around those beautiful cymbals. Mr. Z told Jo sure, anytime, and after a half an hour talking with Mr. Z. Jo pretty much forgot about the job and decided that he wanted to pick out some cymbals.

"I took Jo to the vault area, and he had a little brown bag with him that he wouldn't let go of, but finally he put it down on one of the tables and we started to pick out some cymbals. I asked what size he wanted, and he said to go and get some of those big cymbals, some 20s and 22s, because he wanted to check out those 'red devils.' When I brought him some of the big ride cymbals, he never used a stick to hit them with—he would put his thumb or

Postcard from the historic Storyville Jazz Club announcing a Papa Jo Jones performance (1951)

Ella Fitzgerald with Papa Jo Jones on drums

finger in the center hole suspending the cymbal and then with his other hand tap the outside of the cymbal, looking for vibrations. Then he would say, 'Oh bless my soul, I can see the red devils out there jumpin' around. That's what I want to see—I want to see red devils jumpin' around out there. That's it—I'll take that one.'

"He went along and picked out four or five more cymbals, checking for red devils, and when he saw them, he would take that cymbal. Isn't that something? To this day I've never seen any red devils, but Armand and I would often go to hear Jo play, and without a doubt, he really knew what he was doing when picking out cymbals.

"After awhile I asked him if he wanted to go and get something to eat, but he said no, that he had brought his lunch with him in that little brown bag, and he wanted to eat lunch with the guys in the shipping room. So I said okay, and we walked into the shipping room. He opened up his bag and took out five or six pork chops. He gave us all a pork chop and we sat there and had a pork chop. Can you believe that? I'll never forget that day. Jo stayed till we ate our pork chops, then took his cymbals, and off he went. He was definitely one of a kind, a classic individual who had to do his own thing, and had his own way of picking out cymbals.

"Joe was very unique He had his own way of talking and explaining things, and when he spoke about the red devils on the edge of the cymbal, he was referring to the vibrations and the timbre of the cymbal. He liked thinner cymbals because they vibrated more, and I could really dig it—it made a lot of sense to me.

Legendary Papa Jo Jones, who began his career as a drummer and tap dancer with carnival shows and went on to influence many of the great swing and bop drummers, passed away in New York on September 3, 1985.

Armand Zildjian, Lennie, Papa Jo Jones (circa 1978)

Shelley Manne, Pioneer Banque Club, Seattle, WA (1974)

Gus Johnson rehearsing with the Basie All-Stars at the Palace Theater in Cleveland (1985)

Tiny Kahn (circa 1980)

Sonny Greer, Duke Ellington Band (circa 1940)

Chapter 6

Oldies But Goodies

Before continuing with Lennie's memories, we want to touch on a few of the other ground-breaking drumset players, like Baby Dodds, Davey Tough, and Chick Webb, who influenced a generation of drummers. Also, there will be some brief biographical information.

Baby Dodds (1948)

"In the old days, Jim," Lennie begins, "there were many great clubs in New York where you could jump in, see a Latin band, and then go a few steps and see someone like Gene Krupa. One of the drummers that was before my time and I never got to hear play was Chick Webb. Armand, however, got to hear him play a few times and always raved about the incredible technique, the virtuosity of his playing, and his control on the bass drum. Armand also talked about a recording that Chick made with his band, and I think the tune was 'Liza,' a real up-tempo tune, and he played a terrific solo. Chick had his own band and is known for 'discovering' Ella Fitzgerald, and she sang with his band for many years."

Chick Webb was born in 1909, and throughout his brief life, he fought congenital tuberculosis of the spine, resulting in becoming hunchbacked and almost a dwarf. In spite of this, he formed one of the best bands in the big-band era and was feared by the other bands when the Savoy Ballroom put on its famous Battle of the Bands. In fact, in one battle, Chick's band defeated Benny Goodman's band with Gene Krupa on drums. Lennie mentioned that Chick discovered Ella Fitzgerald, and he became her legal guardian and built his band around her. The tune "Liza" was on the flip side of the famous Decca recording of "A-Tisket A-Tasket." Chick's drumset was somewhat unusual. It was a circa 1938 Gretsch-Gladstone model with a 14 x 6 1/2 snare, 13 x 9 tom, 16 x 16 floor tom, and a 28-inch bass drum. All of his cymbals were Zildjians—12-inch hi-hats, 12- and 13-inch crashes, and a 15-inch Chinese swish. He also used a wood block, a cowbell, and four tuned temple blocks. The drum world lost one of the

Chick Webb (circa 1937)

Ray Bauduc (circa 1970)

early giants when Chick Webb died at the age of 30 on June 16, 1939.

One of the other early drummers Lennie regrets never having seen or heard in person was the great Ray Bauduc, who was born in New Orleans in June 1909. His main drumming style was the New Orleans two-beat, and he kept this style throughout his career. In his early days, Ray worked with many groups including Eddie Lang and the famed violinist Joe Venuti, and besides the drums, he was the featured dancer in a band led by Freddie Rich. Ray joined Ben Pollack's band in 1928, and after that band dissolved, it became a co-op band under the leadership of Bob Crosby. Ray continued his two-beat style with the Bob Cats, even though most bands of that era were into four-on-the-floor. Ray was one of the WFL Drum Company's top endorsers.

"Over the years I was dealing with the artists, I would get many of Armand's phone calls," Lennie remembers. "Now, Ray would call the factory needing some cymbals and I got to know him that way, though I never got to hear him play. Whenever I would talk to Armand about Ray, he would always tell me this story: Armand went to see Ray play with the Bob Cats and was amazed that he didn't use the hi-hat. I think the hats were new around that time, and with his style of drumming—heavy two and four on the snare drum—they probably weren't needed. He sounded great without them."

Ray really added to his fame when the Bob Cats were playing in Chicago at the Blackhawk Ballroom. When the fans demanded an encore, only Ray and the great bassist Bob Haggart were on the stand. They improvised a tune with Haggart whistling and Ray playing a rhythmic pattern on the bass strings with his sticks. The outcome was the big hit "Big Noise From Winnetka." After leaving the Bob Cats, Ray went on to work with Jimmy Dorsey, Jack Teagarden, and others.

In 1960, Ray went into semi-retirement in Texas but did go back to New Orleans on occasion, and in 1985, still with his two-beat style intact, he appeared in St. Louis in a reunion with the Bob Cats. Ray Bauduc, the great two-beat drummer, passed away January 8, 1988.

Lennie continues, "Armand and I used to go to New York in the old days, because our ad agency was there. We'd work on some advertising and then go hang with the cats, and we'd check out Zutty Singleton if he was in town. Zutty played drums with Earl Hines, Fats Waller, and Louis Armstrong. In fact, Armstrong, when recording with his Hot Five, supposedly said to Zutty, 'Come on, Zutty, whip those cymbals pops!' Now, Zutty was a big guy and had a regular drumset, used 14-inch light hi-hats, a 15-inch thin crash, a 20-inch medium-thin ride with sizzles, and he

Dave Tough (circa 1945)

liked to use a 17-inch Chinese cymbal for cooking on the last chorus. One of the things that knocked me out was the fact that he always had a wood block and cowbell attached to his bass drum. And when he took his solos, it was just like, you know, comparing the difference between today's drummers and Zutty—it would be like him playing on one or two chairs. I mean, he could continue his solo and play for five minutes off the woodblock and the cowbell, the rim of the drum, and pat the bass drum with his right hand occasionally. He had so much finesse and dexterity around the drumset that he didn't need a lot of drums or a lot of cymbals and a lot of shit like the kids are using today. His basic ingredient was 'time.' He had the time element down and could play endlessly with a beautiful flow of time and smooth sticking. And to top it off, he was a perfect gentleman."

Zutty was born May 14, 1898, in Bunkie, Louisiana, and at the age of ten he was in New Orleans. He was a great brush artist and one of the influential drummers of early jazz. Zutty was wounded in World War I and returned to New Orleans to play with several of that city's bands, played in St. Louis, and also played in Chicago. Beginning in 1941 he, for awhile, led or played in several bands in Los Angeles, continuing to play until 1970, when he retired after suffering a stroke. Zutty Singleton died in New York in 1976.

To round out this quartet of drummers, one of Lennie's favorites was Elmer J. "Mousey" Alexander, who was born in Gary, Indiana, June 19, 1922, and raised in Chicago.

"A lot of people probably won't remember Mousey, but he was quite the New York drummer in the early days, and I would say, perhaps, maybe in the '60s. He always played with some great musicians, and the one unusual thing about Mousey was that he loved to play on an enormous 26-inch ride cymbal. Can you believe it, Jim? I can't think of many drummers using that big of a cymbal, so it was kinda shocking to see him play on that big 26-inch mother.

Mousey Alexander (circa 1975)

He probably had that cymbal for most of his life. Later he got ill and took up residence in Florida until he passed away.

"I first got to see him in the '60s because Mousey joined Benny Goodman in 1955 and stayed with the band until the early '70s. After touring with Sy Oliver, he worked for Doc Severinsen on the Tonight Show Band, as well as with Clark Terry's Big Band." In 1980, Mousey suffered a massive heart attack, left New York, and moved to Orlando, Florida, where he got the jazz scene jumping, as well as teaching at the University of Central Florida, working with the lab band and the rhythm players. He didn't dig contemporary jazz-rock fusion and promoted a series of traditional and swing concerts in the Orlando area. Mousey Alexander died of a heart attack at the age of 66 on October 9, 1988.

Stan Kenton (circa 1970)

Two versions of Lennie hard at work

Chapter 7

So, You Want a Cymbal Endorsement?

Although the Zildjian Company had a Hall of Fame at the factory, there wasn't much of an official artist relations program in place when Lennie joined the company in 1961. Over the following decade, Lennie and Armand developed what became the premier and world-renowned Zildjian artist relations program. Here Lennie tells the story of how it all began.

"In the early '60s, there wasn't an official artist program and there wasn't a company position to manage the informal artist relations things that did exist. In fact, we didn't have many artist signatures or any kind of an official agreement. A few of the cats had signed an informal agreement that Bob Holly, our ad director, had put together, just so we could use the artist's name for advertising purposes. There were no problems as to agreements in those days because there wasn't any competition to worry about between the companies. Where would an artist go besides to us? By the late '60s, when I was manager of sales and selections, I was dealing with everyone—dealers, distributors, and artists. By that time, I was working with so many artists I had to formulate some type of formal agreement. So, with the help of the ad department, we put something together. The main part of the agreement was just to confirm their relationship with Zildjian and the fact that they were playing our cymbals and would use them exclusively on a TV show, major clinics, things like that. As the number of endorsers grew, many of the decisions as to which artists to sign were left to me, and Armand always trusted my judgment. Along with the artist relations program, I was also involved in a lot of the advertising with the ad companies and doing quite a bit of traveling.

"As the company grew, I felt it was important to get drummers signed up even if they weren't big stars. Get drummers from all walks of life—educators, set players, percussionists, orchestral players, it really didn't matter to me—I just wanted to get them on the Zildjian brand and team. I used common sense, observing what they were doing, where they were playing, and how they could contribute to Zildjian's growth. I wanted Zildjian to be diversified, so in those early days I considered everyone who could contribute something to the company artist program."

As the years went on, the agreement became a little more sophisticated and involved but still never really became a real legal document. The agreement meant that Zildjian could use the endorsee's name in advertising and literature, and it requested that Zildjian be recognized on recordings, which resulted in the company's receiving copies of gold and platinum records. Many of these records were dedicated to Lennie, and he had a wall full of them in his office.

"As the artist relations program became bigger and bigger, more drummers would send in their resumés, many from overseas, and I would read them all and check them out to see what the drummer was all about. If I felt that they were sincere and had some merit, I would

One of Lennie's early Zildjian endorsers, (Lennie's sister) Margie Roman, drummer and vocalist, with husband and pianist, Nicky Fabiano

give them a call. When I took on an endorsee, I would invite them to the factory, set up a program for them, and help them pick out their own special cymbal setup. Over the years, this developed into hundreds of drummers coming by the factory, and as the reputation of the program grew, I became the cymbal guru, with all of the cats wanting their cymbals to be 'specially selected by Lennie D. In fact, a brochure was printed in the early '70s with the title 'Let the Experts Talk to the Experts About Cymbals.' It was full of wonderful photos of me with the great drummers.

"All of this would have been difficult if I wasn't a drummer and if I didn't love what I was doing, plus taking everything very seriously. I was into all types of music; I had no problems working with country-and-western drummers, reggae and Latin drummers, and could relate to all of those different cats. I had to get them inspired and happy with their sound. I needed to stay in touch with these guys to take care of their cymbal needs. For some of our endorsees it became like getting your car tuned up—every six months or so you need to get your car spinning like a top, and these drummers were like that. They liked to get involved with some different sounds, make a few changes—like getting a new suit, looking a little different, feeling a little different behind the drums. That always kept them fresh and their creative juices flowing. In essence I became their cymbal doctor and mechanic for these tune-ups, and all the cats came to depend on me for this.

"As the artist relations program took off, the special selection program also grew to the point where certain cymbals were stamped 'Special Selection by Lennie DiMuzio.' But after awhile this became a problem because dealers wanted to sell cymbals with the special selection stamp on them. Finally, we had to eliminate the stamping because it was creating a lot of problems at the dealer level.

"During all of these years of growing the artist relations program and developing a lot of new products for the company, I continued playing on weekends. I joined a group called The Three of Us, which included my friend Ken Drinan on bass, who was also a great singer (he sounded like Perry Como), and a virtuoso pianist, Nick Lombardo, who was also a talented singer. The Three of Us played in many Boston lounges, including one fine South Shore establishment called Casa Ber rini, an Italian restaurant with great food and a hip crowd where we played for over 15 years.

The Three of Us band: Nick Lombardo, Lennie, Kenny Drinan

He's the guy Buddy Rich, Billy Cobham, Louie Bellson, and Harvey Mason talk to.

There's a little bit of Lennie DiMuzio in almost every great drummer's sound.

Some of the world's finest artists trust Lennie and his staff to select the cymbals they will use. And when they want advice on cymbals, Lennie DiMuzio is the man whose advice they want.

"His ear is impeccable," Alan Dawson says.

"Lennie DiMuzio is the only guy besides me who knows the individual sound I'm after," Louie Bellson says.

Lennie is Manager of Sales and Selection at the Zildjian Company. For seventeen years he has been practically a member of the Zildjian family, working closely alongside Armand and Bob Zildjian.

He is also a professional drummer whose career began at 12 and continued through high school, the armed services, the New England Conservatory, and the Berklee College of Music. He performs frequently in the Boston area.

But the part of his job that Lennie likes most is talking to drummers. So come and talk with him about cymbals. And let him put a little bit of Lennie DiMuzio into your sound.

A promotional flyer created by Zildjian and used as an informational handout at Lennie's clinics

Two of my closest friends, Lou Magnano, a great jazz vibist from Braintree, MA, and Rebecca Paris, one of Boston's finest jazz vocalists, would often come by and sit in. Rebecca had great natural talent in her youth, and today she remains a major performing and recording artist. Unfortunately we lost Lou Magnano ten years ago in a terrible auto accident, and every- one misses his lov-ing, smiling face and great talent.

"Playing was becoming a bit of a scheduling problem due to my workload at Zildjian, along with my gigging on the weekends, but I always felt that it was important to keep up my chops, not only for me as a drummer, but for my position at Zildjian. I would always take new cymbals we were developing to the clubs and field-test them. We would do a lot of sound analysis, and there was a lot of experimenting at that time. Keeping my playing in shape was important for demonstrating cymbals at clinics, and shows, and especially the big showcases that Zildjian was putting on around the country. So, all in all, I felt that the playing aspect was very important."

Rebecca Paris, one of Boston's finest jazz vocalists (circa 1980)

John DeChristopher

Zildjian has also announced its expansion of its Artist Relations and Education programs, together with increased emphasis on new product research and development. John DeChristopher will be joining Zildjian's worldwide artist relations team, working closely with Lennie DiMuzio

Percussive Arts Society press release

The artist relations program was getting bigger, and the advent of rock 'n' roll brought a new dimension, so eventually Lennie needed additional assistance. In the summer of 1989, John DeChristopher joined the worldwide artist relations team, working the U.S. with Lennie and Mike Morse, who was in charge of Zildjian's West Coast office. Johnny D, a skilled drummer, in addition to working with the rock drummers, became part of the product development team reporting to Colin Schofield. At this time, Lennie became the head of the newly created education program department that was established to foster "Zildjian's support of all aspects of the percussive arts," as referenced in the press release shown above.

Colin Schofield, Dave Weckl, Murray Kramer, Mike Morse, Lennie

Some of Lennie's Drummer Friends

Ron Thompson, drummer with Willie Nelson, and Boxcar Willie (1985)

Danny Seraphine of the band Chicago with Lennie at the Zildjian factory (circa 1975)

Lennie, Billy Gibson of Huey Lewis and the News, Billy's dad

Mel Brown of the Temptations

Alan White of Yes

Greg Warner, drummer for Dionne Warwick

Chapter 8

Cozy and Philly Joe: A Pair to Draw From

Cozy Cole

One of the great drummers, Cozy Cole, was born in East Orange, New Jersey, October 17, 1909. He epitomized the rudimental drummer and applied that style of playing to many genres that spanned many decades. Just as Mr. Zildjian was always a well-dressed gentleman, the same could be said about Cozy. In fact, Cozy, was one of Mr. Z's favorite drummers. One of the interesting tidbits about Cozy was his love of learning about the drums. He studied with Saul Goodman of the New York Philharmonic in the '40s and opened a drum studio in the '50s with his good friend Gene Krupa. Over many years, he was a sideman for Cab Calloway, Lionel Hampton, and Louis Armstrong and led a group with Benny Goodman. Lennie picks up the story.

"Cozy used to come to the old factory in North Quincy. Mr. Avedis Zildjian would always try to be around because he really liked Cozy. He was always a Dapper Dan, a very respectable gentleman, and everyone liked Cozy because he was kind and gentle.

"Now, I have a lot of stories about Cozy, but this time I learned a new phrase. He came to the old factory one day and he walked in, and although we knew he was coming, we didn't expect him that early. In those days, as you entered the main door, you had the shipping room, the bathroom, and the vault was attached to the shipping room. Then there was a corridor and you went upstairs to where all the offices were. So Cozy comes in, walks over, and wants to know what we were talking about. When Cozy walked in, Armand and I happened to be standing by the bathroom laughing like crazy, and he wanted to know what was so funny. At that moment Armand happened to be in his shorts and getting dressed. He tells Cozy that he is going to the doctor to get a check-up and says, 'Well, Cozy, sometimes a guy just has to take care of things because you never know what can come up. You know what I mean?' and Cozy says, 'Yeah, I know what you mean. One day chicken, the next day feathers.' This was one of Cozy's favorite expressions for 'one day you got it and next day you don't'; could be your health, your wealth, or whatever. That's where I picked up this saying, and I still use it today.

"We took Cozy out to lunch, then came back to the factory and picked out some cymbals for him. We'd always go and hear Cozy. He very often played Boston's old Hi Hat Club with his great quartet."

Cozy Cole

Cozy was the first African-American musician on a

Max Roach

network TV staff band when he joined CBS in 1943. He was also the drummer on the Broadway show *Carmen Jones*. In the 1960s, when Lennie met him, he had joined Jonah Jones and also had reunited with Stuff Smith and Cab Calloway. That group remained together through the '70s and in 1978 was given an honorary degree of Doctor of Musical Arts at Capital University in Columbus, Ohio. As Lennie has pointed out, Cozy was always a gentleman, and all of his musician contemporaries stated he was one of the best. Cozy Cole passed away in Columbus in January 1981 at the age of 71.

The drummer in the legendary Miles Davis Quintet, Philly Joe Jones, was born in his namesake city on July 15, 1923. After learning the rudiments of music from his mother, he learned the rudiments of drumming from Cozy Cole and Charles Wilcoxon, and got advice from Art Blakey and Max Roach. Philly played everything from rhythm and blues to tunes written by Monk, Bud Powell, and the other greats of the day. In his hometown he backed stars such as Dexter Gordon and Fats Navarro. His bio tells the story of him getting fired from his job as a streetcar driver because he would stop the streetcar and hop off to sit in at a jazz club he'd pass, sometimes playing an entire set and forgetting the riders on the car.

Lennie recalls a couple of stories that seem to hint that Philly never got enough sleep.

"When we were in the old factory back in the '60s and '70s, Philly Joe came out only two or three times to pick out some cymbals. This one time he was playing in a Boston jazz club called Conley's, which was quite an historical club, very popular, and a lot of small groups played there. Philly was appearing there with Red Garland, and I was in the audience, sitting there amazed at his ability and talent. The group took a tune for about 15 or 20 minutes, and then the cats got off the stage and left Philly there to solo. At that time, he had a really small kit consisting of a 20-inch ride, a pair of hi-hats, a snare drum, and a bass drum; that was it. However, Philly must have soloed for about ten minutes. He was sitting against the wall while playing, and he suddenly leaned back and fell asleep. The cats came back onstage, woke him up, led him off the stage and right to

Max Roach, Papa Jo Jones

Max Roach, Lennie

the bar. I was sitting at the bar, of course, and Philly sat down beside me, and I asked him if he wanted a drink, and he said sure. He gave the bartender his order, who returned with a glass of milk and a double scotch. I'd never seen anyone drink a glass of milk with their shot of scotch. Apparently, Philly had a bad stomach, I don't know, but different strokes for different folks." Lennie says that last bit with a chuckle.

After the company moved from Quincy to Norwell, Armand had his new office outfitted with a Steinway piano. He would play during the day and occasionally pick up one of his trumpets and blow a chorus.

"When Philly came to the factory, he would always end up in Armand's office," Lennie continues. "The office had a little bar, the beautiful Steinway grand piano, and a set of drums. We would have a few cocktails and listen to Philly play the piano. He was an accomplished piano player. That's probably why he was such a great drummer. The one day I'm referring to, we fixed Philly up with some cymbals, and after he played the piano, he was getting ready to leave, probably around 4:00 or 4:30, and we went outside and he got into his car. We all went back inside to Armand's office, talked about Philly and some other cats for about an hour. I happened to look out the window and saw Philly's car was still there. I went outside, looked into the car, and Philly was sound asleep—out like a light. I woke him up, made sure he was ok, got him some coffee and got him back on the road. Can you believe it?"

Philly was recognized as an outstanding drummer by *Down Beat* magazine in the late '50s and early '60s, but as some new, younger players came onto the scene, his career began to fade. In the mid-60s he moved to England, did some teaching and playing, but after awhile moved back to New York. He continued playing into the '80s, passing away August 30, 1985. Philly was a trendsetter, especially with Miles, where his rhythm section work with bassist Paul Chambers and pianist Red Garland is historic. Philly and Chambers were also the rhythm section for many of the bebop stars such as Sonny Rollins and Art Pepper. Philly Joe Jones—one of the giants.

I have to insert a little story here, since I worked with Philly Joe in the '70s when I was with Premier drums. Philly called and said he and his wife were going to drive down from Chicago to Elkhart, Indiana, where the Selmer Company was located. Selmer was distributing Premier at that time.

They showed up around lunch time, and I noticed Joe didn't have a tooth in his head—they had all been pulled. I asked him if he wanted some lunch and assumed he would say soup or something soft. Joe said, "I want a steak." I replied, "Joe, forgive me, but you haven't got a tooth in your head." "I don't care," said Joe. "I'm waiting for my new choppers to come in, and I'm dying for a steak." So we went to a local restaurant and he ordered a glass of wine and a nice steak. He eventually finished the whole thing, and every one got a kick out of it.

Papa Jo Jones, Frank Ippolito, Philly Joe Jones

Gene Krupa (standing) and Buddy Rich (1955)

Buddy Rich, Papa Jo Jones, Freddie Gruber, New York, NY (circa 1980)

Chapter 9

Gene Krupa: Got the Drums Out in Front

Gene Krupa twirls

Gene Krupa was born in Chicago January 15, 1909, the youngest of Bartley and Ann Krupa's nine children. Although he started on the sax in grade school, at the age of 11 he picked the drums because they were the cheapest instrument in the music store where his brother worked. Gene's first kit was a set of Japanese drums consisting of a bass drum, a cymbal, a wood block, and a snare. According to Gene, they cost "16 beans." Gene is considered the father of the modern drumset because he convinced the Slingerland Drum Company to make tunable tom-toms. Also, Avedis Zildjian asked Gene to help design the contemporary hi-hat stand. Gene had a heart attack in 1960 but returned to playing a few months later. During that time, he and Lennie met.

"We always had fun when Gene came to town, usually with a small group, and he always came out to the factory. He and I hit it off really well as he was a respectable, warm, loving guy. Easy to talk to, no big airs or a big ego—he knew who he was, but he was always willing to learn more. He just got respect for who he was. We'd be downstairs picking cymbals—not very difficult as Gene knew the sound he wanted and I eventually also got to know the sound he wanted, and it was pretty much a simplified set-up: one 20-inch ride, a couple of crash cymbals, a splash, a swish ride, and a pair of 14-inch hi-hats.

"I'd sit down on a chair and go through the hi-hats, matching up his style, and I learned a lot of tricks on the hats from watching all the cats when they came by. I was playing pretty good then and was able to pick up a lot of the techniques they were using, and all the little fancy things they would do. So, I would sit there and play, and I had a lot of my own ideas—I was all over the hats, underneath and cross-sticking. Gene would sit there and say, 'My God, what are you doing? I've never seen that before. How did you do that?' I would slow down what I was doing and try to break it down so Gene could get what I was playing. He was so enthusiastic about learning some new tricks and beats and some of the things I was doing. In those days, cats weren't playing that much solo stuff on the hats, but I played them so frequently by themselves in my testing that I played them almost like I was playing a full set—up and down, over and under, and stuff like that. Gene, who was always an

Papa Jo Jones presents Gene Krupa with an achievement award at the Newport Jazz Festival (July 7, 1970)

innovator and searching for new things, seemed to really like my stuff, and we spent some time goofing around with licks. Over time we became very close friends."

According to Lennie, great drummers such as Gene and Buddy seldom broke cymbals. Because of their style and touch, they knew how to extract the sound from the cymbals correctly. As a result they returned very few broken ones to the factory.

"Once when Gene visited the factory, I was playing in a very nice club in Boston, and they had a beautiful restaurant, so Armand and I decided to take him there to dinner. The opposite band was playing that night, and as soon as I put out the word that Gene was there, the people started going crazy. They were coming by and Gene was signing autographs, the owner kept coming by and bringing us drinks, and they wanted Gene to get up and play. So we went into the lounge and Gene sat in and played with the band and got a standing ovation. It was a wonderful thing, and he was so congenial and willing to go along with the flow. The cats in the band were thrilled.

"Gene always played Slingerland drums throughout his career, which, I think, was the main reason for the growth of that company. He was always featured in their advertising, and when the big NAMM trade shows would be in Chicago, Slingerland and Zildjian would have parties at the Hilton Hotel in one of its big ballrooms, and Gene would always come and play for the big bash.

A young Gene Krupa (1955)

Gene Krupa and Buddy Rich (1955)

"I have to tell you about one of those parties we had with Slingerland and Gene that was outta sight. It was at the Hilton, and Zildjian and Slingerland were footing everything—the advertisements, the food, the booze, and it was open to all the dealers—everything was on the house. The opening band was the Dick Long Band, a local band, and Don Osborne, a VP at Slingerland, played drums and Gene's quartet was to follow. We had four bars set up around the room and a big food table, with carving meat, you know, buns and rolls—food and booze all night. After the Dick Long Band, Gene's group started to perform.

Jerry Lewis, Gene Krupa, Buddy Rich (1973)

"Bob Holly, who was in charge of our advertising, decided to set up a photo shoot with Gene after the show down on the dance floor. They moved Gene's kit into place, got the dealers lined up, and one by one they would stand behind Gene, get their picture taken, and then move to another table and leave their name. Man, everyone was having fun, the booze was flowing, it was getting wild, and we had a line a mile long. We didn't know there was another

Gene Krupa and Lennie (1970)

convention going on upstairs in one of the smaller ballrooms—a gathering of plumbers and steamfitters. These guys started coming down to our party, drinking our booze, and crashing the line to get their pictures taken with Gene. Meanwhile, I was slipping Gene scotch and sodas and he was beginning to feel the booze. Though he looked good when the photo shoot started, after about an hour or so, we were all falling over the drums. I was holding him up, the plumbers and steamfitters were jumping the line and then giving their names, we kept taking pictures—everything was discombobulated. We were all in the wrappers, and we finally had to take Gene back to his hotel and put him to bed. When we got the proofs, we couldn't identify anybody. There would be a dealer, then a couple of steamfitters, then a dealer—what a nightmare."

Gene was always a hit at the many shows he attended, so we decided to take him along with us to Germany for the Frankfurt Music Fair (at that time the largest music instrument convention in the world). On the plane ride over, Gene was not feeling well. He seemed to be getting really sick. He ended up staying in his hotel room for the whole show, after which we took him back home. He kept feeling sick and went to the hospital. There, after much testing, he was diagnosed with leukemia. Sadly, that was the beginning of the end. He didn't play much after that, and most unfortunately his illness continued to worsen.

Gene's close friend Sonny Igoe

Gene Krupa tribute party in New York City: From left: Lennie, Danny of Manny's Music Store, Buddy Rich's manager Stan, Armand Zildjian, Zutty Singleton at head of table, Maurie Lishon, Frank Ippolito, Cliff Leaman. Far right: Roy Knapp, Bobby Columby (1973)

"All the cats in New York, led by Henry Adler and Manny (of Manny's Drum Shop), decided to throw a big party for Gene. We had an incredible gathering in New York, and many stars came to the festivities. Some that I can remember were Jerry Lewis, Joe Morello, Buddy Rich, Zutty Singleton, Bobby Columby, Cliff Leaman, Frank Ippolito, Roy Knapp, Sonny Igoe, and Papa Jo Jones. It was an incredible party. Less than three months later, he passed away."

On October 16, 1973, plagued with leukemia and emphysema, Gene died of a heart attack. There were two funerals for him, one in New York and another in Chicago. "Armand and I went to the funeral in New York and it was very emotional and moving, with a huge group of people in attendance. For Gene's funeral in Chicago, Armand and I, plus Don Osborne and Barrett Deems, were pallbearers. They decided to ship the body by air to Chicago for burial. On the trip, something happened to the casket—we won't be using the word coffin—the lid or something came open and the body got disfigured or something, so they had a closed-casket service and wake. We met up with Don Osborne, and because it was going to be a tough scene, we had a few pops before the wake and, like, you know, we were getting in

Some of the many guests at Gene Krupa's tribute party in New York City (1973), that included Joe Morello, Buddy Rich, Airto, Papa Joe, Jerry Lewis, Zutty Singleton, Roy Knapp, Bobby Columby, Don Osborne, Frank Ippolito, Cliff Leeman, Henry Adler, Danny Bergour (Manny's Drum Shop) Sonny Igoe, and Cathy Rich.
(Photography and collage by friend and drummer Peter Lanzarone)

The very debonair Gene Krupa at the height of his career

the wrappers, and when we were walking by the casket, Armand said, 'Man, if you think Gene is stiff, you should take a look at us.' That sort of broke up the tension.

"One of the most interesting things that I remember about Gene Krupa is the way he tuned his drums and how much time he spent to get them to sound right. I personally was with Gene one night in Chicago when he was the guest soloist at a big NAMM Convention. He was playing with the Dick Long Big Band in the ballroom of the Hilton Hotel, and the place was packed to the rafters. Gene's drum tech was a dude called Crip. He would set his drums up on the stage and let Gene come up and tune them personally. I went up on stage with Gene and he started tuning each drum in intervals of a third. Then Gene asked me to play the drums while he

Lifelong friends and drumming greats Buddy Rich and Gene Krupa (circa 1971)

The NAMM Show All-Star Band's rhythm section: L-R Armand Zildjian, Lennie, Don Osborne, Gene Krupa, "Boom-Boom" Browning

walked around the stage, listening and coming back to make adjustments on the drums. After that, he asked me to sit down at the drumset and play the set when he got to the rear of the ballroom. As he walked around the rear of the ballroom, listening to the drums, he would yell to me onstage and tell me what to do to correct the pitch. Gene was more concerned about the drum sound from the back of the hall than from up front, whereas most drummers only tune their drums for the stage sound and forget about the sound in the back of the hall.

Gene Krupa at a photo session during the NAMM Convention.
Standing L-R: Unknown guests, Lennie (third from left), Roy Knapp, Marty Lishon, Lloyd McCausland, Fred Hoey, unknown guest (1965)

"I always felt that it was rather unique and different, but Gene clearly knew what he wanted and how to get a great sound. He made those Slingerlands sing, sing, sing.

"Gene Krupa is still remembered as the man who made the drumset a solo instrument, and all the greatest drummers of that era remember him as not only a wonderful man and a great player, but also as someone who brought the drums to the forefront. Gene is buried at the Holy Cross Cemetery in Calumet City, Illinois."

Armand, Lennie, and Don Osborne Sr. (President of the Slingerland Drum Co. (1965)

Chapter 10

Hair Today, Gone Tomorrow

Guy Bognano (sax), Frank DiMare, Armand Zildjian (piano), Lennie DiMuzio (drums)

The heading for this chapter also could have been one of Lennie's sayings, "Let the hair go with the hide." However, this little chapter is intended as a breather from cymbal and drummer talk. Even during the best of times, his hairstyle would never have made it into any fashion magazine, but Lennie's toupee, or rug, escapades are a barrel of laughs.

"Jack Adams, owner of Jack's Drum Shop in Boston, who has already been mentioned, apparently had a collection of real 'bad toupees' of various colors, and when traveling in his convertible with the top down, the wind caused his rug to sort of hover over his head and would flip-flop up and down. What a sight to see.

"Rugs were popular in the early '60s, and maybe I was influenced by Jack Adams, but a cousin of mine who was a hairstylist told me I should let him fit me with a toupee and I'd look fantastic. He said, 'You'll look 20 years younger.' Oh my nerves. So, between my cousin and Jack, I got the name of the fella who made Jack's rugs and went to him and asked if he would make me a rug. He said sure. He was a bass player and made rugs on the side. For about couple hundred bucks I got fitted for a rug. After looking at their rugs, I should have known better.

"First you have to have a portion of the front part of your head shaved; then you need a mirror, a brush, a comb, and some special adhesive tape. Then you need to learn how to position it properly, which was really a pain in the ass—what a nuisance. I get the damn thing settled on my head, and I'll never forget

Rare photo of Lennie sporting his cool rug (1970)

the first time I wore it—it was at a MENC show in Boston. Several people came up to me and asked if I had lost some weight; you really look good, man; you got a new hairstyle. And I said I had got myself a short haircut and found a new barber.

"After the show this particular night, several of us, Mr. Zildjian, Al Moffit Sr., Joe Rache with the Slingerland Drum Company, and others, were going out to dinner. We were parked at the Sheraton Hotel next to the convention center and across the street from the Hilton. I told them to meet me at the front entrance and I would go and get the car out of the garage. Now, it was one of those nights when the wind was blowing like crazy, with little twisters between the buildings, and I pulled the car in front of the hotel and went in to get the guys. They were all standing there by the swinging door, and the wind comes, blows the rug off my head, and blows it down the street. I'm running down the street trying to catch the damn thing, they're all peeing in their pants, laughing like crazy. I finally catch it, pick it up, and bring it back. Two or three of them didn't even know I was wearing a rug. Talk about being embarrassed. You can't put it back on because you need the mirror and all that stuff, so the rest of the night I had to sit there with my shaved head and the rug stuck in my pocket. That was strike number one.

"After that episode, I was thinking about not wearing the rug again, but a couple of months later, my cousin the hairstylist convinced me that I wasn't putting it tight enough on my head and would have to use more tape. So I had another spot shaved on my head, got more tape, and was ready to give it another try.

"The next incident was when I was catching a shuttle to fly to New York. Back in those days there weren't any, you know, those jetways, so you had to walk outside about 50 feet to the plane. There were about 50 or 60 of us lined up, I've got my luggage in one hand and carrying a newspaper in the other. We go out the door to board the plane when a wind gust comes up and blows my rug down the fucking runway. I drop my luggage and paper and I'm running down the tarmac, my rug is tumbling and tumbling, and I must have run about 100 feet to catch it, the people are all breaking up, laughing, and I was sick with embarrassment, sweating, stuck the rug in my pocket, and said to myself that's it, never again.

"The last time I wore the rug, Armand and I were at a convention and we were sharing a room at the hotel. We were out partying, I had the rug on, we got back to the room and went to bed. The next morning I wake up, the damn rug is lying across my face. Armand looks over, picks the rug off my nose and says, 'It looked like a muskrat had died on your face during the night.' I said that's it, I'm not wearing this piece of crap any longer. It was three strikes and you're out. No more rug stories."

Lennie sporting his new hair piece during a visit to Las Vegas with his Uncle Tony Portanova, who was a card dealer, and Armand (1970).

One last hair incident. This was after the rugs. At a Zildjian Day in Dallas, Lennie and I shared a suite and we each had a bedroom. I got up in the morning and walked out to the living room, and Lennie came out of his room with this long bunch of hair sticking out to one side. I started to laugh because he looked like he had stuck his finger in a light socket, and I said, "Lennie, your hair!" He said, "It's okay, Jim, I'm going to comb it." He proceeded to part his hair just above his right ear, leaving a few strands above the ear and then flipping the rest over his bald spot. I laughed so hard I cried.

Buddy Rich (1970)

Buddy Rich (1971)

Buddy Rich at the Statler in Cleveland (1985)

Chapter 11

Buddy Rich: Drumming Legend

Buddy Rich relaxing at home (circa 1967)

"If I had to choose the greatest drummer that ever lived, Jim, I would have to say Buddy Rich," Lennie reminisces. "In any profession the world always remember the giants, and he was a giant in our lifetime. Being with Buddy during my career was certainly an honor and a great blessing. I was very fortunate to be a part of his life, and I will always cherish his memory, the good times, his friendship, and his relentless passion for drumming."

Buddy Rich was born to vaudevillians Robert and Bess Rich on September 30, 1917. At the age of four, billed as "Traps the Drum Wonder," he began a fabulous career that spanned seven decades. Much has been written about Buddy—his caustic, biting tongue and those famous band bus tapes—but this is Lennie's story and his memories.

"Armand and I shared so many of Buddy's incredible performances, and we could hardly wait for Buddy to come to Boston. We would go anywhere to see him play, and for 27 years we couldn't figure out where he got all of his energy, his drive, and his power. Where the hell was it coming from? Sometimes we thought he must have come from another planet.

"One of my first experiences with Buddy at Zildjian was when he drove the band bus to

Star drummer, Buddy Rich—now out of Marines after two years as judo instructor—sits in for that equally great hide beater, Jo Jones, during a visit with Count Basie at California's Ocean Park Aragon Ballroom.

Buddy Rich, Papa Jo Jones

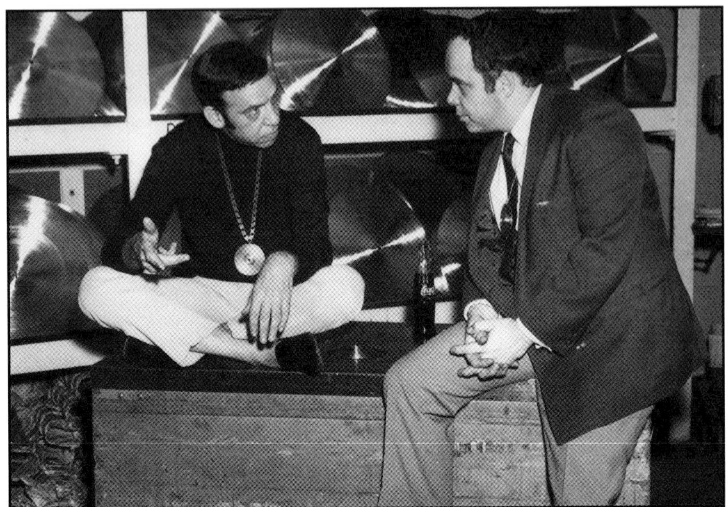

Buddy Rich, Lennie (1970)

the factory. He just wanted to hang out for a few hours and pick out a few cymbals. So, you know, we gave him a tour of the factory, and then Buddy, Armand, and I went to one of the testing rooms and started to pick out some ride cymbals. Buddy always knew what he was looking for. I would put a ride on a cymbal stand and he would play it and say, 'No, not that one,' so I would get another and he would say he wanted more crash or more ping. Or he might say it wasn't high enough, so after awhile, I raised the cymbal stand and asked him if that was high enough. Buddy looked at Armand and said, 'Where did you get this wise guy? Does he think he's funny?' We all broke up, started laughing, and on that day began our lifetime friendship.

Buddy Rich (1970)

"After I got to know Buddy and his playing style really well, it was easy to select cymbals for him. His basic setup never changed: 13-inch New Beat hi-hats, 18-inch thin crash on his left side, 8-inch splash right in front of him, a 20-inch ping ride to his immediate right, and above that an 18-inch medium-thin crash. About five years before he died, influenced by his buddy Mel Lewis, he started using a 22-inch Swish Knocker over his second floor tom. He loved to smack that swish at the end of a chart, letting everyone know the tune was over. He was an incredible cymbal player—he played all over the hi-hats and did tricks with that little 8-inch splash cymbal. Come to think of it, you know, he never changed his drum set-up either—just the name on the drums."

Lennie's Buddy stories run the gamut from one-liners to the band's appearances and some insight into the rapport among Buddy, Lennie, and Armand. Let's start off with one anecdote when Buddy and his band were performing at Lennie's on the Turnpike, a club on the outskirts of Boston where Buddy was featured many times because the owner, Lennie Sokoloff, really loved him.

Buddy Rich testing cymbals (1970)

"Lennie Sokoloff was a frustrated drummer, heavy into drummers, and had a lot of clinics in his club. Buddy performed there quite a bit, and everyone looked forward to it and the place would always be packed. Of course, Armand and I always had a front-row table reserved, and we were right up against the bandstand so we could converse with Buddy—the stage was about a foot off the floor. One time Buddy came out from the dressing room and was ready to get behind the drums. The fashion in those days was wearing boots with high heels, and Buddy had those type of boots on. Armand couldn't resist and he said, 'Hey, Buddy, how are you going to play the bass drum with those high heels?'

Don Osborne, Buddy Rich, Lionel Hampton, Johnny Martin, Armand Zildjian, Lennie (1975)

Buddy looked at Armand and said, 'What the hell you talking about? The shoes don't play the goddamn drum, the foot does. Where the hell are you from?' Armand and I fell apart laughing."

This was also the night that demonstrated the band members' futures were always precarious.

"That particular night, Buddy had just hired a new guitar player. A nice kid, a graduate from Berklee and a good player. Now, Jim, you have to picture this—the guitar player was sitting right in front of Buddy, and his amp was close to the bass drum. The band was into one of Buddy's rip-roaring tunes when all of a sudden Buddy gives a loud whack on the snare drum, which was his way of stopping the band. He stops playing, the band stops playing, and all the cats knew something was wrong. Buddy looks down at the guitar player and says, 'Hey, you—you on the guitar.' The kid turns around and says, 'Yes, Buddy, what's wrong?' Buddy replies, 'Show me in the music where it says help the drummer. Knock it off.' I guess the cat was overplaying and Buddy got pissed and was laying down the law. Everybody broke up.

"We were in the dressing room during intermission. We're rappin'—Armand, Buddy and me—and Buddy calls his road manager, Steve Peck, and tells him to go get the guitar player because he wants to talk to him. Steve brings in the kid and he's standing there and Buddy says, 'Hey, look, next set get that goddamn amplifier away from the bass drum and put it somewhere.' The kid says, 'There's no room on the stage, Buddy. Where the hell can I put it?' Buddy says, 'I said get that amp away from me!' Once again the kid wants to know where to put it, and I can see that Buddy is getting furious. Buddy says, 'I'll tell you where to put it. Put it out in the parking lot and sit on it, 'cause you're fired. Get outta here.' Armand and I almost fell off our chairs. The poor guitar player was totally stunned, didn't know what to do, the poor kid. Buddy dumped him on the spot. He was hard on the players and you didn't dare oppose him. But Buddy was hard on himself as well."

Buddy ran a tight ship, and his ability to snap out one-liners was legendary. He was witty and could zing them quickly. Although he knew the band needed an audience, when it came to the music the band was going to perform, he called the shots. Lennie recalls a couple of instances concerning requests:

"One time a woman came up and asked Buddy if the band would play 'In the Mood,' the old Glenn Miller standard. Buddy got red in the face and said, 'In the Mood'—we don't take requests, ma'am. You'll have to wait for Guy Lombardo to come by to hear that.' Another time a disc jockey came up and asked Buddy if they were going to hear some new music that night, and Buddy said sarcastically, 'What's wrong with my old music?'

Buddy Rich's first clinic performance in Boston, MA (1970) at the Cheri Biltmore Hotel

Buddy Rich; Lennie (standing); Roy Burns, Rogers Drum Co. VP; Ben Strauss; wives; Dick Seibert (1974)

"Buddy was strict with his band and also strict with the audience, and he hated it when people would be talking, you know, conversing when the band was playing. That really annoyed him. Another time he stopped the band in the middle of a tune and looked down at two couples sitting near the bandstand who were gabbing away. Buddy actually waited for about four or five minutes until they looked up trying to figure out why the band had stopped. Buddy said, 'Excuse me, are we disturbing your conversation? If you would like to chat, why don't you four go out in the parking lot where you belong.' The audience broke up—it was hilarious."

The Buddy Rich Band over all of those years played many great concerts, and it would be impossible to recall them all, but Lennie has fond memories of two times when Buddy and his band were teamed with another great group, the Louis Bellson Big Band.

"One particularly great performance was when Buddy's band and Louie Bellson's band were playing opposite each other at the Newport Jazz Festival. Because Newport was close to Boston, Lennie Sokoloff wanted to have a gala event at one of the big ballrooms. He managed to get Buddy's band and Louie's together on the same stage. What an incredible evening. The place was packed to the rafters and both bands tore it up. For the finale, they decided to have both bands play the same chart together. Buddy and Louie were on stage chatting and cutting up, and Louie looked over at Buddy and said, 'Let's have some fun. Why don't we switch sets. I'll play your drums and you play mine.' Well, you know, Louie's set had twice the number of drums and many more cymbals, and Buddy said, 'Hey, Louie, you gonna give me a saddle to ride that set?' It was pretty funny, but they didn't switch sets because it didn't make any sense. Just another example of a great one-liner by Buddy.

"In the '80s there was another event that took place at Lennie's on the Turnpike. Both Buddy's band and Maynard Ferguson's band were at the Newport Jazz Festival, so Lennie Sokoloff managed to get both bands to come down and perform at his club. That was a glorious night, because both bands were tearing down the house, and during one set, Maynard came out and blew with Buddy's band—an incredible performance. But something else happened that night that was unusual. I had invited Terri Lyne Carrington and her folks to be my guests at the concert. We had told Buddy that Terri, she was 11 years old, had played with Dizzy Gillespie, Clark Terry, and other New York cats, and so he decided she should play with his band. Well, Jim, she got up there behind Buddy's drums and really played—she got a standing ovation when she finished. After that night, I signed her up as an endorsee, and Slingerland also gave

Armand Zildjian, Buddy Rich, Lennie at Buddy's 60th Birthday Party in New York City

Terri Lyne Carrington and her father Matt ("Sonny"), one of Boston's finest saxophone players, meet with Lennie at the Zildjian office (1977)

her an endorsement because Buddy was playing their drums at that time. That was a great night for her and her folks, and now, of course, she is a big star, great player, and perhaps the finest female jazz drummer in the world."

Throughout his playing career, Buddy occasionally gave clinics, although in truth it really wasn't his bag. Following is a story about Buddy's somewhat short clinic career.

"Buddy needed some additional money to get his band back on the road as they needed a new bus, new charts, and so forth, that would total some $10,000. The Slingerland boys and Armand and I came up with a solution.

"We decided to put Buddy out on a clinic tour at $1,000 per clinic, up to $10,000. Buddy said that would be great, he would knock out the ten clinics, have his dough, and would be happy. The first clinic was to be staged in Boston at the old Sheraton Biltmore Hotel. We had flyers and posters sent out, we really pumped it up and had a great response. The room was packed. Buddy had brought his combo, and they were going to play a few tunes to open the show. Following that we were going to bring out Donnie Osborne to play with Buddy's group and show off the kid. Donnie's dad was Don Osborne, the president of Slingerland, and Donnie grew up being a Buddy Rich clone, right down to the sweat towel on the bass drum. Donnie was a good player and eventually became Mel Torme's drummer. After Donnie performed, it was time for the clinic. Little did we know—oh my nerves.

"We were all sitting down in front—me, Armand, Jack Adams, Don, Donnie and some other important Boston people. Buddy comes out, puts out his cigarette, stands in front of the mike and says, 'Okay, what do you wanna do? What do you wanna see? Any questions?' It being his first clinic, Buddy was far from being a polished clinician. Finally a kid raises his hand and asks Buddy if he could ask a question. Buddy says yeah and the kid asks, 'What do you think about George Stone's book *Stick Control*?' Buddy looks at the kid and replies, 'I never think about it.' That was it—question answered. The kid shuffles back to his seat and that sort of opened everyone's eyes.

"Another kid asked, 'What do you think about Stanley Spector's new foot pedal?' Buddy says, 'You mean the one that goes sideways and you have to pump it? You don't play it, you have to pump it? I think the guy's nuts. I'd like to see him play it.'

"There were other questions, and Buddy was killing the audience with his answers, and Armand, Don, and I were turning red, and then Buddy says, 'Does anyone want to play the drums?' Now, you know, Buddy wasn't going to talk about technique or how to hold

Lennie and Terri testing some new cymbals

Standing: Sol Gubin, Armand Zildjian, Henry Adler, Ed Shaughnessy. Sitting: Buddy Rich, Sonny Igoe, Lennie (circa 1970)

the sticks—any of that stuff. So a little kid yells, 'Oh, yes, Mr. Rich, I would love to play them.' So the kid goes onstage, sits behind the drums, and beats the shit out of 'em for about five minutes. Buddy is leaning over the piano, his head in his hands, going 'Oh my god.' The kid gets done playing and Buddy says, 'What's your name?' The kid tells him Billy Burke. Then Buddy says, 'Who's your teacher?' The kid says Stanley Spector. Then Buddy unloads on him with, 'You tell him that I told you you stink and you gotta learn how to play the drums the right way. Get outta here.' That ended the talking, Jim. Then Buddy finally played and that said it all.

"We pow-wowed afterward and decided rather than have Buddy do the other nine clinics why not just give him the ten grand and forget about it. So that's what happened—we paid Buddy off and said, 'The hell with the clinics.'

After that incident, Buddy endorsed Rogers drums for awhile until, according to Don Canedy, who was involved with marketing for Rogers at the time, he got mad that CBS refused to record his new band and left Rogers to again endorse Ludwig. Don recalled that the dates were between the early '60s until '66 or '67 . During Buddy's brief time with Rogers, he became friends with Ben Strauss, who had designed Rogers Dynasonic snare drum.

Lennie continues, "So we all went to see Buddy perform at Basin St. East in New York, and, as usual, about ten of us were sitting right up front. Buddy was onstage with the curtain drawn and was warming up and tuning his drums. There was about a three- or four-foot opening in the curtain, it hadn't shut all the way, and we could see Buddy. He was fiddling with the snare drum, trying to tune it and having some trouble. Well you won't believe what Buddy was doing—Buddy was tuning up one of Bobby Grasso's new fiberglass snare drums so he could try it out. It was a great sounding drum, but it pissed off Ben Strauss, the product specialist for Rogers. Buddy was supposed to be playing the new Dynasonic snare designed by Ben. Plus the fact that Buddy was a Rogers endorser at the time. Ben went up onstage, took the Rogers Dynasonic snare drum, and started to tune it.

"He said to Buddy, 'You know what this is?' and held up his hand. 'It's a drum key. Have you ever seen one?'

'Yeah,' Buddy said.

'Well you tune it. You got too many goddamn gadgets on it!'

"Well, Ben tuned up the Dynasonic for Buddy, put away the Fibes drum, and the show went on. Thank god everything cooled off, because it could have gotten ugly. You know what I mean."

As mentioned, Buddy left Rogers and agreed once again to endorse Ludwig drums, which

Sammy Davis, Jr. and Buddy Rich at Buddy's 60th birthday party in New York City

he had done in 1947. There were three Buddy Rich snare drums in their catalog through the mid-'50s. In the early '80s, Selmer, the band instrument company located in Elkhart, Indiana, purchased the Ludwig Drum Company. To get Buddy's endorsement, they agreed to pay him $50,000.

Once again we're back in Massachusetts, and Lennie has another story:

"Buddy and his band were booked into the Cohasset Music Tent in Boston's South Shore, and in the center of the tent was a revolving stage. Buddy came out to perform, and the stage was turning and Buddy started yelling, 'Oh, mister stage-turner—oh, mister stage-turner.' No one answered. Everyone was waiting for the band to start, but Buddy kept standing there. Meanwhile, he's saying, 'Where the hell's the stage-turner?' Finally someone showed up and Buddy said, 'You'd better stop the stage going around or you won't have a band tonight. We don't play on a merry-go-round.'

"In the back of the tent, Buddy had a little mobile home where he would stay and they had a couple of buses for the band. We're sitting in this little unit—Armand, Buddy, and I—we're talking when Steve Peck comes up and says there are a couple of guys from Selmer to see you. Buddy says, 'Oh yeah, send them in.' The minute these guys walk in, Buddy unloads on them. 'Where's my check? My 50 grand? I've been waiting for six months and you haven't sent the damn check.' The Selmer guys didn't have a clue what he was talking about because it wasn't common knowledge, so they told Buddy they didn't know anything about a check. Buddy fires back, 'You'd better find out, 'cause I'm tired of waiting or you can take the drums back and shove 'em.' Something went wrong with the money, and soon after that, Buddy went back to playing an old original Slingerland set that Joe McSweeny, who lived on the North Shore of Boston and owned Ames Drum Company, had put together. Joe was a Slingerland fanatic."

Two more anecdotes before we close out this chapter about Buddy. Lennie recounts how Buddy's drumset got to Zildjian, and another side of his amazing talent:

"Again we're at Lennie's on the Turnpike. Buddy and the band had finished the last set, and he wanted to do some rehearsing because the band was heading over to London to play at Ronnie Scott's jazz club. For some reason there was a problem with freight or something like that, so Buddy gave Armand his drumset, saying, 'I'm not going to lug that set all the way to Europe. I'll get another one over there.' So, after the rehearsal, I grabbed the set, packed it up, and took it to the factory. After Buddy died, we took the set downstairs in the factory and made a memorial for Buddy in the corridor leading to the drummers' lounge. We displayed the drumset along with some wonderful photos of Buddy. It really looked awesome.

"Also that evening, as I said, Buddy wanted to rehearse, and Phil Wilson, the great trombone player, writer, and arranger, had written several charts for the band. Armand, Buddy, and I sat in the audience while Phil rehearsed the band, and Buddy never got up to play. After the band had played each chart about

Buddy Rich (circa 1983)

Sammy Davis Jr. and Buddy Rich at Buddy's 60th birthday party. Buddy's wife Marie is on the left.

three times, Buddy got up, ran down each chart once, and had it nailed. That was part of his talent—after he heard a chart about three times, he had it down—slam dunk. He had an incredible musical memory.

"Buddy was with the Harry James band playing in a very large ballroom on the outskirts of Boston. Armand and I were there sitting up front near the bandstand at a long table against the wall. Buddy came over to our table during intermission and we where just rappin'. Then Harry came out of his dressing room, and Buddy called him over to say hello to Armand and me. In those days we were all smokin', and I had a cigarette in my hand. Harry was wearing a beautiful hand tailored powder blue jacket, a sky blue bow tie, white pants, etc. When he got over to our table, Harry had to lean over me to shake Armand's hand. I tried to move my arm quickly but it was too late and Harry leaned over me and pushed right into the cigarette. He stood there bent over talking to Armand for at least five minutes. When he stepped away, we could smell his sports jacket burning up, and we could see a big gaping black hole on the side of his now scorched powder blue jacket. Harry didn't even see it, or know what happened (maybe he was in the wrappers too?). Harry walked back onstage with Buddy, not realizing he almost went up in flames. Armand and I just fell apart. We could only imagine him bursting into flames on the next smokin' tune."

One final story: Chili Today Hot Tamale

"This last story will kill you fellas, picture this: Way back many years ago, up on Lennie's on the Turnpike jazz club on the outskirts of Boston, Buddy's band was playing and Armand and I took a bunch of friends up there to see the show. Armand, his wife, two of his golfing buddies, and their wives, and I brought along three friends from the company. We had reserved a table right in front of the bandstand and the club was sold out. The club was real small and real packed. Once you got your seats there was no way in hell you could get up and go to the men's room or walk around, not until the band went on intermission. Before we got to the club, we all stopped at the Red Coach Grill for a little toddy for the body. By the time we left the Red Coach, everyone was in the wrapper. By the time we got to the club, everyone was hungry. It just so happened that the specialty of the club was Lennie's famous chili, so we ordered three or four bowls of chili for the table. Everyone loved it.

"Things were going great. The band was smokin' and we were having a ball until the wife of one of Armand's buddies realized she'd had a little too much champagne and that it didn't mix too well with the chili. Things started to rumble and explode and she was turning a little green. She couldn't get up to hit the ladies room because the band was burning hard and, as I said before, it was impossible to move around in the club. So I just handed her one of the empty chili bowls. She leaned over quickly and let it go in the bowl. "Oh my nerves, what a sight"! She couldn't get up from the table so we gave her a bunch of napkins so she could clean up. Then I took the bowl away

LENNIE'S
ON-THE-TURNPIKE
U.S. ROUTE 1, W. PEABODY, MASS.
TEL. 535-9806

thru sun. jan. 17 **MILES DAVIS**

JANUARY

MON.	TUES.	WED.	THURS.	FRI.	SAT.	SUN.
18	19	20	21	22	23	24
25	26	27	28	29	30	31

18–24: OPEN **GUNS and BUTTER**
a demolishing experience

25–31: **BUDDY RICH** AND HIS ORCHESTRA
(recording nites to be announced)

from her and gave it to my buddy Freddie Sargent. Freddie called the waitress over and told her the chili got cold and could she heat it up a little. She looked at it and even said it had a bad smell to it and that it must have gone sour. Well this really knocked us out and we all laughed our asses off. The poor girl hung in there like a champ for the rest of the set. When the band stopped playing, we had to carry her out to get some fresh air. The funny thing is Buddy and the boys in the band saw everything that happened and said it was an action packed thriller.

We're at the finale, and this was a tough part for Lennie to relate, because, as he said, Buddy Rich was his big favorite.

"Armand and I had always wanted to videotape Buddy, and it had been an ongoing project. We wanted to get Buddy into a room, have some video people come in and have Buddy play, just him, and get close-up shots of his incredible technique. In the early part of '87 Buddy was putting the band back together and rehearsing in New York. Freddie Gruber from Los Angeles, a great teacher and friend of Buddy's, was with him. We figured that as long as Buddy was in New York, we would get Paul Siegel and Rob Wallis, who were running Drummers Collective at that time, to come and videotape him. Unfortunately, we got a phone call from Freddie that everything was canceled—the rehearsal, the tour, the taping. Apparently, Buddy had suffered a slight stroke while they were rehearsing, as he was constantly dropping the stick from his left hand. They took Buddy to Mt. Sinai Hospital, where they ran tests and found that Buddy had the beginnings of a brain tumor."

Buddy flew back to Los Angeles and went to the UCLA medical center, where for the next three months they ran more tests and determined he would need surgery.

"That was a bummer, because after the operation, they didn't get all of the tumor, you know, and they started him on chemo and radiation. They did that for about a month, but it wasn't working. Armand got a call from Buddy's wife telling him that if we wanted to see Buddy, we needed to fly to Los Angeles. So, Armand and I flew out, met Freddie, and went up to a big home where Buddy was staying. A very wealthy man, a close friend and jazz lover, had put Buddy up in one wing of the house, and they were treating Buddy there. In a large room they had put in a piano and his drumset—they wanted to boost his spirits.

"I've got to tell you, it was one of the saddest things I've ever experienced. When we got there, we were taken to the wing where Buddy was staying, walked into the room, and there he was, in bed, paralyzed on his left side. He could speak and was still feisty, and he said, 'How are you doing, Zilch?' He always called Armand that. Then he looked at me and said, "How's the kid doin'?' We sat there saying, c'mon, Buddy, you've got a long ways to go. We were all crying; Freddie was yacking away. We only stayed for a couple of hours because Buddy was drifting off. He was really sick and there was nothing we could do. All of the chemo and radiation was tearing him down, and previously he had had some light heart attacks. So, Armand and I caught a red-eye back to Boston, and when we got to the factory, there was a message for Armand that Buddy had died. The end of an era. We felt fortunate that we had got to spend a few hours with Buddy before he died."

Buddy Rich passed away April 2, 1987, of heart failure following surgery for a malignant brain tumor. A giant and a drumming legend was gone, but his amazing legacy continues today. Even near the end, as the story goes, his wit was very much intact, and he still had a one-liner in him. Supposedly, as they were wheeling him in for surgery, a nurse asked him if he was allergic to anything. He responded, "Country-and-western music."

"In closing," Lennie says, "I hope I haven't offended any of the other great drummers that have been a big part of my life, and hope they will agree with me about Buddy. My best wishes to his daughter Cathy, his wife Marie, grandson Nicholas, and son-in-law Steve. I will never forget Buddy, and I continue to miss him more and more year after year."

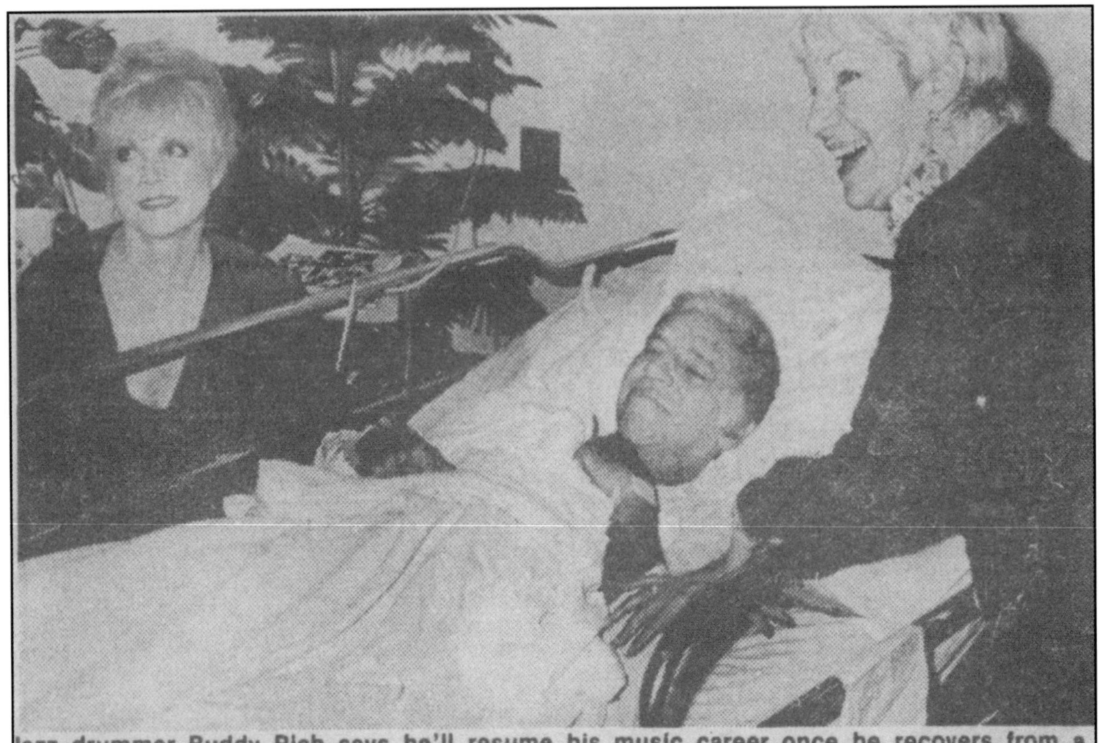

Jazz drummer Buddy Rich says he'll resume his music career once he recovers from a quadruple bypass heart operation. Here he is visited in an Ann Arbor, Mich., hospital by his wife Marie (left) and sister Josephine Corday. "I'm feeling better," he said. "Not a lot better, but better."

UPI PHOTO

Buddy recovering from quadruple bypass surgery vows to return to the stage (1983)

Buddy Rich onstage after his bypass surgery (circa 1985)

Chapter 12

Barrett Deems: He Made Coffee Nervous

To paraphrase "There are a thousand stories in the naked city"—there are countless stories concerning the many drummers who hung out with Lennie.

"We always had a close relationship with Barrett Deems," Lennie says. "He played in Boston a lot, and he always loved to come to the factory. One particular time, he was playing with Jack Teagarden, and Armand and I went down to the joint to see him play. When we walked in, Barrett spotted us and started whistling and yelling like he always did. He could care less—he was always rambunctious and nervous. When the band took a break, he grabbed a snare drum and yelled for Armand and me to come with him. We go outside the club, and we're in the middle of Stewart Street in Boston and Barrett is yakking about the new snare drum he had just picked up and he begins to play the drum. He's rapping away on the drum in the middle of the street, cars are going by honking, people are walking by, and in a manner of ten minutes there must have been 15 people around him. A couple of homeless cats were standing there looking at Barrett. They didn't know him; they were thinking he must be a freak of nature, and all the while Barrett is going crazy on the snare with a cigarette dangling from his lips. We couldn't stop him. After the gig, we went across the street to get a cup of coffee. Barrett walked in with his drumsticks in hand and started playing on the counter, something that had apparently happened before. When the owner saw Barrett doing this, he picked up a meat cleaver and asked us to leave the restaurant. We were laughing like crazy. Barrett was truly a character, but he could play his ass off.

"I mentioned earlier in the book how I first met Barrett along with Armand while at Charlie Alden's drum studio in Boston. Barrett and I became close friends and we continued our close relationship until he passed away in 1998. That's 40 years of a great friendship. Barrett also loved Chinese food and so did

A young Barrett Deems (circa 1944)

Barrett Deems, Gene Krupa, Buddy Rich (1952)

Armand and I, so we always ended up in some late-night Chinese food restaurant in Chicago or Boston or wherever we were. The big problem we always had was that Barrett couldn't sit still. He would always start playing on the dishes and cups with the chopsticks, banging away until the waiter would come over and throw us out. Besides Barrett knocking great time, he had a lot of great tricks with the sticks. He could play the snare drum with the normal right-handed grip, and after a few minutes he would immediately flip the sticks over to a left-handed grip without stopping or dropping anything, then back to the right-handed grip. He would bounce the sticks off the cymbals and catch them in the air and twirl them around his fingers. He was quite a showman but he mostly kept great time, and that's why all the band leaders loved him."

I had the opportunity to meet Barrett when I was with Premier Drums back in the '70s. A bunch of us were at the jazz club in the old Blackstone Hotel where Barrett was playing with his group. Lennie had told me many great things about Barrett and also mentioned how he loved everything drums and drum gear. Premier had just come out with an innovative new foot pedal and I showed it to Barrett. He said he had to have one. I jokingly told him I had heard that he had about fifty pedals and that when he was down to only one I would send him one. Barrett got a kick out of this, and, of course, I sent him one the next day.

"Later in his career Barrett married a beautiful young dancer named Janie who he met while playing floor shows (cabaret) in Chicago. They got along great, and she was always with him. She was very devoted to Barrett and helped him a lot with his music career. She was so sweet she even helped him carry his drums and get them set up onstage for his gigs. Once Armand and I were in a lounge talking to Barrett before a gig and lo and behold she brought his drums in and began setting them up onstage. Armand asked Barrett why he had his wife lugging his drums around. Barrett replied, 'She's not only my wife, but she's my manager, agent, roadie, she plays great saxophone and flute, she has her own band, and she goes everywhere with me. She even handles the payroll, and watches all the bread. Armand said, 'Thank God!' and we all had a laugh."

Barrett Deems (1970)

Louie Bellson, Bob Stone, Barrett Deems (1985)

Lennie continues with another story. "We were at a trade show in Chicago in the mid-'60s at the Hilton Hotel. Most of the companies had double rooms, they were fairly large, and the companies would bring in their equipment and demonstrate it. The dealers would go from room to room and check out the stuff. Now, Barrett had just signed up with an Italian drum company, Miatzi drums, and they were new on the scene. Barrett was downstairs in the lobby talking to Armand, me, and a few guys, and he wanted us to see the drumset.

Janie Deems, Barrett Deems, Lennie

The set was supposedly especially designed with some new innovations and hardware. So we said sure, we'd be happy to check it out, and went with Barrett to the Miatzi room. Barrett was very excited, just a ball of fire. He goes over and picks up some sticks, gets behind the drums, and yells, 'Dig this sound,' and begins to bang away, beating the hell out of the drums, slamming away, when all of a sudden the stool broke. Barrett falls over backward, knocking over a cymbal stand and everything. He's on the floor and we had to pick him up. He almost killed himself, and he's yelling and screaming that he's going to sue Miatzi, that the drums are a pile of shit, and making a big scene. It was hilarious. He was a crazy cat, and there were always plenty of laughs when we hung out with him."

A last story: "One time Armand and I went to hear Barrett and his Dixieland band at the Gaslight Room near the Chicago airport. His bands were always great, and it was fun to hear and see Barrett play. This particular club had a lot of popcorn and roasted peanuts on the floor, on the tables, and things like that. So, when Barrett wasn't looking—he was off the stage for a moment—we filled up his hi-hat cymbals with peanuts. He started playing and the hats wouldn't 'chick,' and the peanuts started falling out, and Barrett laughed his ass off. He was swearing and started throwing peanuts at Armand and me. The band picked up on the jive and started throwing peanuts, then the audience started throwing peanuts, and it ended up everyone was throwing peanuts at each other. It was crazy! It was a funny scene and we were just as nuts as Barrett."

Barrett Deems was born in Springfield, Illinois, March 1, 1914, and he was best known for being Louis Armstrong's drummer. Armstrong always called him "The Kid" and once said Barrett's drumming style 'made coffee nervous.' He played with many groups such as Joe Venuti, Jimmy Dorsey, and Mugsy Spanier, along with having his own big band in Chicago, and was still playing at 80-plus years and referring to himself as the oldest teenager in the business. He died September 15, 1998, of pneumonia at the age of 85.

Barrett Deems (1993)

Chapter 13

Clinics to Die for—and We Almost Did

Like most of the major companies in the drum and cymbal business, Zildjian presented many clinics over the years. Top artists would appear at conventions such as PASIC or MENC and give of their time and knowledge to assist the many students and others who were eager to learn and improve their playing. Most clinics achieved the goal of spreading the drumming gospel—and then there were others.

"One of the funniest was when Slingerland, along with us, had Joe Cusatis, who was playing with Peter Nero and now is the owner of the Modern Drum Shop in New York, do a major clinic at an MENC Convention," Lennie remembers, laughing. "Joe had told us that he had done a lot of clinics, but I don't think he had done a major one in a big hall in front of a large audience. At that time, he had a big black mustache that hung over his lips, and he had a habit of squiggling it from side to side, and he's standing out on the stage, twitchin', as I introduced him. He stood in front of the drums and really didn't know what to do. I could see he was getting a little nervous, stuck for words, but he finally started talking and things got going. Joe said, 'The first thing we're going to talk about is chops. You kids out there have got to get your chops in shape. You've got to work on your chops constantly, at least two or three hours a day, and without chops, you aren't going to be able to express yourself. Read those things I've written out for you, and they are great for your chops; they will build up your chops and will prepare you for everything.'"

"Some guy puts his hand up and asks Joe if he can ask a question, and Joe says yes. So the guy asks, 'What kind of chops are you talking about? Lamb chops, kidney chops, or pork chops?' The audience fell apart. Everyone was laughin'. I was red in the face and Joe was turning all kinds of colors. It was hysterical. He stormed off the stage, but finally cooled off and came back on and played an incredible solo that made the day and the audience loved him."

Mel Lewis was playing at the Village Vanguard every Monday night in Greenwich Village in New York. He was in top form and at the top of the game, doing a lot of recordings, and was considered to be one of the great jazz drummers. He was a great artist for Zildjian, but he had not done many clinics. He asked me if Zildjian would sponsor his presentation at the PAS national convention and, of course, I said we would. So the company sent him to PASIC for the clinic.

Joe Cusatis and Lennie checking out some cymbals

"The room was packed for the clinic. I'm there with Armand and I say to Mel that it is time to go on, and I introduce him. Mel goes to the mic and the first thing out of his mouth is, 'How many of you guys like rock 'n' roll?' About thirty to forty kids put up their hands. So Mel said, 'Listen, all you guys, I want to tell you right now—I hate rock 'n' roll, I'm not going to talk about rock 'n' roll at all. So if you want to stay here and listen to how to play the drums properly, I'll talk to you. But if you think I'm going to talk about rock 'n' roll, you might as well get up and leave.'

"So, half the room got up and left. Oh my God, it was so embarrassing. Mel said, 'The hell with them. I'm not going to talk about rock 'n' roll.' That kinda blew that clinic, but Mel always spoke his mind."

Another rather spectacular clinic was at a Florida MENC where the clinics were sponsored by Slingerland, Rogers, and Zildjian, and Roy Burns was the featured artist. Slingerland decided to bring in Mickey Sheen because he lived in Florida and it would be inexpensive for them. No one knew whether Mickey could do a clinic, and it seemed no one cared, so they sent him in. Lennie picks up the story:

"No one knew who Mickey was, but Armand and I knew that he was a pretty good big band drummer. We didn't have a chance to talk to him before the clinic, so we didn't have a clue as to what might happen. The night before, Roy had really torn it up and had closed his

Left to right: band director, Armand Zildjian, Lennie, Mickey Sheen, Sandy Feldstein, Roy Burns, Mickey Sheen clinic in Florida (1970)

Joe Cusatis, Lennie DiMuzio (1975)

performance with a tremendous 15-minute solo. Now, Mickey was a Gene Krupa clone, set up his drums just like Gene, and dressed in a black tuxedo with white stockings because that is what Gene would always wear."

Roy Burns shed some light on why Mickey dressed like Gene: Mickey had worked with Sal Mineo, who played the part of Krupa in the movie *The Gene Krupa Story*. Mickey was so taken with Gene that after this experience, he would always emulate Krupa, right down to the way he dressed.

"Mickey came out and told the audience that he couldn't follow a great artist like Roy Burns with that type of drum solo, so he was going to talk about different segments of his life and how they influenced his drumming. Now, there was a huge audience, maybe a couple thousand people, so when Mickey proceeds to start playing on the wing nuts, it got pretty quiet. The trouble of it was that he had soft mallets in his hands, so we couldn't recognize any of the rhythm patterns. He played about a four- or five-minute solo on the wing nuts, the hi-hat clutch, and various metal stands and stuff like that—didn't hit any drums or cymbals. Roy was sitting with Armand and me and I think Sandy Feldstein was there also. We all thought, hmm..., that wing nut thing was pretty clever.

"Then he sat down behind the drums and started playing a heavy four on the bass drum. He tells the audience he discovered that boxing was good for drumming and that it helped him with foot work and stuff like that. Then, he wipes his nose with one

Jazz drummer Jimmy Cobb

hand and starts throwing punches at the drums—wham, thump, a right cross, a jab, an uppercut—it was wild. He stops that, four thumps on the bass drum, he gets up from behind the drums, picks up a pair of sticks, and walks up to the mike. This time it's fencing, and he talks about position and stance and how all of that helped him as a drummer. He takes one of the sticks, assumes a stance of one leg in front of the other and begins to fence with the cymbals—slashing away, stabbing the cymbals, dancing around the drumset.

"Well, now we're starting to snicker, the audience begins to laugh, and Mickey goes into his next act. This is turning into a comedy routine, and we're wondering if this guy is nuts or what.

"He gets behind the drums, starts thumping four on the bass drum again, and he tells us that at one time he wanted to become a surgeon and that helped him with his brush work. Mickey picks up his brushes and for two or three minutes makes carving motions on the snare drum like it's a cadaver. Now everybody is laughin', but he still isn't through.

"Thumping the bass drum again, this time he's going to take us around the world, and he ends up with flamenco dancing. Can you believe it? He's dancing around the set, slashing away with his hands at the cymbals, and now it's pandemonium. Everybody is breaking up, I mean, this guy is jumping around going crazy, we're on the floor laughing, and suddenly he stops. He was serious about what he was doing. He looked at everybody breaking up, grabbed his sticks—pissed off—walked off the stage, and disappeared. We never saw him again that day or ever again. Then, many years later, we heard he had died from a nervous disorder. That was, without a doubt, the most bizarre clinic I have ever seen. I wish we would have had a video camera."

I must admit that as I was writing this story, I was laughing so hard I had to stop and regain control. I wish I had been there.

10th ANNUAL GRETSCH DRUM NIGHT . . . The big annual event held on May 1st, at Lennie's-On-the-Turnpike, West Peabody, Mass . . . Among the top drum stars who participated in the big percussion demonstration were, left to right: Alan Dawson, Elvin Jones, and Jimmie Cob.

10th Gretsch Drum Night Draws Record Boston Crowd

A record turnout for the 10th annual Gretsch Drum Night filled Lennie's-On-The-Turnpike in West Peabody, Massachusetts, as jazz fans poured in from all over to see the famous drummer "battle royal" on May 1.

president, stated that this year's 10th m stone was the best for participation, eagerly looks forward to planning the n Gretch Drum Night for the coming ye

Alan Dawson, Elvin Jones, Jimmy Cobb at the tenth annual Gretsch Drum Night (circa 1975)

Freddie Sargent, Norman "Scotty" Scott, Phil Delio, Armand, Joe Morello, Lennie at Wurlitzer Music, Boston, MA, clinic (1975)

Mel Lewis during his last performance

Armand Zildjian, Ed Shaughnessy, and Lennie at Wurlitzer Music, Boston, MA, during a clinic (circa 1977)

Chapter 14

Little Big Horn and a UFO

GRETSCH-GLADSTONE DRUMS
ANDREA FLORIO 1944

This chapter is a little break from cymbal selection, artist relations, and the like. It concerns a drummer named Andy Florio, a big band drummer and actor from Los Angeles, and great storyteller. Naturally, he was Lennie's friend.

"Andy was something else—a real character and a funny guy. He was a drummer in LA, had played in some big bands, did casuals, and would always hang around our booth at the NAMM show. We'd go to lunch and talk a little about cymbals, and then he would tell us stories about his life that, I guess, you know, were real. Most people thought he was a weirdo and wouldn't give him any credit, but underneath it all he was a pretty talented guy.

"He was part American Indian, and he said his grandmother was hiding on a hill close to where Custer was ambushed in the Battle of Little Big Horn and she knew the true story. [J.C.: Custer and his men were killed June 1876.] Andy had this Indian blood in him, and every time he came near a horse, he had to jump on and ride it. Because he could ride, he got a lot of bit parts in the movies, such as *The Ten Commandments, Quo Vadis,* and *Geronimo.* He gave me photos of him with an Indian headdress on, and he had made a lot of bows and arrows. In fact, he made drumsticks out of arrows and made headdresses for the studios. He was talented.

"Andy was married to Zacky, who played sax in Phil Spitalny's all-girl orchestra. She would come to the show, hang out with us, and although she was a good player, she was also missing a few spark plugs. We called her Wacky Zacky. The drummer in Phil's orchestra was billed as Viola and Her Seventeen Drums. Now, most of her drums were toms across the front, and she'd do a drum solo as part of the show. Sometimes they'd all go to dinner with us, and Andy always had lots of pictures to show us, plus the stories. Viola was a great drummer.

"The most bizarre story was when he would go into his UFO sighting. Andy claimed this happened when he was driving in the desert either from Vegas to LA or the other way around, I can't remember. Anyway, he was in his van, had his drums with him, when all of a sudden a UFO was hovering over him and followed him for about 15 to 20 miles. It came down close to him. Andy was like, you know, in hysteria. He stopped the van and got out. As he was looking at the UFO, it shot a beam that hit his elbow, burned his arm, and burned a hole in the van door. Then while he was telling the story, he would roll up his sleeve, show us the scars, and say they proved he was shot at by a UFO. He reported his story to an agency concerned with UFO sightings, so he did have some documentation. But no one believed him, and everyone thought he was a little nuts about this UFO thing.

"The time period on Andy is probably from 1965 to 1980. One time when he came to the the big NAMM show, something happened to his back as he was going to step from the floor into our booth. Andy pitched over like he was picking something up and started yelling, 'Lennie, Lennie, my back.' We ran over and had to literally pick him up and set him down

Promotional picture taken during Andy Florio's acting career (1969)

in a chair. All the time he was yelling get a doctor, get a doctor, but he had some pain pills that eventually let his back relax. What a scene. Whenever Andy and Zacky were around there was always something off-the-wall happening. I can only say Andy was a great guy, but he hit one too many rim shots. He went for a walk one day and I think he was abducted by an alien and never came home. That was it."

Andy Florio pictured with one of his many makeovers

Andy Florio, Barrett Deems, Lennie (circa 1985)

JEWOPs Cartoon drawn by former Disney Cartoonist Fred Edlund

Jim, Lloyd, Lennie,
Cape Cod, MA (circa 1995)

Chapter 15

Rack of Lamb for Two for One

Jim Coffin, Lloyd McCausland, Lennie

Probably the most famous or infamous group, depending upon the situation, ever formed in the drum business is the JEWOPs. Now, before those of you who lean toward being politically correct get bent out of shape, the acronym is not an ethnic slur; it stands for Junior Executives Without Power. Okay? Calm down. At a party during the first PASIC in 1976, at the Eastman School of Music in Rochester, New York, in the middle of the frivolity, the idea of such a group gave birth. There were many people at that "earthshaking party" and the first JEWOP group included not only Lennie, Lloyd McCausland, and me, but also Bobby Nelson (Zildjian), Marty Lishon (Frank's Drum Shop), Bill Carpenter (Remo), and Carol Calato (Regal Tip). After that initial assembly, T-shirts were made and our theme, "We never pay for anything," was established. The sponsors of the group were Joe Calato, Regal Tip owner; and Maurie Lishon, Frank's Drum Shop owner; and I think that they ended up paying for the shirts. After a few years, the JEWOPs became just Lennie, Lloyd, and me; although there was talk of forming the JEWOP-ettes, but for some unexplainable reason the women who wanted to be in that group refused to do the initiation requirement.

Lennie covered the East Coast, I was working for Selmer/Premier in Elkhart, Indiana, and had the Midwest, while Lloyd with Remo took care of the West Coast. We would have a JEWOP meeting at the various trade shows, PASIC, the Mid-West Band Clinic in Chicago, and other such conventions. In fact, it was at the Mid-West Band Clinic where the title of this chapter came to be.

Jim Petersczak, Lennie, Peter Erskine, Lloyd McCausland, Jim Coffin, Dave Weckl, Vinnie Colaiuta, and his wife Darleen (circa 1986).

Jim (center) with Lloyd and Lennie after receiving the PAS President's Award (1999)

We usually tried to have at least one dinner at the restaurant on the 95th floor of the Hancock building, where listed on the menu was rack of lamb for two. Lennie told the waiter he would have the rack of lamb, and Lloyd said so would he. The waiter, looking a little puzzled, stated that it was a rack of lamb for two people. They both said in unison, "No, we want a rack of lamb for two for one." After a few more minutes of explanation, the waiter left, shaking his head. (And, no, I don't like lamb.)

Lloyd and Judy enjoying the lamb dinner

In those early days we had a lot of fun getting on each other about receiving publicity. Whenever one of us would be mentioned in one of the trade magazines, the other two would immediately copy the news article and write some rather obscene remarks on it and send it to all three, which demanded a reply from the publicity party. If someone got out of line and tried to get more power due to publicity, that JEWOP was threatened with having to turn in his shirt. Occasionally, outsiders would get involved with the JEWOPs. One memorable incident involved photos Bill Kurth took of Lloyd sleeping poolside at a MENC meeting in Miami Beach. Bill was working for the Music Education Group, and he sent copies to Lennie and me, which led to a letter sent to Lloyd demanding blackmail money.

For a brief time we went international by adding Roger Horrobin, advertising manager for Premier Drums, to our Enclave Adjutants; he would be a part of the group at PASIC. Roger was based in Leicester, England. A brief JEWOP story with Roger is in order. Lloyd and I, along with Roger, were attending two conferences that were almost back-to-back, so we decided to make a side trip to New Orleans because Roger had never visited that city. Also, we could check in on Freddie Kohlman, the great Heritage Hall Jazz Band drummer who was playing Premier drums, Remo heads, and Zildjian cymbals. As an added benefit, we would be there for Halloween. In New Orleans they really celebrate that holiday. Very bizarre.

Remo Belli and Lloyd McCausland (circa 1970)

Lennie, Jim, and Lloyd discussing one of their many financial ventures

Lennie, Lloyd, Jim (circa 1975)

Halloween afternoon Freddie said he wanted to stop in at the Famous Door and see the house band clarinet player. So while he was chatting, we three sat at the bar for a small toddy. Behind the bar taking our drink orders was a beautiful woman, statuesque with a great figure and a see-through blouse. We were the only guys at the bar, so we immediately struck up a conversation. Things were going great, when Freddie came up behind us and said softly, "Before you guys get too excited, that she am a he." Whoa! Seems the clarinet player had taken her home one night after the gig was over, and during the exploratory session, found something unexpected. We took our leave.

That night Bourbon Street was packed and we didn't have a clue who or what we were looking at since the cross-dressing was rampant. One guy had a snake mask over his head and was walking back and forth down the middle of the street sticking out his tongue. We finally decided it was time to return to the hotel but popped into a bar on the way for a nightcap. When Roger went to the restroom, two ladies came in and sat close to us at the bar. Lloyd and I thought why don't we try to fix up Roger with one of them. I said, "Good evening, ladies." (Pretty snappy, huh?) They looked over, and the nearest one responded in a very low bass voice, "Good evening." The night was over.

Instigated by Lloyd McCausland, investments were one of the JEWOPs' biggest endeavors, which included investing in a horse-training facility in Sacramento, California; battery-powered automobiles (in 1981); and a house in Claremont, California. I don't want to go into detail about the three schemes, but the horse-training facility was part of a California teacher investment program; the battery-powered car fiasco happened through a Boston ex-drummer friend of Lloyd's who had an investment firm in Las Vegas (does that tell you anything?); and the only one that made us a little money was the house in Claremont—and if it hadn't been for my uncle Willie Coffin, who was a plumber in Big Bear and fixed the place up so we could sell it, that investment would also have been a disaster.

I'll never forget Lennie telling Lloyd, after he had sent us our business cards laminated as a luggage tag: "Big deal! Coffin and I send you 5,000 bucks apiece, and so far we've gotten one free meal and a laminated baggage tag paid for by Remo. You're investing like crazy, wearing new suits, and grinning a lot. We demand an accounting."

The car investment deal was with Micro-Tech, and in one of the company's advertising propaganda sheets it stated General Motors estimated it would be selling 200,000 electric cars by 1990, with it's first battery-powered commuter car by 1985. In fact, Lloyd's Vegas friend told us to pick out our Cadillacs. Yeah, right!

Jim, Kathy Coffin, Lennie

Jim, Lloyd, Lennie, at Lloyd's retirement party at the NAMM Show in Los Angeles, CA (2004)

Fortunately, one scheme that Lloyd came up with turned out to be only talk and a lot of laughs. Around Lloyd's home in California were many rabbits, and at one of our "business" dinners he came up with the idea of Bunny Burgers. This was to be a multi-pronged marketing plan involving the raising of rabbits and using their fur for Bunny Mittens, their meat for Bunny Burgers—sort of like a McDonald's approach—and their droppings for fertilizer used to raise earthworms. Both Lennie and I told Lloyd what he could do with that idea. Here's a synopsis:

"Butch, are you out of your goddamn mind? You trying to sell a kid on eating a little bunny rabbit and wearing little bunny mittens? What are you going to use for a mascot, Bugs Bunny? We could have Elmer Fudd in an ad saying, 'How about eating a wascally wabbit.' And the earthworms—c'mon." That ended that nonsense. But we still laugh about it.

Occasionally over the years one of us would be asked by a friend if he could join the JEWOPs. Our rejoinder would be that if we would ask the other two, it would appear that we would be looking for power, so we couldn't do it. At one PASIC the three of us were together when the well-known music publisher Sandy Feldstein asked if he could join the group. Sandy was always well dressed, and we told him that anyone who could afford Gucci shoes was too rich for us, so we turned him down. Speaking of Sandy, Lennie said I should tell the following little story about JEWOP retribution.

The JEWOPs (Junior Executives Without Power) at the Midwest band Clinic 1976. Left to right: Lennie, Lloyd McCausland, Bobby Nelson, Marty Lishon, Jim Coffin

This took place in the '70s when I was working for Selmer and Premier drums. Sandy, Jim Sewrey (who was with Ludwig at that time), some others, and I gave a percussion clinic at Iowa State University in Ames on a Saturday, and we all stayed at a local Holiday Inn. The next morning, I went to the motel's restaurant for breakfast and it was packed with families. The only available table was near the kitchen. Just as my food was delivered, I looked out the window and Sandy was getting into a taxi. He spotted me, stopped the driver, got out, and walked into the restaurant and headed for my table. As he got to the table, the waitress asked him if he wanted anything, and Sandy replied in a loud voice, "No, I just came in to kiss Jim goodbye." He leaned over, kissed me on the mouth, turned and walked out, got into the cab, waved, and left. Every head in the restaurant turned toward me, and the waitress went into the kitchen and shouted, "You won't believe what just happened out there. A guy just kissed another guy on the mouth!" Man, I scarfed down my breakfast, and as I paid my bill, I could hear people whispering, "That's the guy the other guy kissed." I vowed to pay Sandy back.

A few years later, I was in Canada conducting a band that was sight-reading high school jazz band arrangements. In the book were two of Sandy's charts, and I had noticed that he had snuck into the room and was sitting near the back, not realizing I had seen him. When we were done playing a chart, I turned to the audience and said, "A good friend of mine is Sandy Feldstein, who has two arrangements in

Bobby Nelson, Marty Lishon, and Lennie (circa 1975)

the book, and I want to make sure we read them down before we run out of time." Turning to the band, I asked them to turn over a few charts and pull up Sandy's arrangement. We played the intro and the first chorus when I stopped the band and turned to the audience and said, "Sorry, this isn't up to Sandy's usual standards. Band, pull up his other chart." This time, right after the intro, I again stopped the band and said, "This is even worse than the other one." Then I pointed to the back of the room and said, "Sandy, will you please stand up." Like I said—retribution!

Before we close this chapter, here are two more short incidents that involved the three of us. One year PASIC was held in San Antonio, and we were staying at the Hilton Hotel that was across from the convention center and overlooked the famous River Walk. After the displays closed around 5:00 p.m., we would meet with other companies' personnel in the hotel bar, which had as part of its decor a statue of a horse with a saddle and bridle. One evening, more fun-filled than most, we decided Lennie should take a ride on the horse. We helped him up onto the saddle and then proceeded to push him and the horse across the floor toward the exit of the bar. Everyone was cheering and yelling, "Ride 'em, Lennie," and the bartender went bonkers. He came running out from behind the bar, got in front of the horse, trying to stop us, all the while hollering he was going to call the cops. That threat put a bit of a damper on Lennie's Kentucky Derby ride, so we helped him off and, with discretion being the better part of valor, promptly left and went to dinner. After eating, we stopped off at the bar; the horse was back in the paddock. We quietly had a nightcap and went to bed, laughing all the way.

One summer, on the grounds of the Norwell factory, Zildjian held a big bash complete with a huge tent, food, drinks, and performances by some of their endorsees. It was a gala affair. The JEWOPs had decided that the next day we would hold a meeting on Nantucket Island, the ancestral home of the American Coffin clan. We had made reservations at the Jared Coffin House on the island, and the next morning, early, Bobby Nelson was going to drive us to Hyannisport to catch the ferry over to Nantucket. The party lasted most of the day, and attempting to get Lennie and Lloyd to go to bed was a real challenge, which I won't go into. We did make it to the ferry, and Lloyd and I were on the upper deck taking in the scenery, discussing the previous day, when we noticed Lennie was missing. Lloyd said he would look for him, and after about fifteen minutes came back and stated Lennie was sound asleep on the baggage in the ship's hold. After we docked at the Straight Wharf, Lloyd and I departed on the passengers' gangplank—no Lennie in sight. Finally, in the midst of the baggage being unloaded, there was Lennie, looking a little green, coming down the gangplank. We rented a car,

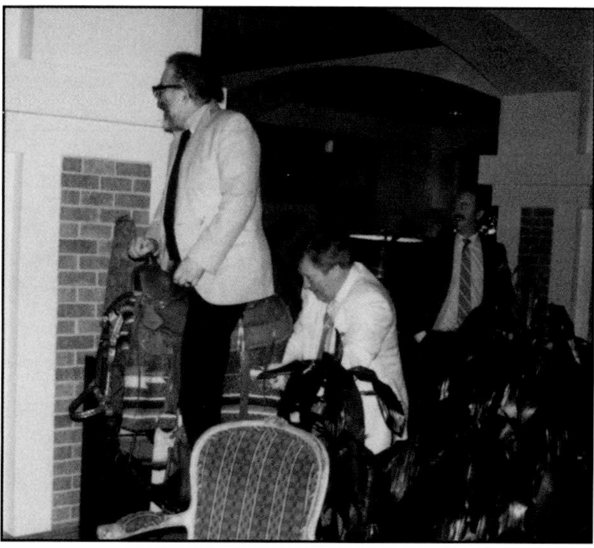
Lennie and Lloyd in San Antonio, TX, during a PASIC Convention (1988)

and Lennie slept in the back seat for most of the afternoon while Lloyd and I went sight-seeing around the island. All in all, it was one of the JEWOPs' more famous meetings.

One of the fun things we three liked to discuss was how everyone seemed to take the JEWOPs so seriously—thinking that when we were together we were working on some nefarious business plot. The simple truth was, we were three friends who, through our business affiliations, became very close and enjoyed each others' company. Certainly, we talked about our jobs, the drum business, music, drummers, PAS, and NAMM, but for the most part it was friendly conversation—including many stories and jokes.

All of us have been heavily involved in PAS, with each receiving the President's Industry Award—Lloyd in 1995, Lennie in 1997, and me in 1999. I first joined the PAS board of directors in 1970 and spent a two-year term as secretary of the executive committee in the late '90s. Both Lennie and Lloyd have been on the board of directors for many years, with Lloyd being a major factor in the establishment of the Percussion Marketing Council.

We can't count all of the other organizations we've worked with, attending meetings and conferences—MENC, IAJE, NAMM, Midwest Band, state music conferences, the Frankfurt Fair—many plane flights, hotel rooms, meals on the run, cocktail parties, entertaining dealers, late nights and then early mornings getting to the displays and standing all day. As Lennie would say, "Oh, my nerves."

In the mid-'80s all three of our companies, Zildjian, Remo, and Yamaha, worked with musicians who performed at Disney World in Orlando, Florida. We went to Disney World several times, and Fred Edlund, who was the repairman in charge of the percussion instruments, became a good friend of ours. Occasionally, we would receive envelopes from Fred with artwork on them by some of the Disney artists. Unfortunately, they couldn't sign their names because of a Disney rule. In fact, they did the drawings only as a favor to Fred. Sadly, Fred was driving to work one day, felt something in his chest, pulled over to the side of the road, and died of a heart attack. He was young, I think in his early forties. But in 1987, before his death, he had one of the artists draw the *Congratulations* illustration that appears on the last page of the previous chapter. It's a great drawing, and the little lamb says it all. Thank you, Fred.

Throughout the years, we worked very hard for our respective companies, fighting many battles and putting out a lot of fires. We have made many friends, are proud of our many successes, and have learned to live with a few failures, but our greatest joy is to be recognized and to hear the words, "Hey, there are the JEWOPs!"

Mickey Toperzer (retired drum shop owner), Mickey' wife Shirley, Lloyd McCausland, Lloyd's wife Judy, Jim Coffin, Cape Cod, MA (circa 1993)

Chapter 16

Kenny Clare: A Swirling Dervish

Kenny Clare warming up on his new Remo practice pad set (1978)

Kenny Clare, a gifted percussionist, was born in London, England, June 8, 1929, and died at a young 55 December 21, 1984. His brilliant drumset career included playing in the bands of Jack Parnell, Johnny Dankworth, and Ted Heath and co-leading a band with fellow drummer Ronnie Stephenson. He also did another two-drummer stint with the famous Clarke-Boland Big Band. As a first-call studio player in London, Kenny played on recording sessions for TV and radio as well as film soundtracks. In addition to touring with Tom Jones, his recording dates included Ella Fitzgerald, Joe Pass, and Stephane Grappelli.

The following anecdote is one of Lennie's favorites. I'll never forget a dinner party that included the JEWOPs, other Zildjian personnel, and Louie Bellson, who was sitting across from me at a long table. Lennie was in rare form, on his feet, arms waving, and demonstrating the following story. It is in the top ten of Lennie's stories.

"Kenny Clare used to come across with the Johnny Dankworth band that featured Johnny's wife, Cleo Laine—she was the featured headline star. This time they were touring the states and I always looked forward to Kenny coming over because he was an incredible player—a great player—and a close friend of Buddy, Louie Bellson, all the

James Blades, Clinic Presentation, London, England (1973)

Drum clinic in London with Kenny Clare, Lennie (1973)

great players. Now, Kenny, you know, was one of the top recording artists in England, and he was very busy in the studios when he wasn't traveling. Because of being a recording artist and having a variety of jobs, studio and big bands, he always had a lot of cymbals to deal with, and occasionally I would send cymbals over to our English office for Kenny, to fill in the missing sounds he needed cymbals for—but getting it sent to him wasn't like hand-picking them at the factory. So, whenever Kenny came through the United States on tour with the band, he always made a point to call me, make an appointment, and come up to the factory. He always brought the huge selection of cymbals that he had—could be a few years' worth—cymbals that were broken, cymbals that were worn out, and things he had to change or update. Kenny always looked forward to the visit and would bring a couple of bags of cymbals with him.

"This particular time when Kenny came to the factory, he was playing in downtown Boston in one of the theaters with the Dankworth Band and Cleo Laine. We had a beautiful day at the factory, selecting cymbals pretty much all afternoon, exchanging a lot of stuff, updating his cymbals, and we ended up with a bag full of cymbals. I mean, my God, it must have had 15 or 16 cymbals in it, and we didn't realize how heavy the bag was. Now, you know, Kenny wasn't a big guy, maybe 5'5", on the thin side, a small type of person.

"The plan was for me to drive Kenny back into town in time for a rehearsal that was, I would say, probably set for five o'clock. Now, we had forgotten that was the height of rush hour in Boston and the theater that Kenny was supposedly playing in was right smack in the heart of downtown Boston—right in the middle of the goddamn traffic. I put Kenny's cymbal bag in the trunk, we got in the car, headed for Boston, the theater was on a main street, the traffic was bumper to bumper. One of our cymbal testers, Kenny Hadley, was driving. We got there about 3:30 or so and thought we had plenty of time. Oh my God, things did change. We were stuck in traffic and weren't moving at all. Kenny was getting nervous and didn't want to blow the rehearsal because he already had some troubles with the band. He said that they would can him if he didn't get to this rehearsal, so he must have missed a few other rehearsals.

"Well, we finally got to the theater and it was the wrong theater—Kenny was mixed up—can you believe it? The right theater was to our left about five or six blocks away, but with the traffic and one-way streets, we could only

English studio percussionist with Barrett Deems and Kenny Clare at BBC Recording Studios (circa 1975)

make right-hand turns. So, we had to go around the block. The traffic was barely moving, and when we got a little closer, we could see the theater. By this time an hour or so has gone by, it's quarter past four, we got around another corner, and Kenny was getting uptight, starting to panic. Then he says, in his fine English accent, 'Lennie, stop the car, mon, I'm going to walk the rest of the way.' I told him he couldn't walk the rest of the way—the cymbals were too heavy. He said, 'No, mon, I ken make it.' I said wait another ten or fifteen minutes, but he said he could make it.

"So we stopped the car, I got out, went around the back, and opened the trunk. Kenny bends over into the trunk and pulls the bag out and tries to throw it over his shoulder. While trying to throw the bag over his shoulder, there were so many goddamn cymbals in the bag, he started spinning around like a top. Kenny must have spun around four or five times. The cymbal bag breaks, all the damn cymbals go rolling down Stuart Street, people don't know what the hell is going on, cars are beeping their horns, the fucking cymbals are clashing and banging on the street and sidewalk. It was a horror show. Kenny is absolutely panicking, trying to pick up the cymbals. I'm trying to get them together. I said what the hell are we gonna do now? I tell Kenny to get in the car and we'll just sit this out. He yells, 'No, mon, I'm gonna walk.' He grabbed a bunch of cymbals, put 'em in the broken bag, put the bag in his arms, and started carrying the bag down the street to the theater. I'm telling you, he was staggering down the street and I was behind him in traffic [Lennie is laughing like crazy as he is telling this], and by the time he got to the theater, he was clinging to the side of the wall with one hand, trying to hold the bag in the other hand, huffing and puffing. He was ready to drop dead.

"We were able to pull my car over to a garage that was close by and worked our way over to help Kenny with the cymbals, but by the time we got inside, it was about a quarter past five and they had already run down a tune. Kenny was really upset. Dankworth fired him on the spot and said, "you might as well go home, Kenny—you're not going to play tonight." That broke Kenny's heart, and at that point we didn't know what to do. We stayed with him to help him chill out, and we went across the street to a bar and had a couple of pops. We went back to the theater, and after things calmed down a bit, Kenny explained the problems we'd had with the traffic and such, and Dankworth said, okay, forget about it. So he played that night and the rest of the tour. That was such an off-the-wall day and night. I'll never forget it. Kenny Hadley and I still talk and laugh about that day. Today Kenny is one Boston's finest big band drummers, with his own 15-piece big band featuring jazz vocalist Amanda Carr.

A young Tony Williams (circa 1975)

Tony Williams during a clinic in 1986

Chapter 17

Love Those Ks

Tony Williams during a Zildjian Company visit

Lennie with Tony Williams (1985)

Of all the cymbals in the line, the K Zildjians were probably the most desired by jazz drummers. Many hours and days were spent in development and working with a variety of players. In doing so, Lennie discovered a few tricks along the way.

"I met Tony Williams for the first time in Boston when he was playing with Miles Davis at a club called Paul's Mall. It was the hot, swinging jazz spot in Boston run by Freddie Taylor, a big jazz lover and promoter. [After Paul's Mall, Freddie began booking and promoting jazz artists at Sculler's, a very successful Boston jazz club.] This had to be in the early '70s. Tony was no more than 17 or 18, and was developing a reputation as a great young jazz drummer. When I first walked into the club a few hours before the show, he was playing the piano, composing a few tunes, and I introduced myself. This was around five or six o'clock. The group was going to do a sound check, so I told him I had a bag of specially selected cymbals I wanted him to try and see if there were any he would like to use. He said he would try them out that night.

"So, I returned to the club around eight o'clock and caught the evening show, listening to Miles and the group, but Tony only tried a

Tony with his mother and father

Tony Williams during a clinic performance

couple of the cymbals. I think in those days Tony was really influenced by cats like Max Roach, Alan Dawson, Roy Haynes, and Elvin Jones, and he was into the old-fashioned vintage-type Ks. As you know, during that time period we didn't really have many cymbals in that category, so most of the stuff I showed Tony was the newer cymbals that were bright and shiny, and, naturally, finished off. As I said, he was into the older, classic cymbals, funky-looking, maybe handed down from one drummer to another. Because there wasn't anything he really liked, he continued to play the older Ks, picking up more of them over the next ten years of his career. When we finally had more stuff to offer, Tony came out to the factory, and that's when we struck up a close relationship with him. We outfitted him with a bunch of new Ks, ran some ads featuring him, and he became the most influential K Zildjian drummer. It was rare for Tony to do a clinic, but when he did, the place was always packed. I'll never forget his clinic at Wurlitzer's Music in Boston, when someone asked him to play the brushes. Tony said he never uses brushes because they were invented by a pissed-off bartender who hated loud music and drummers. Everyone laughed and that relaxed the audience. Then Tony went on to play his butt off, and he blew everybody away, as usual."

As we move ahead a few years, Zildjian continued to work on the new "old" K line of vintage cymbals, and we were getting many more great players of the day to use the product.

"Steve Gadd was one of the gifted and unique players who had an incredible influence when we were preparing to put the K Zildjian line back on the market, around the end of the '80s," Lennie recalls. "When Steve would come to the factory, many times we would end up in Armand's office, where we would have maybe four or five prototypes of cymbals we were working on. They would be lying there for an R&D session, and this one time we had some that were partially lathed and had just come out of the hammering department and looked pretty beat up. They were in the very raw stage and were probably a spin-off of the

Tony Williams (circa 1996)

Steve Gadd giving a clinic at
Bill Crowden's Drum Show, Chicago

Lennie and Steve Gadd

Earth Ride cymbals we had just put on the market. The Earth Rides only came in 20- and 22-inch sizes, and we were thinking about making some smaller sizes of the Earth Rides, relating them as the new vintage K line we were talking about putting back on the market.

"Steve spotted one of them and asked if he could try it and what had we done to them. We explained that they were only hammered, not lathed or finished, and I put some on a cymbal stand. Steve played them and he immediately loved them because they fit his style—extreme dryness. Now, when you eliminate the lathing, it dries out the cymbal, giving it a very heavy, pin-point definition with a stick. He said, 'They're perfect and absolutely what I want; a good, dry sound; a good stick sound; and they won't get in the way of the crash cymbal. Also, they will give me the extreme ride beat I've been looking for.'

"So we gave Steve one of those prototypes, and after six months to a year, we had cats calling in wanting to know about that new cymbal he was playing. Steve goes on tour and he bumps into a lot of drummers and they also see him on TV. That cymbal stood out like a sore thumb because of how it looked—beat up—not shiny and not a traditional-looking Zildjian cymbal. That became a trademark for Steve and led us into the new K line. He is still playing that type of cymbal today."

Many times when Lennie would be working with one drummer to help him with his cymbal

Steve Gadd, Lennie, Gregg Bissonette, Al Miller

Lennie, Adam Nussbaum, Ed Soph

needs, he would get a line on another player who would turn out to be a great asset for the company. Lennie describes another instance of a particularly important drummer he connected with.

"Adam Nussbaum, an all-time swing master, was hooked on the K line, and he would come to the factory to work on getting his sound. He always called me the 'good doctor.' He and I would work with the R&D engineer, Paul Frances, and go through the ritual of taking some metal off the cup area or thinning out the crown. Through the lathing process, we could thin or thicken the metal, and we used to do that a lot with Adam. When we were doing this with him, the new line was growing. Adam also hipped me to another player who would be a big help with the Ks.

"Around 1994, Adam said I should check out Bill Stewart, who was playing great. So I went to check him out, and I think he was playing with John Abercrombie at the time. Now, Bill was a quiet guy, not pretentious, and he was a collector. He had a selection of old Ks he had purchased at several hock shops, some from overseas—he loved the old vintage stuff—so he brought them to the factory. Some of those old Ks were probably 50 to 75 years old, and I considered them a little played out—suffering from metal fatigue. They still had a decent sound, they weren't very loud—on the subtle side—they just weren't alive and vibrant. Once again we were dealing with a unique player who was looking for a dryer sound, and those vintage cymbals were perfect for what he wanted. Well, come to find out, it was very difficult to match up cymbals like that because those old cymbals take on their own personality and have their own individual sound.

"That particular day it was very difficult to please Bill with what we had available. We didn't have much in the K line to show him, so Paul Frances and I realized that for him we were going to have to make up something special. We told him we would make up some prototypes for him to check out and that we would have him come back to the factory. In the meantime, I said to myself, we've got to come up with something for Bill today. Now I kinda knew what he was looking for, because the old vintage Ks had a little bit of a buzz to them, and if you put them up to your ear, you could hear it. Also, by using a magnifying glass, sometimes you can detect some very small, almost invisible cracks around the cup area or around the trademark—those are the most vulnerable areas for a little crack to start. I took one of Bill's cymbals, and using my magnifying glass, I did find some hair-

Zach, Sue, Mya, and Adam Nussbaum

Bill Stewart (2006)

line cracks, so I grabbed two or three cymbals in the size he was looking for, like a 20-inch medium-thin ride in our K vintage line with special hammering. I took them down into the factory, put them on the anvil, got a hammer, smacked them hard, and cracked the metal in two or three different places.

"I didn't tell Bill what I'd done but said I had found some old vintage cymbals that I had stuck away and wanted him to hear them and see if they were close to what he was looking for. We put the cymbals up on the bandstand. He sat behind the drums and started to play them and fell in love with them. He said, 'That's what I wanted, Len. I wanted to hear that bit of a buzz. And they've got a little bit of that dirty sound, gets a little rough, and doesn't have that high ping sound.' Bill wanted a little undisclosed stick sound with a little bit of growl in it, as we say, and it worked out fine. Bill left happy, and Paul and I got a big kick out of it because it bailed us out for that day.

"Bill came back about three months later and we told him what we had done. But he was still playing them and liked them. As we went on, we discovered some other creative ideas in the hammering process that helped us find what he was looking for in his ride cymbals and we were able to add those to the line. Bill became a valuable and very influential endorser for us and the K vintage line."

Steve Gadd and Lennie (circa 1981)

Another late night with the fabulous JEWOPs.

JEWOP partners in crime: Johnny Lee Lane, Lennie, Neil Grover, Dean Anderson

Chapter 18

From the Sublime to the Ridiculous

Lennie in one of his many famous disguises

Of all the chapters in the book, this one really stretches the imagination, even though it is all true. This chapter deals with some of the close encounters Lennie has had with some of Hollywood's TV stars.

First, the sublime:
Although many know of Lennie's drumming skills, most might not realize he has written articles for PAS, has judged contests, was listed in *Who's Who* (25 years ago), and invented and patented the *Flextrol*, a device for developing finger control. Lennie authored an article, "The History of Cymbals," for Eastman School of Music professor emeritus John Beck's *Encyclopedia of Percussion* (Garland Publishing Co.). JEWOP Lloyd McCausland also had an article in the encyclopedia, about plastic drum heads. In addition to the above, Lennie has, over the years, belonged to MENC, IAJE, Massachusetts Educators Association, the Berklee School of Music Advisory Board, Mid-West Band Organization, Texas Music Educators, and the National Band Association. And, as mentioned in a previous chapter, he was on the PAS board of directors for many years as well as the recipient of the PAS President's Industry Award in 1997.

To top it all off, he was on a popular TV show.

What's My Line?: Lennie, a TV star
It is difficult to imagine Lennie on a TV show like "What's My Line?" when he is bright and alert, but after no sleep and a long flight? Well? Heeere's Lennie!

"My TV appearance on 'What's My Line?' was almost a horror show. The show was shown the last week of June 1970 but was taped in New York in either March or April. Armand and I had been to a show in California that closed on Sunday night and the taping was the following Monday morning. We took a red-eye flight from

Record American, Boston, Wednesday, June 17, 1970

Bostonian Robert Allen, who designs laundry bags, is a guest on Channel 5's What's My Line stanza of this Thursday night, and Lennie Di Muzio of Cambridge, who manufactures musical cymbals, will be seen on the same show a week later. Both programs, I need hardly point out, already are on tape.

Lennie on "What's My Line" TV show

Lennie DiMuzio, Armand Zildjian

LA that got into New York at around three or four in the morning and I had to be at the TV studio at eight. We were exhausted from the show, got to the hotel, there was nothing to do, so we stayed up and had a few pops. By the time we got to the studio, I looked like a wreck. They had to do a dry run, and there were a lot of contestants. I had written to the show five years prior to getting accepted—that's how many people were writing in to get on the show. Wally Bruner was the master of ceremonies, and on the panel was Soupy Sales, Anita Gillette, Arlene Francis, and I think Jim Backus. I went back stage after I did my dry run, and Armand, who had been in the Green Room and had watched it on the monitor, said that when I came on I looked like something the cat dragged in. I could hardly keep my eyes open, couldn't talk straight, but I did get through it.

"The taping wasn't until the afternoon, so I did get a chance to go back to the hotel, lay down, and finally get myself presentable for the show. To continue on with the scenario, everything went okay. They weren't guessing what I actually did for a living because I was classified as a cymbal tester. So, there I was, questions were being fired at me left and right, and believe it or not, Soupy Sales is an ex-drummer, and his son, Hunt Sales, is a fine drummer living in Texas. Hunt loved to play a 24-inch ride, and he would call the factory and ask for that big ride. So I would occasionally send him one and over the years we became good friends.

"Okay, Soupy did know a little about manufacturing, and, you know, a little bit about what I was on the show for. About halfway through the questions, they were able to zero in and start to pinpoint exactly what I did for a living and narrow it down. So, Soupy finally figured out what I was all about and he told Arlene Frances and she asked, 'Do you manufacture cymbals, those things that you clang together?' And I said yes. So, with all that hoopla, you know, and all that there, they were all clapping and yelling. They asked me if I had brought any cymbals with me to demonstrate, and I had. I had brought the smallest pair of finger cymbals and a pair of 26-inch crash cymbals. So I performed onstage, and it was hilarious. I picked up those 26-inch cymbals, and I was so tired I could hardly lift them. But I managed to smack them once, and it brought the house down. It was quite a show. I got a lot of little gifts—I think $100, and they paid for the airfare and stuff like that, plus some cosmetics for the bride. So that was pretty much the whole scenario. Armand was backstage and thought it was hilarious. He met Clayton Moore, the movie star who played

Hall of Fame Banquet

Karen Hunt receiving plaque from Jim Campbell

Steve Houghton and Lennie DiMuzio

A highlight of the convention was the Friday night PAS Hall of Fame Banquet honoring educator and orchestral timpanist **Alexander Lepak**, composer and jazz pioneer **Shelly Manne**, notable teacher and author **George Lawrence Stone**, and drumset virtuoso and band leader **Tony Williams**. Other honors included the Outstanding Chapter President Award to Marshall Maley of the Virginia Chapter of PAS; the 1997 President's Industry Award to Lennie DiMuzio, of the Avedis Zildjian Co.; the Outstanding PAS Supporter Award to Steve Houghton; the Outstanding Service Award to Karen Hunt PASIC Logistics Coordinator; and the PAS Award of Appreciaton to Theresa Dimond for her role as PASIC '97 Host. Following the banquet Terry Gibbs with U.S. Navy Band Commodores Jazz Ensemble appeared in concert.

PASIC '97 PHOTOGRAPHY BY LISSA WALES & TERESA PETERSON

Lennie receives the 1997 Percussive Arts Society President's Industry Award

the Lone Ranger. He was also on that day, and we got to hang with him and shoot the shit. Armand was joking with him, cutting up—we had a ball."

Lennie the TV star. If Soupy Sales hadn't been there, and with Lennie's tap dancing ability, the show still might be going on. Enough of the sublime. Now to the ridiculous.

Lennie and Armand model clothes:

"This happened at a trade show in Chicago in the 1960s. At the time the company was rather conservative with expenses and we didn't have the luxury of having our own hotel rooms. Armand and I would double up in one room and the other guys would share rooms as well. We were out partying, going from one suite to another, and before you know it, we're halfway in the wrapper and it was getting real late—maybe three-thirty, four o'clock. At a show, you have to get up pretty early and be on the floor by nine o'clock. So we take our clothes off, go to bed, and bingo—the alarm goes off. We jump up, saying we've got to get to the floor, put our clothes on, run to the elevator, and get off at the lobby. Suddenly, I notice the sleeves on my coat are a little long and so are my trousers, and the suit didn't seem to fit right. I wonder what the hell is going on. Then I look at Armand, who is standing beside me, and his pants look like he was waiting for the flood of the century—they were way up above his ankles—and the coat sleeves were way up to his elbows. We looked at one another, started laughing, and realized we had put on each other's clothes. We had to turn around, go back to the room, and change our clothes. It was hysterical."

The nose knows:

Lennie had many disguises that he donned on various occasions. At any given moment he could appear as a Rabbi, a Mexican bandito, a priest, a cowboy, and so on. One of Lennie's most well-known disguises was a special nose. Attached to a pair of eyeglass frames was a rubberized facsimile of a male's protuberance. (For the faint of heart, we don't mean to offend. Its just that after our work for our respective companies, and our love of drums, cymbals and music, laughing and enjoying ourselves together with our friends was our greatest pleasure.) So, here we go. At a comedy roast held after Lennie received the PAS President's Industry Award in 1997, then Warner Bros. Publishers president Sandy Feldstein, during his personal roast of Lennie, gave Lennie a nickname befitting of his disguise, and it forever stuck, and the disguise itself came to be known by all as "The Nose."

We never knew when The Nose would appear. Many times, it showed up at some surprising point during the PASIC banquet. One year I was the banquet speaker and in the middle of my speech, out came The Nose. I'm standing on the podium trying to say a few words that are supposed to be serious, while addressing the somewhat formal crowd, and I glance into the audience and see The Nose! Another one of the funniest times The Nose appeared was when PASIC was held at the University of Tennessee in Knoxville during the '70s. The display day was over and several of us stopped off at the bar at the Holiday Inn where we were staying, for a quick pop before going to dinner. The group included Lennie, Dick Richardson, (president of Musser mallet instruments at that time), Norman Goldberg, (president of Studio 49 instruments), Maury and Jan Lishon (Frank's Drum Shop), and some others I can't remember.

Drummer friend, Jan Lishon, Lennie, Maury Lishon, Johnny Lee Lane

Lennie DiMuzio Caught Speechless

Anyone who has spent time with ***Lennie DiMuzio, Director of Orchestral***, knows that he has the "gift of gab". Lennie can always add to the conversation even if it's in a foreign tongue that's not quite recognizable.

But last month at the ***Awards Dinner*** for the ***Percussive Arts Society, Lennie*** was left speechless as it was announced that he was the ***recipient*** of the ***1997 President's Industry Award***. Nearly brought to tears before a standing ovation, ***Lennie*** graciously accepted the recognition he so much deserved.

As emotional as the moment was, ***Lennie*** miraculously recovered to be the life of the party given in his honor that night.

Lennie receives the PAS 1997 President's Industry Award

Marty Lishon, Franks Drum Shop, Chicago, IL

The waitress came to take our drink order. (Norm was just eating an apple, not having a drink). She was going around taking our orders, and the last person she came to was Lennie, who had just put on The Nose. He turned around to place his order. She took one look at The Nose and left in a serious huff, and refused to put in our drink order. Dick went up to the waitress to cool things out, offered her a nice tip, and asked her to please serve our drinks. Nope, no drinks, not from her or from the other waitresses. Not only were there to be no drinks, they invited us to leave. Dick took his money back and we left. We didn't know it at the time, but we were told later by others working at the bar that those particular waitresses working that shift were lesbians, so they didn't appreciate our humor or The Nose. (Norm complained he had been thrown out of the bar for just sitting there eating an apple.)

The capper to this story is that Halloween was that weekend, and at the same Holiday Inn that Saturday night, they were having a costume contest, complete with a band and refreshments. Marty Lishon, the son of Maury Lishon, was there and borrowed The Nose from Lennie and put it on. A woman, who was dressed up as a nun, was standing next to Marty and promptly bit The Nose, much to everyone's amusement. Then Lennie put on The Nose, he walked around the crowd, sat in with the band, and won the contest! Ironically, the celebration for the contest winner was held at the very bar mentioned in the last paragraph.

In the following story The Nose gets a come-uppance. Lennie kept up a steady stream of laughter while telling the following anecdote:

"This happened after a huge clinic show in New York. One of the artists performing was the great rock drummer for Guns N' Roses, Matt Sorum, who always dressed the part. The day was over and a large group of the performing clinicians and some of the drummers attending the show went back to the hotel and we had a nice little party in the hotel lounge. We always happily entertained the artists after any show, and especially after the big performances. Drummers love to hang with each other and the place was jumping. Of course, I had The Nose with me, and while I was sitting with the cats, I would occasionally put it on. Now, Matt Sorum was sitting at the bar with a beautiful girl and he called me over to his table. I took The Nose off and walked over to Matt, and he said, 'Lennie, I want you to meet my girlfriend, and I want you to show my lady The Nose. So I put it back on. Everybody was laughing, and she said, 'Well, I've got something to show you.' She had a tight, low-cut blouse on—and she pulls down the blouse, and out pops her, ahh, rather large boobs—and both of them had nipple rings on 'em. I almost peed my pants. I managed to say, 'Oh, bless my soul.' There she was, standing at the bar, showing me that she could top The Nose, and Matt says, 'Lennie, I thought you would get a kick out of that, you know what I mean?

Final score: Boobs—2, The Nose—1.

Matt Sorum and Lennie

Lennie in another of his disguises at an industry halloween party with his daughter Cecilia.

Señor Lennie

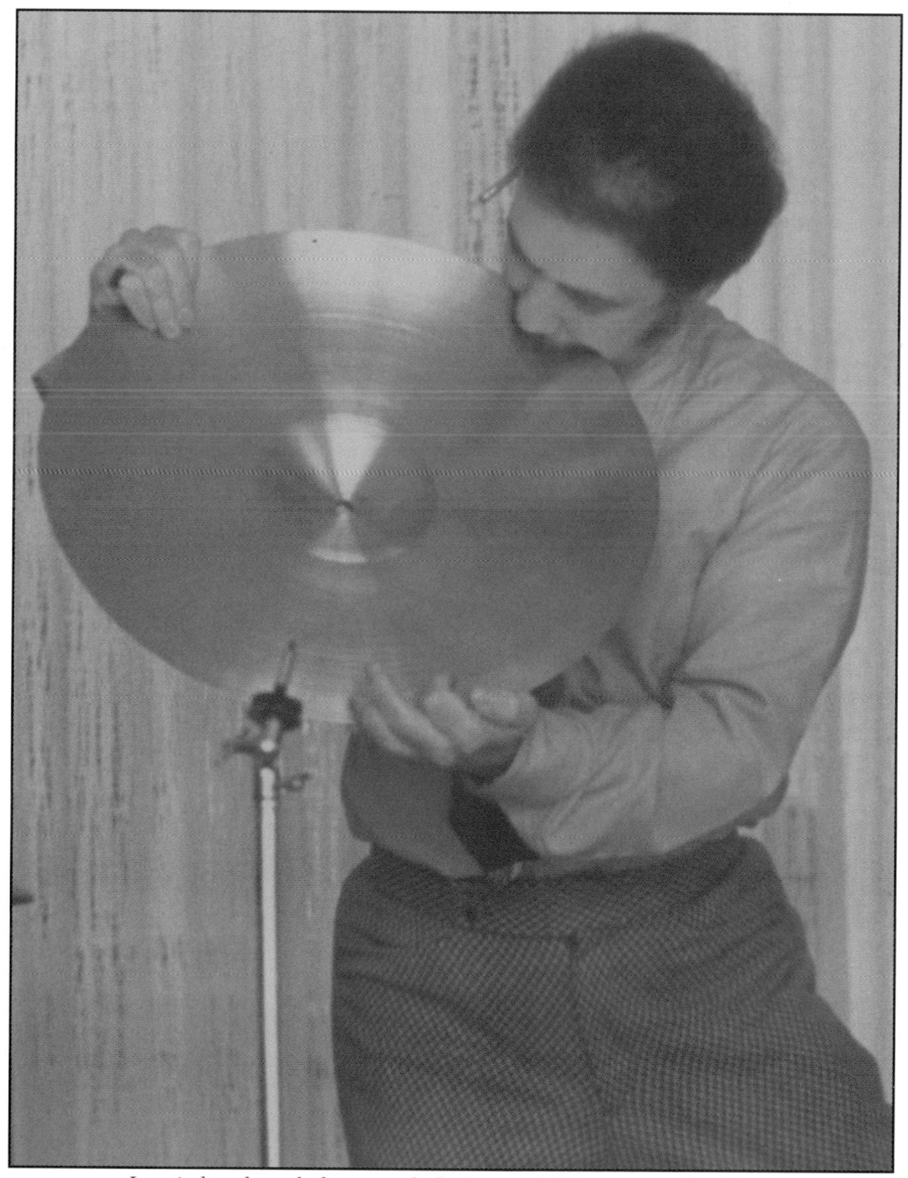

Lennie loved cymbals so much, he just couldn't get enough of them

Picture of Frank Sinatra autographed for Lennie during a concert at the Worcester Centrum, Worcester, MA (circa 1975)

Chapter 19

Irv Cottler: Bootin' Ol' Blue Eyes

Irv Cottler

Irv Cottler, "Mr. Steady," was not only called the best in the business by Frank Sinatra, but also he toured with bands such as Red Norvo, Jimmy Dorsey, and Les Brown, who all liked Irv's rock-solid time. After he moved to Los Angeles, his sense of time made him a first-call studio drummer, and he got the pick of the best jobs. In addition to TV commercials, he played on popular shows and movies such as "Mary Poppins," "The Jungle Book," "The Smothers Brothers Comedy Hour," "The Milton Berle Show," and "The Dinah Shore Show." Irv joined Sinatra's touring band in 1962 and continued with the band until his death. He also performed on practically all of Sinatra's Reprise recordings.

"Irv was a good friend of Armand and mine," Lennie recalls. "Whenever he came to Boston with Sinatra, he would always come to the factory, and he was very particular about his ride cymbals. I can see why, because he was backing up Sinatra and he had to have the right cymbal sound, the right projection, and everything had to be perfect. So, he was very fussy about his ride cymbals, and Frank loved his playing style.

"Well, Irv had bought me a ticket to see Sinatra up at the Worcester Centrum, up in Worcester, Mass., and I went backstage before the show and Irv introduced me to Frank. I did have the opportunity to shake hands with him, and I got an autographed picture from Frank

Las Vegas drummer Joey Vespe, Irv Cottler, Angie Del Abodia, percussionist, Chicago Symphony Orchestra (circa 1970)

that's hanging on my wall at home. Just before the concert started, there must have been, ooh, man, 25,000 people there, packed to the rafters. They had put the stage in the center of the auditorium, and the seats were around the floor going up to the balcony. Like I said, it was packed, and Frank always had a lot of bodyguards; they were sitting on the edge of the stage and facing the audience. I was sitting right down in front, you know, right alongside the bodyguards. Well, as Frank entered the auditorium, pandemonium broke out—people were going crazy, yelling, and cheering. But at that time, right in back of me, maybe about ten rows back, there were a lot of people screaming and yelling, and I could hear them saying, 'Get a doctor. Get a doctor quick.' With that enormous amount of noise, no one could really hear these people that were yelling for a real medical doctor.

"So, some woman comes running up to the stage, and one of the bodyguards grabbed her and she had to explain that there was a guy on the floor and it looked like he was having a heart attack. Frank, at that point, had just climbed onto the stage, which had been roped off like a boxing ring. The bodyguard got to Frank and told him what had happened, and Frank grabbed the mike and tried to calm the people down. He kept yelling, 'Please, stop, quiet please. We need a doctor. Is there a doctor in the house? Is there a doctor in the house?' That must have gone on for about five, six, seven minutes before the people, you know, started to realize that Frank was serious about the situation. Finally, when they were able to subdue the noise level, you know, the people were all pushing and all upset in back of me because there was that guy on the floor. Soon some police showed up and carried the guy out on a stretcher, and they went on with the concert. God, it was kinda weird, and I'll never forget that scenario. It was another one of those crazy nights.

"I just wanted to say a little about Irv because he was such a unique player."

In the '70s, when I was with Premier drums, Irv became an endorser. Frank was performing at the Sands in Vegas, and I got a call from Irv to fly out and catch the show, which I did, and met Irv just before their rehearsal. Frank, when he went to Vegas, took Irv; Bill Miller, the pianist and musical director; plus a lead trumpet. The rest of the band was filled out by local Vegas players. As Lennie said, Frank was always surrounded by bodyguards, and I was walking ahead of Irv to go backstage when these two giants came toward me. Irv yelled, "It's okay. He's with me." The gorillas stopped but kept a watchful eye on me. Frank came out while the band was getting set up, and Irv introduced me. Unlike Lennie, I didn't get an autographed photo.

There were stories about Frank not being able to read music and so forth—all hype for the unwashed. Anyway, Frank went to the piano and began to play the changes on one of the tunes he was going to sing. Later, he stopped the band and told the second alto to play a certain note stronger because that is what he listened for. For the evening show, I remained backstage, and while the comic finished his routine, Frank came out of his dressing room. He took a look at me, recognized me, and walked toward a long mirror hanging on the wall, stood in front of the mirror, slapped a hand on each side of his face, and said to himself, "I don't know how you do it, baby." He went onstage and knocked them dead. After the concert, Irv and I were invited to a dinner party where I got to sit next to Barbara, Frank's wife.

I have one more tale concerning Frank. You met my uncle Willie, the plumber, in the JEWOPs chapter, and when I told him about meeting Frank Sinatra, he said, "Oh, Frank and I are old friends." I was incredulous and said, "C'mon, how could you know him?" He went on to tell me that when he lived in Palm Springs, Frank was having a party, and either Barbara or a lady guest had dropped a ring down a sink. Willie was on call, so he went over to Frank's house and retrieved the ring. Frank gave him a drink, paid him, and then Willie went home. Uncle Willie and Frank Sinatra—amazing!

It might appear that this story was more about Frank Sinatra than Irv Cottler, but when Lennie and I worked with Irv, it was when he

Sonny Payne, who performed with Frank Sinatra in the late '50s, performing in My Music Room in Spokane, WA, during the Harry James era (1968)

was primarily with Frank. Irv was a no-nonsense drummer, who came on the gig and did his job with no theatrics, no showboating, just making every note count and everyone else sound good.

That's why Frank always wanted him, because he knew that each fill and each chart would be nailed. That doesn't mean Irv wouldn't take a stand. Billy May liked to tell the story of Irv straightening out singer Bobby Darin. On one chart, after Irv had played a drum break on the seventh and eighth bar of the intro, Darin stopped the band and went over to Irv and said, "This is how I want those bars played." Irv stood up and said, "You sing the songs, I'll play the drums, so fuck off." That took care of that. Lennie and I had nothing but respect for Irv—a great drummer and friend.

Irv was born in New York City February 13, 1918, and died August 8, 1989, in Rancho Mirage, California.

Harvey Mason and Lennie selecting some cymbals in the Zildjian Vault (circa 1978)

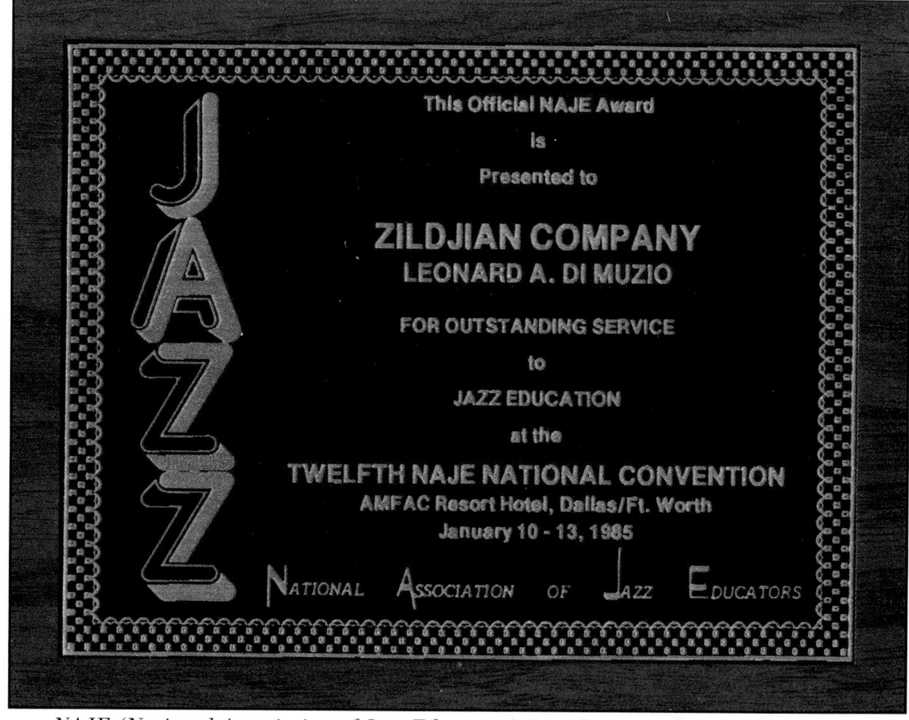

NAJE (National Association of Jazz Educators) Award presented to Lennie in 1985

Louie Bellson (1954)

Louie Bellson (circa 1970)

Chapter 20

Louie Bellson: A Double Kicker

Louie Bellson (1965)

Louie Bellson, called "the world's greatest drummer" by Duke Ellington, was born in 1918 in Moline, Illinois. At the age of 15 he started using two bass drums, unknown at the time, and at the age of 17 he won the Slingerland National Gene Krupa contest after competing against 40,000 contestants.

"Louie goes way back with the Zildjian Company and was always treated like the star that he was," Lennie reminisces. "He was very close friends of the Zildjians and became a very good friend of mine. In the early days he was very popular and played with a lot of great bands, like Duke Ellington, Count Basie, Tommy Dorsey, Harry James, cats like that. He also had his own combo and came to Boston quite a bit.

"There was this one particular time when Louie came to Boston with his small group and was booked into the Regatta Bar in the Charles Hotel, a very exclusive and expensive hotel. Naturally, Louie always sold out the room. And I was there, as usual—I wouldn't miss a night with Louie. There was a large parking garage across from the hotel, and for some reason I pulled in there rather than using the hotel's garage. After parking the car, I walked across the street, went into the hotel, and met Louie before the show. We had a bite to eat and got our business squared away. Louie performed—packed the joint, standing ovation. After the first set, he took a break and signed some autographs and things like that. He played the second set, and after that was over,

Louie Bellson, Pearl Bailey (1968)

Louie Bellson

it was around 12:00 to 12:30 then, standing around, talking, more autographs. Then Louie and I got together downstairs with a few of the guys in the band, and now it was around one or a quarter after. I told Louie I had to go and that I would call him in the morning and we'd pick up where we had left off.

"I walked across the street and the damn parking garage was closed, locked up for the evening, and I hadn't seen the sign that was standing off to the side of the door. Of course, they never put it where you can see it. It said that the garage closed at twelve o'clock and if your car wasn't out by twelve, you would have to come back in the morning to get it. No way I could get my car. I was pissed off. I didn't know what I was going to do. So, you know, I thought I'm going to have to go back to the hotel, get a room, and stay in the hotel for the night. So I go back in and Louie is still talking with some of the guys in the band and Louie said, 'What happened'?' And I said, 'Louie, I can't get my car out of the garage because it's closed down, so I'm going to have to stay in the hotel tonight. Let me go to the desk and see if there are any rooms available.' So I walk to the desk and Louie comes over with me, we're standing there, and the lady at the desk says, 'We do have some rooms available; they're $225 a night.' Louie says, '$225 a night? My God.' And I said 'Yeah, that's a lotta dough isn't it, Lou?' And he says, 'You're not going to spend that kinda money, Lennie. Stay in my room. I've got an enormous room. It's a big suite and the bed is like a bowling alley. Don't worry about a thing. I've got some pajamas, the whole damn thing. Pearl won't mind, and I'll explain it to her in the morning.'

"Louie was married to Pearl Bailey at the time, and he was joking, you know. So anyway, I stayed with Louie that night and he did have a beautiful suite. He gave me a Japanese bathrobe that Pearl had given him and a pair of silk pajamas. Man, I felt like the king of, ahh, what do you want to call it? The Queen of Sheba. God, it was great. Louie was so hospitable; it was just a wonderful thing. The next morning Louie and I get up and he gets a call; it's Pearl. And Louie says, 'Pearl, I want you to say hello to someone.' So I get on the phone and she doesn't know what the hell to make of it. She says, 'What are you doing there, Lennie?' I said I slept here with Louie last night, and she goes, 'Oh, my nerves. What has happened to Louie?'

Louie's piano player, John Brunch, Armand Zildjian, Louie Bellson, Lennie (1970)

Lennie, Louie Bellson, Armand Zildjian, 1970

Louie Bellson, Eddie DiMuzio, and Lennie DiMuzio at a recording session, 1975

"So I said, 'No, Pearl, the garage was locked up across the street and I couldn't get my car. I couldn't take a taxi way back to the factory, and Louie wouldn't let me rent a room, and he thought it would be a wonderful thing if I just stayed with him. So I did, Pearl, and believe me, he's still the straight cat that you married, so don't worry about a thing. Everything was just wonderful.' So she got the biggest kick out of it, Louie got a big kick out of it, and we were laughing our asses off and it was a beautiful thing and Louie came to my rescue." (Pearl and Louis were married for 40 years. Pearl passed away August 17, 1990, in Philadelphia.)

Louie has performed and/or recorded more than 200 albums as a leader, co-leader, or sideman with some of the greatest artists in the music world. He is also a great composer and arranger and an author of many books on drums and percussion. Although he is primarily known as a big band and jazz combo drummer, Louie is interested in all areas of the drumming world. Lennie recounts one time when he got Louie exposed to some really live rock 'n' roll.

Lennie, Dean Anderson, Louie Bellson, Armand Zildjian, Skip Hadden, and Berklee students during a Berklee College of Music visit to the Zildjian factory

"Louie was in town and visiting the factory. Sometimes he would come in a day early just to work on his cymbal selection. We worked a lot with Louie throughout his career and we made a lot of special things for him over the years.

Clinic/performance in Toronto Canada L-R: Armand Zildjian, Louis Bellson, Steve Smith, Steve Houghton, Lennie and band director, 1995

He was always so gracious, so polite. Louie is an incredible person and we all love him. On this particular day, he was at the factory and the Grateful Dead were playing downtown at the Boston Garden. I was on the phone with Mickey Hart and he wanted a couple of cymbals, so I told him I'd be glad to drop by, check out the concert, and bring some cymbals down. So I was planning on going down there that evening, and Louie didn't have much to do other than a little rehearsal that afternoon. They were going to open the following night. So Louie said, 'Lennie, why don't you come to my rehearsal and afterwards I'll go to the Grateful Dead with you.' He said that he'd never seen a major rock 'n' roll concert, and there was nothing bigger than the Dead. So I said, 'Louie, you got it; we'll do it.' We went to the rehearsal and Louie knocked that off in a couple of hours, and about eight o'clock we went to the Boston Garden and,

Louie Bellson, Peggy DiMuzio, Pauline DiMuzio (1975)

Steve Gadd and Louie Bellson Clinic Performance

bingo, we knocked off a couple of backstage passes. We went backstage and Louie met all the cats, and he loved it as he didn't really have an opportunity like that, and he was really looking forward to it. Well, I'll tell you, the Grateful Dead packed them in, about seventeen, eighteen thousand, and if anyone has seen the band, you know, they start playing—nothing's rehearsed—they just get on and start playing. One of the guitar players, it could have been Jerry Garcia or Bob Weir, would start a guitar theme or riff or something, then embellish it or extend it and almost make it a tune, and then the drummers would join in and, bingo, now they've got it cooking, and the place gets really rocking. So that went on for maybe, you know, a half-hour, like people who know the Dead, their tunes are not short tunes. The intensity in the hall, the sound level, and the cheering and yelling, after an hour it became unbearable because we were onstage right behind the band. It was getting difficult to hear the music properly, you know, or comprehend what was going on. So we waved goodbye to Mickey and he threw us a kiss and all that there, and he was absolutely thrilled to see us, and Louie was thrilled. We left and I took Louie back to the hotel. He had a wonderful evening. It was a treat for Louie."

As if seeing the Grateful Dead wasn't enough rock 'n' roll for Louie, Lennie recounts another story after the two of them had chosen some cymbals for Louie.

"Another time Louie came to Boston and was playing downtown with his combo. He came in a day early, came to the factory, and we did the cymbal routine, you know, selecting some new cymbals. Louie had a free night, so I picked up my daughter Thèrése and we all went out to

Bun E. Carlos of Cheap Trick

dinner. Now, there happened to be a rock 'n' roll band playing at the Boston Garden, and this time it was Cheap Trick, and Louie said he would like to see them. The drummer was Bun E. Carlos. We went backstage and I spotted Bun. He waved and then he saw Louie. Bun absolutely flipped out. He couldn't believe that Louie, you know, a drummer of his stature, would come to see him play a concert. Every time I've spoken to Bun afterward he has said that, perhaps, maybe, it was the highlight of his career to have someone like Louie come to see him play."

Joe Morello, Louie Bellson

Most of the drummers who would go to the Zildjian factory to select cymbals would, at one time or another, want something special for their cymbal set-up, something that would set them apart. Louie was no exception. One of his suggestions was truly a great idea, but a little ahead of its time.

Mickey Hart, Billy Kreutzman of the Grateful Dead

"This was many years ago, and Louie called me at home, one or one thirty in the morning," Lennie says, chuckling. "He was on the road somewhere, and he said, 'Lennie, I have an incredible idea.' So I said, 'Okay, Louie, what have you been thinking about?' So he says, 'You know when a drummer sits down behind the drumset, he's got one pair of hi-hats. Wouldn't it be nice to have another pair of hi-hats over somewhere, maybe in front of the drumset, but not in the shape of a pair that is round. How about making them with just a cup and two protruding lips out about seven or eight inches, and have them in a closed position so you would get sort of a dead sound, but yet you could play a beat on them.' So I said, 'Louie, you're the man, we'll do what we can.' We made a set for Louie out of 16-inch cymbals by cutting off maybe four or five inches off both sides of the cymbals, just leaving the cup area and four or five inches coming down lengthwise. Unfortunately, it didn't work out—not enough sound—so it wasn't practical. But I must say, Louie's idea wasn't that far-fetched, because about four or five years later, drummers started using a second pair of hats attached to their set on the right side, in the closed position, giving them a permanently closed hi-hat to play on the other side of the kit. So Louie was without a doubt an instigator in contributing to a second pair of hats attached to the drumset."

It appears that Louie didn't let the failure of his idea for a second hi-hat stop him from coming up with other ideas. One cymbal idea that Zildjian did realize for him ended up in their catalog and had some great sales for the company.

Billy Kreutzman, Mickey Hart (circa 1980)

Wedding of Francine and Louis Bellson (1992)

"Louie used to play a big 22-inch swish cymbal on the right-hand side of his drumset, getting that high, crunchy sound—Chinese sound—that was great for closing a tune or riding a hot chorus. One of the times when he came to the factory, we talked about the swish cymbals, and he asked, 'Is there something you could do to lower the pitch of the swish cymbal?' Now, the swish cymbal that Louie played had a turned-up edge and it got a weird sound. So we decided, instead of turning up the edge, leave it flat, about two inches from the outer edge, and flat all around the perimeter of the cymbal. The cymbal would have its normal shape of the cup and bow, a regular configuration, but the outer edge would be flat. Well, that certainly lowered the pitch, and instead of that high, crunchy sound you got a low, funky sound. We marketed the cymbal as a Pang cymbal, promoted it, and although it wasn't a big seller, it was innovative and worked well for some drummers. The Zildjian company sold Pang cymbals for about 20 to 25 years. But, eventually, with changing styles of music, we replaced it with other models that were created."

Louie has received many honors, including induction into the Modern Drummer's Hall of Fame and the Percussive Arts Society's Hall of Fame, in addition to the American Jazz Masters Award from the National Endowment for the Arts. He also received an honorary doctorate from Northern Illinois University.

"Louie was probably one of the greatest jazz educators of all the drummers of his generation," Lennie continues. "He participated in so many of the Zildjian showcases, so many festivals, and so many college band workshops. Louie was a wonderful teacher for both the students and the pros."

Louie continued performing, presenting clinics, and receiving awards throughout his career. He also remarried. On September 26, 1992, Francine Wright became Mrs. Louie Bellson at a beautiful ceremony in San Jose, California. Francine took on the duties of being Louie's manager, doing his PR work and assisting him in all aspects of continuing his drumming career. At the 2005 winter NAMM show in Anaheim, the Zildjian Company celebrated Louie's 80th birthday, along with Roy Haynes and Earl Palmer. It was a special evening for three special people.

As difficult as it might be for some to imagine, Louie maintained an impressive schedule of clinics and performances well past his 80th birthday. This was a testament to his love of music and the drums. As one of the friendliest and most well-loved drummers, he was never too busy to talk and flash his well-known smile. Louie Bellson was truly one of the drumming world's giants.

program, the proposal, what kind of sales figures we were looking at, and how we were going to present it to the Martin salesmen. While we're talking about all of this, the plane makes a few stops. After about, maybe, you know, three or four stops, we look out and thought we were at the right airport. We got off the plane, went into the lobby, sat there for about 15 minutes and no Bobby. After another half an hour, still no Bobby. So I say, let me go get the luggage, Armand. I go over and ask the porter and he says there wasn't any luggage. After I say there has to be some luggage, the porter asks where we were going. I tell him Nazareth, PA, and so the guy says, 'Oh, man, you passed that—it was two stops ago.' Jim, we missed the goddamn airport. We phoned Bobby, who was waiting for us at the Nazareth airport, and he wanted to know what had happened. After we told him, he said, 'Grab one of those cabbage cutters and fly back to Nazareth.'

Lennie and Les DeMerle

Ed Shaughnessy

"So we went out to the shuttle people, and they said there was a plane leaving in about a half an hour but we'd better hurry and get on board because it looked like a storm was coming in. Armand and I said that we'd take a shot at it. We got on that shuttle, got up in the air, and the pilot went right smack dab into the storm. That was one of the worst flights I've ever been on; the plane was dropping all over the sky like leaves falling from a tree. Whew, that was scary. Well, we finally landed at the Nazareth airport and Bobby was waiting for us. Everything was late, but we finally took care of business and everything turned out well."

Lennie is going to tell another story, this one about his good friend and drummer, Les DeMerle, now living in Florida and still kicking ass. Les played with several big bands, but at the time of this story he was living in Los Angeles and fronting his own band. Les was a very demonstrative drummer, quite a showman, and tended to feature many drum solos.

"We were out at the winter NAMM show in Anaheim, this was in the '70s, and Les and his

Les DeMerle

Vinnie Colaiuta

band was scheduled to play under a tent opposite Ed Shaughnessy's Big Band. The weather was quite warm. It was a major event, and a very beautiful day. Armand was in a new white suit that had to cost him four big ones, and I was in some sharp-looking clothes too. We always dressed up for those type of occasions. We were right down in front. Ed's band finished and then Les and his band came on stage, with Les in a bright red jumpsuit. The band started playing. Les was a fucking maniac that day—every other tune a drum solo. He saw Armand and me down front and then he really got psyched, the juices started flowing. On the last tune he must have taken a solo that lasted at least 15 minutes. He was burning up the lumber, sweating and playing his butt off. His jumpsuit was dripping wet; the crowd gave him a standing ovation. Les jumps off the drumset and throws a big hug around Armand and me. Everybody is yelling, 'yeah baby.' We were all laughing, and when Les stepped back, Armand's new white suit was redder than a bloody mary. The dye from the jumpsuit had all washed off onto both our suits.

Lennie, Vinnie Colaiuta, Kai Eckhart

It was hysterical. Armand was swearing, we were all laughing, and we both had to go change immediately. What a crazy night that was. In fact, later that night we found Les sound asleep on the hopper in one of the men's rooms."

No No-Doze Needed for These Two Guys

Both Armand and Lennie are noted for falling asleep at the most inopportune times. I'm going to tell this one. It was the day after Zildjian Day in Dallas, and we were all on our way to what is now the University of North Texas for a clinic by Vinnie Colaiuta, who had been one of the artists. On the way up in the car, Vinnie and Jay Wanamaker, who at that time was working with me at Yamaha, were trying to cut each other on who could play the fastest rudiments. They were pounding on the dashboard and the seats, driving everybody crazy. The clinic was held in a small auditorium for all the North Texas drumset students. We set up Vinnie's kit, he warmed up a bit, and then the students came in. Armand and Lennie were sitting in the middle of the second row, and I was in the third row over to the right. After the introduction, Vinnie began to play, and he was tearing it up. You never know with Vinnie, but that day he was cooking on all cylinders, playing everything. His chops were incredible, and the solo went on for more than 15 minutes. I was mesmerized, but something told me to check out Lennie and Armand. There they were, heads lying on the backs of their seats, their mouths open, cutting Zs like crazy. And Vinnie wasn't playing softly. In fact, at times he went off the Richter scale. I motioned to a couple of

Vinnie Colaiuta, Colin Schofield, Greg Bissonette, Lennie

Vinnie Colaiuta, Peter Erskine, Terri Lyne Carrington (Oct. 1983)

students sitting behind the two sleeping beauties to give them a nudge and wake them up. And, just as Vinnie stopped playing, Lennie and Armand bolted up, looked around rather dazed, and began to applaud. I don't see how anyone could have taken a snooze during Vinnie's playing, but the dynamic duo accomplished that feat.

This sleeping bit happened quite often with those two. Lennie elaborates:

"You know, Jim, Armand and I went to hundreds of clinics—most of them great but some of them were repetitive and boring. We'd been up late and so forth; you know what it can be like. So we took a little snooze during the clinic, and after the clinic—many of the clinicians were our artists—we'd go up on stage, give them our best wishes, say what a fabulous job they did. 'You really tore the place up, great representation for Zildjian, we really appreciate what you did.' We could say all these nice things to the artists, but we could not always speak specifically about their presentation because we had been napping and we didn't always catch all the licks the cats were laying down. What's a little nap between friends."

Vinnie Colaiuta, Steve Gadd, Lennie, Al Miller

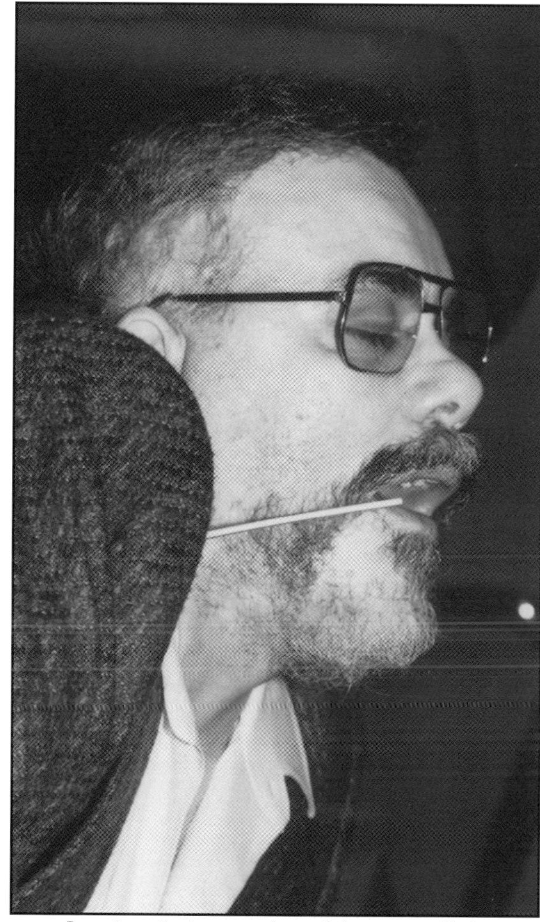

Lennie enjoying another of the many clinic performances he has attended

I can just imagine what is going through the minds of those Zildjian drummers who gave clinics and remember that Lennie and Armand said those exact words to them after their clinic—wondering if they slept during their performance. Other even more amazing sleeping stories follow in subsequent chapters. Can you imagine what Buddy Rich would have said if he had caught Lennie and Armand napping?

Lennie in The Mask hanging out with Armand Zildjian at a PAS Halloween party (1990)

Bobby Grausso, inventor and owner of the Fibes drum company. (1977)

Percy Brice, New York jazz drummer.

Chapter 22

A Potpourri of Cobham, Rich, Mr. A. Z., W. Newton, and Joey Lead Boots

Rab Zildjian, Armand Zildjian, Lennie, and Billy Cobham

Armand and Lennie visited many, many drummers in their years together, but the following story is special because Mr. Zildjian Sr. experienced a new type of drumming and had a great time.

"The reason I mention Billy Cobham is that there was a time when we did a beautiful ad on him. It was when he was in the prime of his career and was really hot. He was with the Mahavishnu Orchestra, in the '70s, and he was blowing everybody away with an approach to the drums that no one had ever seen. I'll never forget the night Buddy Rich was playing at a small joint in Boston; I think it was the Charles Playhouse, and Billy was playing down at the Jazz Workshop, also in Boston. Both bands were playing the same night, and first Armand and I went to see Billy and his band, and it was really incredible. He had such a phenomenal cymbal set-up in those days. And I guess you could say that he was a little ahead of his time, because he wasn't playing rock 'n' roll; it was more fusion than anything. And he had those incredible runs around his enormous drumset, and he would just knock your socks off.

"We stayed for a couple of sets and then Armand and I kept saying, 'Hey, you know, we're going to have to go and see Buddy. It was kinda funny because in the back of our minds, we were going to compare Billy to Buddy. It really wasn't fair because they were two different types of drummers. Buddy was playing with Jimmy Smith on organ and I think Illinois Jacquet on tenor—it was just a trio. Armand and I sat there and watched Buddy play with

Billy Cobham in Las Vegas, NV at his first clinic for the Zildjian Company (circa 1980)

Rudy Collins, Billy Cobham, Armand Zildjian, bassist Tim Landers

this trio, and he did a lot of work using brushes—this was one of the first times that I had seen such incredible brush work. They played the tune, 'Sweet Georgia Brown' at breakneck speed and Buddy played the whole tune on brushes and then took a long solo on brushes. And, you know, we just looked at one another and said, my god, Billy probably wouldn't even think of playing the brushes. But it just 'sanctioned' the fact that Buddy was untouchable, and it was such a beautiful thing.

"It was a great thing with both of those cats in town and showing off probably the best drumming you could ever want to see. Billy was a very strong part of Zildjian's advertising, and Armand and I put this incredible ad together. It showed a picture of Billy sitting in an easy chair, holding three or four cymbals up close to him, and it was called 'Sitting Pretty With Billy Cobham.' It was a classic ad."

Billy was born in Panama on May 16, 1944, and his parents moved to New York when he was eight years old. He was familiar with percussion instruments at an early age and really got into drums while playing in the St. Catherine's Drum and Bugle Corps. His musical credits are legendary—from Horace Silver to Shirley Scott, Miles Davis to the Grateful Dead, and of course Mahavishnu to Spectrum and everything in between.

Dizzy Gillespie, Lennie, George Wein

"We decided to put Billy out on some clinics. In fact, it was the first clinic we did with Billy and it was probably the first clinic he had done. It was out in Las Vegas at the Musicians Hall, and we timed it after a NAMM show in Anaheim. So we all flew out to Vegas, and the nice part about the clinic was that Mr. Zildjian came with us. The hall was packed with all of the Vegas drummers, and Billy did his thing. And Mr. Zildjian was in awe of Billy because he had never seen that type of drumming. Mr. Z was always just involved with the old-timers and never had the opportunity to see this incredible fusion drummer who everyone was raving about. So Mr. Z had a beautiful time there and Billy gave a great clinic. It was a big chapter in Zildjian history because Billy was at the top of the heap at that time. And he continued to stay up there for many, many years."

As long as we're in Vegas, there is another story concerning celebrities, drummers, and drum battles. And, of course, Lennie and Armand are again part of the main cast of characters.

"We always had a lot of musical stars visit the factory in addition to drummers. In the early '70s, Wayne Newton and his drummer Johnny Sciarrino were performing in a big Boston night club called Blinstrub's. Well, they came to the factory and we picked out a set of cymbals for Johnny and also gave a few pies to Wayne because he was dabbling with the drums and loved it. Wayne was also a good musician, in addition to his singing career. Both he and Johnny were thrilled to be at the factory, and that night we all went to Blinstrubs, spent the evening with Wayne, and had a ball.

"A few years later, Larry Linkin, the president of Slingerland Drums at that time, gave Wayne a set of drums, and we gave him a set of

Lennie, Armand Zildjian, Louie Bellson

Dizzy Gillespie selecting his own personal 22" swish cymbal

cymbals. After Slingerland, Larry was the president and CEO of the NAMM organizations for many years. Slingerland sponsored a series of drumming contests throughout the country, and the finalists were to perform in Las Vegas in one of the big hotels. Armand and I flew out there to be involved with the festivities. Slingerland brought out Louie Bellson, and he and Wayne had a battle of the drums onstage. Armand, Link, and I were the adjudicators for the contest and we were all onstage.

"Another time, Armand and I were out in Vegas to hang with Wayne Newton and also the drum shop owner Mo Mahoney, who also gigged in Vegas. Now, Mo was going to take us to a show and the drummer was Joey Vespa, a good show drummer and a nice kid. Joey was in the dressing room, so we went to check him out, and as we got closer to the room, we heard this thumping on the floor like someone was dancing. We go in and there is Joey behind a practice kit working on foot control using a method book. We looked down at his feet and he was wearing lead boots. Armand looked at Joey and said, 'What the hell are you doing with those lead boots on?' Joey said, 'You have to have something heavy on your feet to develop the muscles, build up your ankles. I spend hours with lead boots on.' Armand and I just looked at each other, smiled, and were afraid to ask Joey what he did for his hands. We had never seen anything like that before, except for a few eccentric innovations like square drumsticks, three-tipped plastic drumsticks, and a sliding foot pedal...oh my nerves."

Lennie with Larry Linkin (past president NAMM Association)

Louie Bellson (seated), Mo Mahoney (Las Vegas drum shop owner)

Back to the factory to add a few more well-known visitors. "Many instrumentalists and vocalists liked to play around with the drums, so over the years we had many visitors to the factory. One in particular was Stan Getz—in spite of what we did to him at the Blessed Sacrament church. Mel Torme was another, and he was a very close friend of Buddy Rich and wanted to play the same cymbals that Buddy used—had to be identical. Another great cat was Dizzy Gillespie, who came out several times and wanted to pick out his own swish cymbal. Diz loved the swish sound and actually made all his drummers play his special swish cymbal in his bands. Diz had a set of drums in his home and we outfitted him with cymbals. Another frequent visitor and one of Armand's big favorites was Maynard Ferguson and his band."

Zildjian employee Jimmy Wesson, Wayne Newton, Armand Zildjian, circa 1972

Publicity photo of a young Wayne Newton

Wayne Newton drummer Adam Shendal, Wayne Newton musical director Don Vince, Lennie

Wayne Newton, Ray Weinstein, Louie Bellson during a drum battle (1985)

Chapter 23

Some Short Cameos

Ronnie Vater, Chad Smith, Alan Vater (circa 2003)

This chapter contains some of Lennie's shorts stories. It is not that the following individuals are not important—they definitely are—but for this chapter, Lennie's recollections are like quick snapshots covering a period from the '60s to the '90s.

Making the Boss Pay and Escaping Death

"Al Moffit Sr. was one of my favorite drum reps. He was a great character and one of the top salesmen for the Slingerland Drum Company for many years. In fact, his son, Al Jr., is a Zildjian rep and handles all the drum corps responsibilities for the company. He grew up in the drum corps world, graduated from the West Point Academy, and is a very good rudimental drummer. Now, Al Sr. always hung out at the Zildjian booth at the NAMM show, and he liked to have a good time. We'd go out to dinner, he knew a lot of people, and introduced me to a lot of reps and things like that there. And he was a sport, always willing to pick up the tab.

"Many times at the end of the day at the NAMM show, I'd hang out with Al and six or seven of the Slingerland guys. We'd be sitting in the hotel lounge having a few pops when their president, Bud Slingerland, would drop by and sit down with us. Now, Bud would never put his hand in his pocket. The old adage—he had deep pockets and short hands—fit Bud to a tee. He'd sit down and have two or three pops with the guys and never throw a dime on the table, never pick up the tab. That really pissed off the salesmen. But Al was smooth, knew what to do, knew the drill, and he would always get Bud's room number, and when the tab came, he would sign Bud's name to it and just pass the bill to Bud's room. He used to kill us with that. The sales guys told funny stories about Bud. One story was that Bud was so frugal that he went out and bought a tractor lawn mower and would mow the lawn in front of the Slingerland factory himself. This is kind of unusual for a president and owner of a company today, but Bud was old school and that's how he built the business; hard work and watching the pennies."

Al Moffit Jr.

Lennie, Gregg Bissonette

In this next episode, Lennie takes one of those short power naps we mentioned earlier, though this time it might have saved his life.

"One time Al and I were at an MENC show outside Philadelphia, and in the evening he took me to a town, I think it was New Kensington, and it was definitely run by the mob. Al had some accounts there, and in the town was a jazz club. Now, Al wanted to take me to that club, so we drove out about 25, 30 miles to this small town. We got to the club and it was cool, yeah, it was a nice little spot, good music. You could see all the characters that were hanging out there playing cards, and they were definitely dubious characters. Al knew the piano player who was in the band. We hung out with him, and then, you know, after the show was over, we had a couple of pops and then headed home. Al drove a big Cadillac—he always had a Cadillac—and I was really beat, so, like, I jumped into the back seat and fell asleep. Al was going down the highway and it started raining out—it was a bad night. Now, I was pretty much sound asleep when all of a sudden bing, badda boom, badda bing, bing, bang. I fell off the back seat onto the floor, and the car starts spinning around, and spinning around, and God, we went right off the goddamn road and luckily hit a guard rail. Thank god Al was able to bring the car to a halt, because we were so close to going to the happy hunting ground it wasn't funny. I was all shook up, Al was banged up a little, and the car was totaled. We sat on the highway and we must have stayed there at least an hour to an hour and a half before the police showed up. Al gave them all kinds of bullshit stories about who he was, he was related to the governor and I was the governor's cousin, and we were just coming back from, you know, New Kensington, and we were out to that hot club, and I think that the police knew the connection with the club, and they probably thought that maybe we were pretty heavily known in the political area. So they drove us back to the hotel and had a tow truck come out to get Al's car. Later I said, 'Oh, Al, man, did we luck out.' And he said, 'Yeah, the road was really slippery. All of a sudden the car just started to fishtail and spin out. And that's what happened. Honest.' I laughed and said, 'Yeah sure, Al, I believe you.'

"Al came to the factory a lot, he was a great salesman, and we had a lot of fun hanging out together."

Lennie's Daughter Thèrése and Zildjian Accessories

"Another short story. Joey Kramer, drummer for Aerosmith, has been a good friend of mine

Gregg Bissonette

Lennie and Joey Kramer, circa 2000

for years. I got him on the Zildjian team at least 25 to 30 years ago. He'd come to the factory in one of his cool sports cars. He had many, and I think this one was a Maserati. We would go down to the cymbal vault and pick out some cymbals. Joey would let me select everything because he relied on my judgment. He was a very heavy hitter and a big-time rock 'n' roll star. Joey lives in my hometown of Marshfield, MA, and had a big cabin cruiser that he docked at the Green Harbor Yacht Club, which is five minutes from my house. What a rig—it must have been worth mega bucks. At that time, Joey didn't know that I also belonged to the club. All the members used to drool over his boat and ask me for guest passes to the shows.

Aerosmith's Joey Kramer

"I used to tell everyone at the club that my daughter Thèrése was in a national advertising campaign for the Zildjian Company with Joey.

"Zildjian had a marketing campaign to introduce their clothing and other paraphernalia by advertising beach blankets, beach umbrellas, and other cool stuff. They wanted to display the products on a real beach and not on a studio set, so I came up with the idea to use my beach at Green Harbor. Also, they would not have to hire a model because they could use my daughter Thèrése, who is a professional drummer and is gorgeous. So we got all the beach equipment plus the clothes and accessories all set up. The photographer was there and shot the ad with Thèrése, Joey, and A.J. Pero, the drummer for Twisted Sister. I often mention that ad session to Joey and A.J., and they remember the session and photos. It ended up being a great campaign for Zildjian."

Some Special Dancers (Thèrése Isn't Amused)

This is one time when having daughter Thèrése in tow might not have been such a good idea. But I think a story about a father and daughter's relationship might be a nice change.

"Gregg Bissonette was out on tour with David Lee Roth when they came through Boston to play a gig in Worcester, MA, at the Centrum. Thèrése and I went up to catch the show. Gregg was in his prime and Roth was a huge act at the time. I had backstage passes and all that special guest stuff, so after the show we

Thèrése DiMuzio, A.J. Pero, Joey Kramer (circa 1980)

went backstage and met all the cats in the band. We were in the dressing room and they had a big spread, and Gregg said that we should hang around because it was going to get interesting. So I kinda put two and two together. David Lee Roth was kinda wild in those days, if you recall, Jim, and he was always surrounded by beautiful women. After hanging for about an hour or so, a couple of chicks come in and they're talking to all of the cats in the band, and before you know it, they put some music on and the place is rocking. Now, these girls were moving and grooving and they were actually strippers. The girls start dancing around, you know, and start stripping and Thèrése started saying, 'Dad, c'mon, you've gotta get outta here—you know this isn't good for you. Mom will get mad.' I said, Thèrése, you know I've seen nude girls before—what are you talking about?' And she said, 'No, Dad, you know you can't stay here.' Then Gregg comes over and says, 'C'mon, your dad has seen a lot of this stuff in his lifetime, so leave him alone.' [So jump back, Thèrése.] The girls just did some dancing and stripping, and everybody was hanging, having a ball. I became good friends with Gregg and his dad, Bud, and we are still good friends today. They're both beautiful cats."

Those who know Lennie and have been around him late at night can appreciate this little gem that illustrates his knack for storytelling.

"This must have happened at the NAMM show in Anaheim about five or six years ago because, you know, I hadn't been to the show for quite a few years. It was a late night, naturally, all out to dinner, checking out some of the shows, and I was heading back to my room at the Hilton. Just about ready to enter my room when I hear this commotion in the next room—the cats were really cutting up. Whoa, it was a big bash, so I looked into the room and they started yelling 'Hey, Lennie, c'mon in, c'mon in, baby.' So I walked in there—it must have been one, one thirty, and I was kinda beat, you know, hanging and all that crap, kinda in the wrapper—and who was in there but Chad Smith, the drummer for the Red Hot Chili Peppers, and the Vater crew from the drumstick company.

Gregg Bissonette

"Before I tell the party story, let me tell you a little bit about the Vater Company. The two brothers, Alan and Ronnie Vater, own the company and are old friends of mine. In fact, their factory is located on the South Shore of Boston, close to Marshfield. Many years ago, probably 25–30 years ago, I was good friends with their dad, Clary, who unfortunately died quite young. He was a wonderful guy and he used to make drumsticks for Jack's Drum Shop in Boston. He then branched out on his own and bought a little manufacturing shop and started making sticks for lots of folks. At one time he even made sticks for Zildjian, but Zildjian wanted to grow things into a serious drumstick business so they invested in developing their own operation in Alabama. But regardless, as I said, I've always been good friends with Clary, Alan, and Ronnie, and Chad is one of their top endorsers.

"So I'm in the room and everyone is telling jokes and they asked me to, you know, start telling some jokes. There was no room to sit down—everyone is pretty much standing up—so I'm leaning against the door and I start running down my itinerary of old jokes. I'm knocking 'em dead, one after another. And then someone else would tell a joke, then another cat would tell a joke, and then I started to tell some more jokes, and then Chad said, 'Hey, Lennie, didn't you just tell us that joke about five minutes ago?' So I said, oh yeah, I guess I did, okay, I'll tell you another. I started and then they all yelled, 'Lennie, you just told us that joke.' I said, 'Man, I've got to get outta here, go to bed, I'm repeating the jokes over and over again—oh, my nerves.' Everyone was laughing, and that was the first time I had met Chad, and he's never forgotten that particular night, because every time we see each other, he always says, 'Lennie, remember that night when you kept telling the same jokes all over again? Man, you were killing us—you kept telling the same jokes and kept falling asleep.' "

Chad Smith wearing a lemon meringue pie (his favorite pie), carefully placed on his face by Lennie at a NAMM show party

Dennis Chambers, Casey Scheuerell, Thom Hannum, Gregg Bissonette, and Lennie "Dr. Poo Poo" DiMuzio in rare form. A typical and very common after-the-gig hang at a Chinese restaurant (1985)

Chapter 24

Gabriel, Blow Your Horn, and a German General

Maynard Ferguson (circa 1990)

Armand Zildjian was into music and especially loved the trumpet. He always had one in the trunk of his car. Being outgoing, he wouldn't hesitate taking his trumpet out and playing—in the parking lot, anywhere—he was going to do his thing. He also liked playing the piano and occasionally would get behind a set of drums. But the trumpet was his favorite.

"Maynard Ferguson was without a doubt one of Armand's favorite trumpet players, along

Lennie's daughter Cecelia with Maynard Ferguson

with his band," Lennie remembers. "He loved Maynard, and Maynard always had a roaring killer band, and whenever Maynard was in Boston, we would always go to hear him. If we were on the road, we would try to find out where the band was and try to go and see him. Armand played a little trumpet and was really influenced by Maynard.

"Now, one time, Maynard was playing down on the Cape about forty miles from the factory, in a Chinese restaurant, Johnny Yee's, and the band was featured there. We got a front-row table. Maynard starts out the set, and he was hot, tearing the house down. Armand would get very excited, especially when Maynard was blowing those hot, rip-roaring solos. We were sitting there, Maynard was blowing great, and Armand would be going through all his gestures, making believe he had his trumpet in his mouth and blowing the chart, you know, and he'd be whacking me and pushing the table. Every time Maynard would get into another solo, Armand would be jumping around, banging on the table. He got so excited he pushed me right off my chair. As I fell over, I hit the table, the table fell over, I'm on the floor, it was the end of the number, and everyone thought Armand was beating me up.

"The band stopped playing, the drummer and Maynard come over and ask, 'Are you guys okay? What happened?' We said, 'The band just drives us crazy and everything is really okay. We're just enjoying the music, and you guys are blowing the roof off.' As the night went on, Maynard would point to Armand and at his horn and finally he got Armand onstage, gave him a horn, and Armand stood in the back, in the middle of that great trumpet section, and actually played with them. He blew some crazy notes and some clunkers, but he also played some notes right on. It was hilarious, and both Maynard and Armand loved it. We always had special cymbals made up for Maynard's band, and we signed up just about every one of his drummers."

I must interject here that while Zildjian would always supply the band with cymbals, Yamaha would supply a drumset. It came about this way: Maynard has a music school in India and he needed some equipment, so Lennie picked out some cymbals, I supplied a Yamaha drumset, and we think LeBlanc supplied some horns, because Maynard played a LeBlanc trumpet. After that, Maynard insisted that all the drummers had to play Yamaha. Now back to Lennie:

"When Maynard came to Boston, he would always come to the factory on the bus, all the cats would get off, they would take a little tour, then we'd have some food and have a ball. We'd go to the gig and enjoy the band and the evening with Maynard. Once when the band was playing in our neck of the woods at the Cohasset Music Tent, we arranged that the guys would come to a cookout at Armand's

Armand Zildjian, Maynard Ferguson, Lennie

*Lennie, Maynard Ferguson,
Matt (sax player), Lennie's daughter Thèrése*

house, which was in Hingham, aside of Cohasset. Armand had a beautiful pad on the water with a little boathouse, a dock, and a large piece of land. The tables were all set up, and we were ready for the cookout.

"The band showed up about one o'clock that afternoon, we were cooking steaks and lobsters for all the cats, and Maynard was due in about three. He was flying in from LA, but his flight got canceled and he wouldn't land till around five-thirty or six. Because of that, we didn't think that Maynard would be able to make the party. Armand's pad was on the bay directly across the water to the dock at Logan Airport, about four or five miles away. We thought the best way was to launch Armand's boat and go over and pick up Maynard at the dock. So about five or six of us got in the boat and started toward the airport. About halfway across, the fog comes in real fast. We couldn't see a thing. We were pretty much stranded out there, and whoever was driving the boat said we couldn't make it and had to go back. We turned around, and when we got back, we phoned Maynard and told him to take a cab. He showed up around seven-thirty, and the concert was scheduled to start at eight. We get the band (the cats were feeling no pain) on the bus and rush Maynard to the theater. We were all looking bad, had steak and lobster stains all over our shirts; it was summertime, we looked a mess. But we got Maynard there in time and the concert went well. What a day that was!

"We were always there for Maynard and the band. We attended his 65th birthday party in New York at the Blue Note. Ed Sargent, who was Maynard's right-hand man, would always phone me with the band's itinerary, and when they got a new drummer, I would make a special selection of cymbals and ship them to the band. This went on for about 30 to 35 years. Over the years there were some classic concerts at Lennie's on the Turnpike—owned by Lennie Skoloff, a part-time drummer and jazz lover [Skoloff passed away in 2004]—sometimes with both Maynard's band and Buddy's band on the same stage.

"Another cat that Armand loved was the great Harry James. In the early days when Harry was traveling with his band, they would also perform at the Cohasset Music Tent, and Armand and I would always be there. One time when they were playing at the Tent—Lee DeMerle was on drums—it turned out to be a funny evening. After the concert, we were all

Maynard Ferguson (center) with a school brass section while teaching in India

Lennie, Ed Sargent (Maynard Ferguson's manager)

out in the parking lot and Armand got his trumpet out and began to play one of Harry's famous tunes, 'Cheri, Cheri, Bin.' All the people started yelling there's Harry James. I was holding them back, saying that Mr. James would sign some autographs, and I yelled over at Armand and said, 'Mr. James, will you sign some autographs?' Armand said sure and came over and signed some autographs. They also asked Les to sign some autographs. Pretty wild."

Concerning signing autographs, here's a bit of a funny note. This happened when I was working for Selmer in the '70s. I was at O'Hare Airport walking toward my plane when two little older ladies came running over to me and said, "Oh, Mr. Ives, we just love your singing." I thanked them, and then one asked me if I would autograph a piece of paper for them, because the girls back home wouldn't believe that they had met the famous Burl Ives. Sure, I said. I asked them their names, wrote a little something, and, with a big flourish, signed *Burl Ives* and dated it. Off they went, chattering down the concourse, looking at the paper I had signed. I'm sure glad they didn't ask me to sing "Jimmy Cracked Corn." In Japan I was known as Kentucky Fried Chicken—but that's yet another story.

Not Only Germany, But Also Japan

"We're going to finish out this chapter with a tale featuring a drummer and a very funny comedian. This took place many years ago out in LA when Armand and I went to one of the biggest drum shops, Bob Yaeger's Hollywood Professional Drum Shop. All of the cats hung out there, they all knew Bob, and he was a great guy. He later turned it over to his son, Stan, who took *Hollywood* out of the name, and it is still active today. In the old days that was the place to go and you never knew who you would run into. So, Armand and I were talking to Bob, hanging out, and this guy walks in dressed in a German military outfit. He looked like the Gestapo—had all the gear on, smoking a cigarette and walking around. I'm checking the guy out and it was really funny, Armand and I are breaking up, and I said to Bob, 'Who's that cat, man? Some weirdo just came in and he's dressed like he's going to war, you know, like the Second World War with Germany.' Bob said, 'Oh, man, that's Charlie Callis, the comedian.' Charlie was living in LA in those days and was doing bit parts, was on TV, and had a great act, a really funny guy. I went over and said hello to Charlie. He put his hand out and started talking in this fake German. 'Yo, you big a hotzin,

Maynard Ferguson

Harry James (1979)

gesudthein, bowsonheizien, mackasznel.' So I started talking back to him with my special German accent. 'Yavol, mein heirzen, youvax-inishen, machanixin.' We were carrying on this conversation in fake German bebop, Bob and Armand are dying laughing—God, it was a funny scene, I'm telling you. Charlie and I became good friends, and many people didn't know that Charlie was a good drummer. He loved to have his own personal cymbals, and I used to send him some and he used to put the drums in his act. I think that if Sid Caesar hadn't been around, Charlie would have been the big headliner. Sid was noted for his imitations and dialects and stuff like that. Charlie was also very funny and he used to do his tongue routine where he'd throw his tongue out and it must have been at least eight inches long."

My experience with Charlie took place in the late '80s at a NAMM show in Anaheim before the convention center renovation. Our Yamaha drumset display was in a room off a long entrance hallway leading into one of the main rooms. We had about six to eight kits displayed, with Zildjian cymbals, and some men from Hamamatsu City, Japan, had just walked in and were looking at the drums. Charlie walked in and asked if he could play one of the kits. I knew he could play, so I said sure, and Charlie got behind one of the sets and began to play a Krupa/Rich type of solo. I went over to the Japanese interpreter and explained who Charlie was. They all began to smile and bow. After a few minutes, Charlie stopped playing, looked over to the Japanese, and said, "It's all right about the Arizona." Whoa! When Charlie had begun to play, the room had filled up, and all of the onlookers started to laugh along with the Japanese, who didn't know what the laughter was all about after Charlie's Arizona quip. I slowly started to move away from the Japanese when Charlie began to play again. He continued to solo and then stopped again, peaked under one of the cymbals, and said, "Has my laundry showed up?" I left the room.

Lennie, Maynard Ferguson

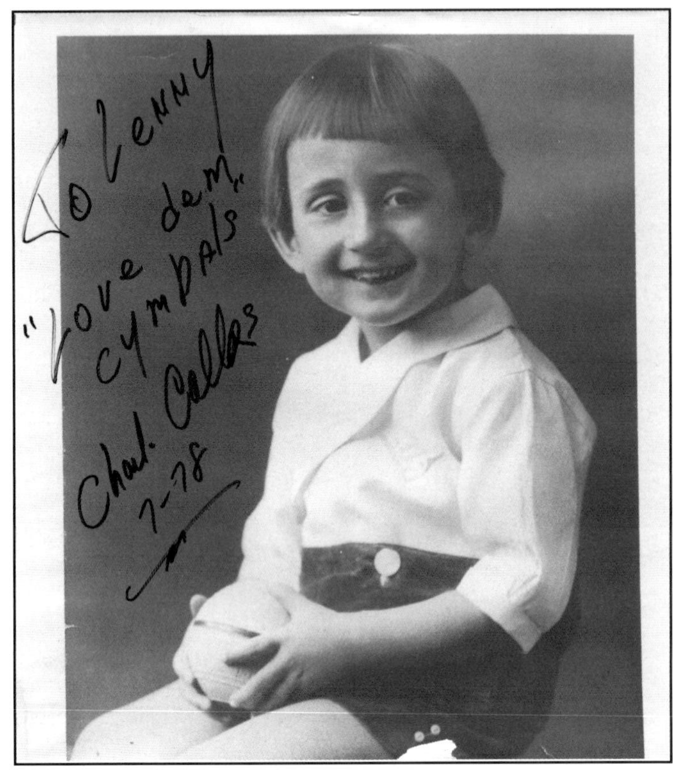

Charlie Callas

Zildjian rep Dan Costa, Maynard, Lennie, Amanda

Don Menza (Maynard's lead sax player), Lennie. Bill Morgan

Danny D'imperio performing with the Maynard Ferguson band in 1975

Some of Maynard Ferguson's Drummers

The late Roberto Petaccia performing with Maynard Ferguson

David Throckmorton, Lennie

Thérèse DiMuzio, Marco Marcinko, Lennie

Jeff Hamilton (circa 1982)

Ray Brinker

Armand Zildjian, Maynard Ferguson, Lennie (circa 2002)

Maynard Ferguson, Lennie, March 18 (1999)

Chapter 25

A Couple of Dozing-Off Stories and a Big Surprise

As you are aware, dear reader, some pretty bizarre things happened during Lennie's sojourn with the Zildjian Company, many of them dealing with sleep or lack thereof. Here is another story about a car, only this time it was Armand who was in the land of nod.

Where Was the Emergency Brake When It Was Needed?

"This happened around '65 or '66, Jim, and Leon Chiappini, who joined Zildjian a year after me and was one of our main cymbal testers for over 40 years, had a gig playing drums down on Cape Cod. This job Leon had was playing at a male impersonator strip joint, and he would come into work and tell us all about the groovy-looking dishes onstage. And the main act, Leon swore, you could not tell the man from a girl. Her name was Katrina or something. He said that when 'she' got dressed up, she was a perfect specimen of Miss America. Now, Leon kept raving about her and said that we had to come down and check out the show. So Armand and I went down to see what was happening.

"There was one act following another and then Katrina came out, and without a doubt she was gorgeous. You know what impersonators can do with their bodies and their makeup. She did her thing and it was terrific. She was talented and put on a great show. After the show was over, Leon invited her to sit with Armand and me. She sat down between us and we checked her out from head to toe. Believe me, there was no way you could tell that 'she' was a guy. And on a bad night, I'm telling ya, the last chance to go steady, and if you had a few pops, you would never know what could happen if you got caught up in a late-night chill-o-rama with her/him.

"So we had a few pops, watched Leon play the show, and then we all left. The three of us were

Lennie playing a little drums at the office (1965)

Max Weinberg

in my car driving back to the factory to drop off Armand. Armand fell asleep in the front seat. We got about halfway home when I had to pull over because I had to take a whiz. I jumped out of the car, ran over to the other side, and didn't realize that I had left the car in gear and it started rolling down the goddamn hill. Leon was in back of me in his car and he jumps out and yells, 'Lennie, your car is rolling down the hill!' Meanwhile, Armand is sound asleep, so we had to run like hell after the car. Leon managed to catch it, open the door, and jump in the front seat and pull the car over to the side of the road. About that time, Armand woke up and wanted to know what was going on. We told him we had just stopped for a whiz and that everything was cool. If he only knew."

The Amazing Snooze

It always amazes me—Lennie's ability to shut out loud music and fall asleep. I guess this section is aptly named.

"You know, there was a time when my daughter Thèrése worked for about five years as a cymbal tester for the Zildjian Company, and she would hang out and come to the concerts with us. To this day, she always reminisces about the time we were sitting right down in front at a Bruce Springsteen concert and Max Weinberg was the drummer. This happened in the late '70s and, as you know, Bruce's concerts were always long. He was known for this, and this one in particular, I guess, went for about four hours. Well, I got through maybe about an hour of the concert before I fell asleep right in front. Thèrése said that it was such a powerful concert that they were actually taking kids out on stretchers and someone collapsed right in front of us. And I'm sleeping—dead to the world. Can you believe it? They're carrying people out and I'm off in la-la land. Max was a great player, you know, and today he's doing the Conan O'Brien show on late-night TV, with his own band and kickin' ass."

A Happy 50th Story

This is one I wish I could have attended. They never did things like this where I used to work. The year is 1983, and Lennie is turning 50. The guys at Zildjian have masterfully managed a surprise birthday party and really manage to put one over on Lennie till the moment of surprise.

"It was a Friday afternoon, and a very attractive young lady comes to the factory and asks to speak to Lennie DiMuzio. The receptionist calls me to the front desk, and I couldn't fathom what this beautiful girl was doing asking for me. She said that she was working for a publication and was sent to write a story

Lennie's 50th birthday party

on the Zildjian Company. Also, she was instructed to speak to me about artist relations and all the drummers, and get a tour of the factory. I took her on the tour, through the factory, the melting room, everywhere, and the guys were tripping over themselves because, as I said, she was quite attractive. Everyone was getting a big kick out of it because I really took it seriously and had no idea what they were laughing about.

"When we got through with most of the tour, she said that she had heard about a very special drummers' lounge that Zildjian had, and she'd love to see some of the photographs and the artifacts, and would I mind showing it to her. Of course, I said I would be more than delighted. So I took her to the drummer's lounge, which was a beautiful place, had a lot of gold and platinum records on the walls, great photos, two drumsets, and a tremendous array of cymbals, as well as a little bar for cold drinks. We walk into the room and all hell breaks loose—everyone starts singing happy birthday. There was a bunch of guys hiding in the room with the lights out. Bingo, they snap the light on and everyone is singing and yelling Happy Birthday. Then they put some belly-dancing music on and the girl starts to do a dance. She was an exotic dancer from a Boston area night spot. The guys had worked out a deal with the owner of the club to have one of the dancers to put on a surprise birthday show.

"Her top was off and she had some words painted on her chest: 'If you catch me, you can have me. Happy birthday, Lennie.' All the guys were yelling 'C'mon, Lennie, catch her, catch her.' She's dancing around and the guys are hollering 'Go after her, go after her.' Naturally, I had to behave myself and of course it was all for the fellas to tease me a bit and in good fun. It was a beautiful thing they did for me that day. In spite of the hoopla, everyone was respectful to the girl. She did her dance and everyone politely thanked her and gave her a round of applause and she left. Then we all had a toast with some champagne and a great time together. It was an incredible 50th birthday party, and I was so grateful to all my friends for putting on the bash. Those were the good ol' days."

Lennie working the hi-hat

Alex Acuña, Steve Gadd performing at a PAS convention

Lennie and Alex Acuña during a winter visit to the Zildjian factory

Chapter 26

More Tales, With Some That Defy Description

Alex Acuña

While attempting to meet drummers' needs for cymbals, Lennie ran across some things logical, some things weird, and some things just plain bizarre. This chapter runs the gamut, with some surprising endings.

They're Not Just for Drumsets

As Latin and world music started to gain more notice, Lennie began to work with artists who required cymbals for sounds other than the standard jazz drummer's ***ding-dinga-ding-dinga-ding***. It was an interesting challenge, and Lennie was looking forward to solving their musical requirements. However, there was an unexpected incident that occurred before getting started.

Lennie with Alex Acuña's wife

"Alex Acuña, at least 20-some years ago, was living in New York but had a gig in Boston," Lennie commences. "Alex's wife and two kids were going to fly up from New York and I was to pick them up at the airport and drive them to the factory. Alex would drive out from playing in Boston, and we would hang out, pick cymbals, and go to dinner in the evening. So, I picked up the family at the airport, not sure which car I had at the time,

Lennie, Alex Acuña, Colin Schofield

probably a two-door Chevy Impala that didn't have a lot of room in the backseat. The kids were in the back and Alex's wife in the front, and we had to drive to Norwell. We were getting close to the factory when one of the kids—I think it was his boy, Jair, who at the time was about six or

Alex Acuña's children

seven years old—suddenly got carsick. He kept telling his mom that he was going to throw up. She was saying we're almost there. I'm saying

Walfredo De Los Reyes, Alex Acuña

another five minutes and we'll be there. We took the last turn to go down towards the factory, and Jair couldn't hold it any longer. He was standing up in the back, and just as we pulled up by the front door, he threw up all over my neck. It was running down the back of my head and neck, and I was jumping up and down. Alex's wife was reaching back and trying to use a handkerchief. It was too late—the damage was done. We pulled up at the factory—what a mess. She ran into the office and got some paper towels, and naturally we had to clean up the car. I went in and took a quick shower because I smelled like an old barnyard goat. That was my first meeting with Alex and the family, and I must say it was rather different.

"That afternoon we picked out some specially selected cymbals for Alex, and our association with him went on for many years. In the middle '90s, Alex wanted some special cymbals for Latin and studio work, because in addition to playing the drumset he did a lot of percussion work. At that time, we didn't have a lot of cymbals for Latin and ethnic drummers, so we began working with Alex, who had some great ideas. In fact, he was the primary influence in creating a line of Latin American cymbals for Zildjian and coined the brand name Azuka. These cymbals were also designed for striking with bare hands. They had an unusual taper on the outer edge so as not to cut the hand when struck. They were very thin and very explosive. The Azuka became a nice addition to the cymbal line."

Many players and groups were always looking for sounds outside of the usual ride, crash, and splash cymbals. Lennie often got caught up in some strange cymbal selection situations.

"I've got to tell you a funny story about a group that visited the factory. It was back in the '70s, and the Mothers of Invention—long hair, long beards, the whole damn thing—came out to pick out some big gongs. They wanted to add some big sounds to their group. We had a small vault off to the side of the main vault where we kept all the gongs. This story will kill you. There were about six cats in the band, maybe five, plus a couple of roadies, whatever, and we all went into this little room. Can you imagine? The room, maybe 20 by 20 feet, no windows, and certainly no air-conditioning.

Frank Zappa and the Mothers of Invention visit the Zildjian factory (1968)

"After about a half-hour smacking gongs, someone busted out some suspect smoking materials and they all started hitting up. I wasn't into that stuff, but between hitting the big 36- and 40-inch gongs, in a small room with no air or windows, everybody started laughing, and the sound was so goddamn loud, that every time one of those gongs was hit, it was like standing aside a 747 taking off. Man, after another 10 or 15 minutes, I was choking to death and my ears were totally blown out. I finally just gave up and ran for the front door. That was tough duty."

According to Lennie, one of the most interesting drummers who visited Zildjian was the Grateful Dead's Mickey Hart.

"He came out several times with Billy Kreutzman, who was also drumming with the band. Mickey was so enthusiastic and interested in the manufacturing side that he would stay as long as five hours because he wanted to see every facet of the cymbal-making process. He wanted to see how the cymbals were cast; the melting-down process; the copper and tin ingots; through the rolling process; through the ovens to get the metal heated up; stretched in the big rolling mills; put back in the ovens; brought out again; cups put in; after cooling down, on to preliminary pressing and shaping;

A young Mickey Hart (1965)

and so on and so forth. Mickey was really intense and into sound. He thought that if Zildjian could make some bells for him, some special marimba bars, special gongs and crotales, various types of metal plates, anything that would create a sound, it would give Zildjian another dimension and identification as the greatest metal workers in the world. We did try to cover some of his requests, but we really were not physically equipped in the factory in those days for Mickey's ideas.

Billy Kreutzman and Mickey Hart

"But as time went on we did move toward making some of the sound effects and other unique things Mickey suggested, and many of these became part of our permanent line."

You Want What?

"This story is really out there," Lennie starts off. "Many years ago, Jimmy Vincent was the drummer for Louie Prima and played in his band until Louie passed away. Jimmy lived in the North End of Boston in Little Italy, was a great drummer, sort of a Buddy Rich clone, and on Louie Prima's band would take very long solos. Whenever Louie and his band would play in Boston, he always performed in the North End, and just about every Italian would go to hear Louie's band. Jimmy would come to the factory, I got to know him really well, and we would make a cymbal selection. One time he made a very unusual request, but first you have to know that Jimmy, during his drum solos, liked to cut it up and be a little

Mickey Hart (circa 2000)

weird. Now, he would put on a gorilla mask and play for a minute, take off that mask and there would be another one underneath, play for a while, take off that mask and underneath would be another one, and so on. He would do that for about four or five masks and drive the people crazy. It was really funny.

"So Jimmy was thinking of something unique and funny, and he asked us to make him some square cymbals. Square cymbals, Jim. Can you believe it? Anyway, we said okay—we'd try anything. In order to make square cymbals, you have to cut down big cymbals into smaller cymbals by cutting off the edges. Armand and I took it upon ourselves to try it because it was a challenge, so we made four or five square cymbals. Unfortunately, when you cut off the outer edges to make them square, you kill the sound wave and have no sound whatsoever. I called Jimmy and told him there wasn't any sound because sound travels in a circular motion—similar to dropping a pebble into water and seeing the ripples. Sound relates the same way as the circle gets bigger and bigger—

Jimmy Vincent, seated (drummer for the Louie Prima Band from Boston) in Las Vegas (circa 1971)

Duffy Jackson, Harold Jones

that's how sound generates. So that didn't work out for Jimmy, but he was happy that we tried, and we became friends for many years. By the way, after Louie Prima died, Sam Butera, Louie's sax player, kept the Louie Prima band going for years. He is still blowing his ass off in Vegas, and Jimmy is still grooving right along, retired and also in Vegas."

Over the years, Lennie and Armand would see a lot of cymbal set-ups, and the following story is about one that was a little different.

"In the late '60s, Harold Jones from San Francisco, who later became a very good friend, was on the Basie Band when they came to Boston. He called us and we invited him out to the factory, and we had a great time with him talking, getting up to speed, learning about his career, and then we went downstairs and selected some cymbals for him. Harold was mostly interested in ride cymbals, as he didn't use too many crash cymbals at that time. He just wanted a couple of rides—20-inch, medium-heavy and a medium—a couple of crash cymbals, and a pair of 14-inch New Beat hats. It wasn't too difficult to please him.

Harold Jones, Count Basie Band

"So we went to the club to hear the band and see Harold play, and we were sitting down in front when he came out and got behind the drumset. I looked at Armand and said, 'How in hell can he play those cymbals in that position?' The ride cymbals were pretty much perpendicular to the floor. He had one ride on his left and another on his right, a crash on his far, far right, and his hi-hats. That was it! In order to get the cymbals to suspend at that angle, you would have to tighten the wing nuts down ungodly tight. The cymbals were almost straight up and down. Harold sounded great with the band, but the fact of the matter was, we could hardly hear the cymbals since they were chocked on the stand and they had no resonance. With cymbals at that angle, all you're gonna hear is the tip of the stick hitting the cymbal, and you can't crash a cymbal properly in that position. The crash will have not spread. Besides, you almost have to jump up to hit the upper edge and you can't do that because it would take you off the seat and it would be very awkward. It was very unorthodox, and when Harold got off the stand and sat down with us, the first thing I said was, 'Harold, how the hell can you play the cymbals at that angle?' He said, 'Oh, really, I can play them.' I said, 'I know, Harold, but we can't even hear them. You can't hear the cymbals; all we can hear is a stick ping. And you're playing with a big band, you need spread.' He didn't take offense to what we said; he was always very polite and a groovy cat, and he said, 'Really, you can't hear the cymbals?' And Armand said, 'No, really, Harold, we can't hear them, and how can you crash them? When you get to the end of a song, you need to be able to swipe the cymbal sideways to get a big beefy big band crash.'

"I think that Harold might have been influenced by some of the small-group bebop drummers of those days—Art Blakey, Philly Joe, Roy Haynes, the cats that played in small groups. That cymbal position is not too bad in that setting because you don't really need a lot of sustain and spread when you're playing with a small band. But with a big band, it's very different. You need the cymbal presence. Harold really appreciated all that information and he did start lowering the cymbals and tilting them on a better angle so he could get more crash and sustain out of his cymbals.

"From then on Armand, Harold, and I became great friends. I always tried to see him when he came to Boston. He came to the factory many times and he just loved to chat and hang out, and very much into the drum thing. One time Armand and I were in the shipping room when Harold came out, opened the door, and yelled, 'I'm here!' He took a vodka bottle out of his bag, rolled it across the floor, and said, 'Okay, fellas, it's time for a break. A little toddy for the body.' So, we took a break."

Chapter 27

Tommy Thompson, Crotales, and the Tokyo Symphony

Tommy Thompson

Even before Lennie got heavily involved with the manufacturing of symphonic cymbals, he worked with some of the top orchestral percussionists. This story begins back when Zildjian was still located in a factory in Quincy, and it has a few twists and turns.

"Tommy Thompson was an outstanding cymbalist and percussionist with the Boston Symphony Orchestra and worked part-time for Zildjian," Lennie says chuckling, thinking ahead. "Tommy was a real character and one-of-a kind. One of the jobs he had was to tune the crotales, and occasionally I had to help him. These crotales were small, thick disc-like cymbals that had a two-octave spread, starting from middle C. Naturally, the crotales needed to be tuned perfectly, and Tommy used his perfect pitch and a Strobeconn, which is a mechanical tuning device.

"Bob Zildjian had designed some unique rudimental educational charts, including a cymbal chart, with percussionist and writer John Noonan, a professor at Indiana University. Now of course Tommy was good friends with Bob Z., and he told Bob that he felt the cymbal chart should be revised. [The cymbal chart we are referred to here was a special piece of literature for developing cymbal technique.] Bob said fine, that I should get together with Tommy and do the revision. When Tommy came to the factory, his neck and back were all bandaged up. I said, 'Tommy, what the hell happened to you?' He said, 'Oh, man! I fell asleep on the radiator last night and I've got third-degree burns on my back.' Maybe he was in the wrapper, I don't know, but when he got sleepy, he leaned against the radiator while he was dozing off and badda-bing, badda-bang.

"I must say that Tommy was a character. I went to his apartment to work on the cymbal chart. He lived alone, and you never knew what you would find in his apartment. We sat

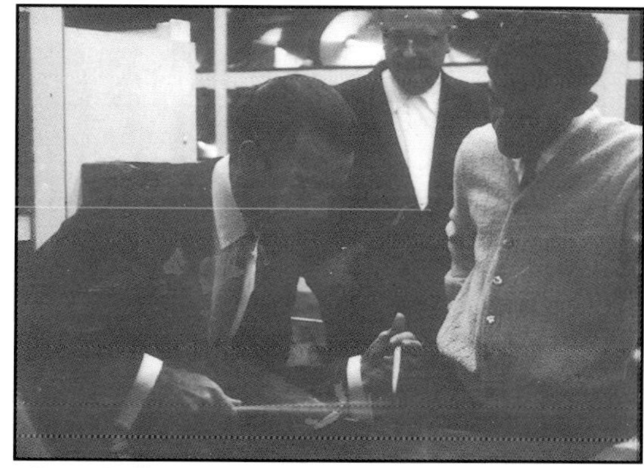
Louie Bellson giving Tommy Thompson and Lennie a drum lesson at the factory

Backstage — Ethel Noonan receives professional assistance from Ellington drummer, Dave Black, l, and husband John Noonan — who can also roll a mean "paradiddle."

Dave Black, Ethel Noonan, John Noonan.
John wrote the first cymbal playing method chart for the Zildjian Company.

down in his kitchen, and Tommy suggested that we have a glass of wine and maybe some food. He opened the cupboard doors above the stove and I saw at least 100 cans of Franco-American spaghetti. Can you believe that? Also, there was a whole bunch of cans of Campbell's tomato soup. He took down a can, opened it up, and went to pour it in a pan, missed the pan, it hit the stove and splattered all over the floor. I'm laughing and Tommy gets mad and said to hell with the soup, let's have a TV dinner. He went to the refrigerator, pulled out a frozen dinner, opened up the oven door, and inside was a frozen dinner that he had put in there about a week before—it was all green and moldy. That took care of dinner. So we just continued to drink the cuckoo juice and forgot about revising the rudimental chart.

"About an hour went by when there was a knock on the door. In came a tuba player and a young female violinist. They walked right by us, said hello to Tommy, and headed for a bedroom. They were in there for about a half hour, and we could hear the bed squeaking and thumping against the wall. I said, 'Tommy what the hell is going on in there?' Tommy said, 'Forget it, man. I rent the room to the cat for 20 bucks a night once a week.' I fell apart and said I can dig it—different strokes for different folks. I figured I better leave before I had a nervous breakdown, so I split.

"Tommy called me the next day and told me that the Tokyo Symphony was playing in Boston and he wanted to bring the percussion section to the factory. I told Tommy to bring the percussionists out and we would introduce them to Mr. Avedis Zildjian and Armand. Tommy arrives with four or five cats from the orchestra, we greet them at the door, give them a tour of the factory, and end up in the shipping room, and Tommy starts to demonstrate some of the cymbals. Now before I go on, you have to know that Tommy loved jazz, especially Duke Ellington and was a good friend of Duke's drummer, Sam Woodyard. Tommy always used jazz lingo, never really spoke 'straight,' always used his own cool jive talk. Just as Tommy is starting to demonstrate the cymbals, Mr. Zildjian walks in to join the group. Tommy introduces Mr. Zildjian to the Japanese and everyone started bowing. They are all bowing and saying, 'Oh

Woody Herman and Tommy Thompson of the Boston Symphony Orchestra in the vault circa 1963

yes, Mr. Zildjian, Mr. Zildjian.' I started bowing, Armand also started bowing, and we all must have bowed for about five minutes. Then Tommy picks up a big pair of 24-inch cymbals and starts to demonstrate while talking all this jazz lingo: 'Like, man, you've got to get the groove going, you've got to get the edges placed in real cool, get this cymbal laid over that, and keep moving with the arms. Keep the sound moving and watch the swing.' It was hilarious because Tommy had his own lingo and the Japanese didn't have a clue as to what he was saying. They just kept bowing and saying, 'Ahh-so, vely good, Mr. Thompson.' I was falling apart.

"Mr. Zildjian and Armand were going to take everyone to lunch. As we're getting ready, I tap Tommy on the shoulder and ask him the name of the head percussionist. He says, 'Like, you know, baby, Chinganakanoya." So I say okay, Tommy, and we go to lunch. We're sitting there talking and I'm saying Mr. Chinganakanoya and he isn't answering me. So I say Ching Shing, and he looks over at me like I'm from another planet. Again I say, Mr. Chinganakanoya. Armand is breaking up and Tommy has a big grin on his face and Armand whispers in my ear, 'Lennie, man, his name isn't Chinganakanoya. Tommy made that up. His name is something like Osake Yakamoto.'

Harold Thompson Services Tomorrow, BSO Percussionist Killed on Pike

Services for Harold Thompson, 53, of 80 The Fenway, Boston Symphony Orchestra percussionist killed on the Massachusetts Turnpike in Brighton, Monday night, will be tomorrow at 2 p.m., in the Waterman Chapel, Kenmore square.

Police said Mr. Thompson was inspecting his car after it hit an abutment, and was struck by a truck.

Mr. Thompson was credited with inventing or improving several percussion instruments and had an extensive collection of cymbals illustrating the history, production and uses of the instrument. He had been compiling an instruction text on percussion instruments.

He joined the Boston Symphony in 1953, under Conductor Charles Munch. He had been the orchestra's cymbals specialist since then. At yesterday's rehearsal, Erich Leinsdorf, present conductor, paid tribute to him.

Mr. Thompson was born in Akron, Ohio. He began serious study of the percussion instruments at the age of 12 under Charles Wilcox, a Cleveland jazz band and theater drummer. He later studied at the Cincinnati Conservatory, and was a member of the Cincinnati Symphony for eight years before joining the Boston orchestra.

He leaves his wife, ~~Elaine~~ Eileen, two daughters, Karen and Nancy, and a sister, Mrs. Janet Hyde of Schenectady, N. Y.

Tommy of the big bang

Symphony loses one of its finest

By MARGO MILLER

Harold Thompson was perhaps the most visible player in the Boston Symphony. He was a tall, bulky man with a ruddy complextion under his crewcut and he played cymbals. Percussion players move around a lot tending their batterie of the stage. Sometimes they carry their music around and always they are counting.

But they are always in the right place at the right time. You would see Tommy come to rest before a stack of cymbals, slide into the hand straps, lift the metal discs, check the coductor. Tommy's large frame, nodding to the beat, then hefted the cymbals, crashed them before him and arms arcing outward made cymbals and Symphony Hall ring to the echo.

This was the big bang of cymbal playing, its razzle-dazzle heroics. There were of course other techniques, as the music might demand: The clash and abrupt stifling of sound, or the wash-wash of cymbals scrubbed against one another tight and dry, or the gay, warm jangle, funny and loose, or the feathery, mysterious shimmer.

Tommy did them all. He was a master colorist, working with the 18-inchers up to the big ones, two feet across, that took quite a man to control. "He was one of our finest artists", says Vic Firth, B.S.O. timpanist, who was speaking for music in general.

Thompson, 53, was fatally injured last Monday on the Brighton part of the Massachusetts Pike. Inspecting minor damage to his car, he was hit by a truck.

At the B.S.O. concerts, they played Gluck's Dance of the Sacred Spirits. "Well I guess something with cymbals would be out of place," said a lameter. "Goddam senseless accident."

Another: "Tommy was a wild man but a very gentle wild man."

Who took his trout down Maine. "I never got a line out like that," reminisced Robert Zildjian whose firm in Quincy makes cymbals and who regards Thompson as he Menuhin of the instrument. "He thought like an artist. And he knew the answers before the question was asked. A certainty to everything, like the time we went to a store to look at those life preservers, those life rings you inflate and you put your feet in. And Tommy blew one up in the middle of the store and began telling me how you could float down stream casting."

Tommy was a belote player and master of the bluff. Players who didn't know his card stratagems would find Tommy taking hands on very little, "just for the hell of it."

And he gave. To B.S.O. conductor Erich Leinsdorf a letter by Daniel Webster. To B.S.O. archivist Laning Humphrey, two Norse figures with poleaxes, "something he'd found."

He was generous about other players' innovations, calling the Globe once to have us send a reporter over to see a new bass drum which Vic Firth and Leinsdorf had had made in London. Or writing to tell us that Artie Press, not Tommy, as reported, had come up with the ironwork to sound King Henry's sword in Boston's "Lohengrin" recording.

Zildjian: "We make cymbals for universal taste. We've learned a lot from Tommy and he learned from us. With him, it would be cymbals for special problems, or cymbals for some buddy wanting a special sound. He had a sensitivity to sound beyond the normal ear and what you don't often see in percussion, an all-round musician."

Charles Munch got Tommy for the Boston Symphony, in 1953. Zildjian thinks this cymbal sound changed the whole essence of the B.S.O. Tommy played Pops, too, and it was he who "auditioned" the beat-up portable which his collegue Charlie Smith plays in "The Typewriter."

Tommy was a talker, in a gravelled, highish voice. It came out sometimes with boyish amazement ("How about that!") and often in floods of jazz talk. Tommy, born in Akron, trained at the Cincinnati Conservatory and cymbalist with the Cincinnati Symphony, had begun at 12 with the jazz drummer Charlie Wilcox. He knocked about, playing medicine shows, cabaret, the pit for opera and ballet and musicals.

And here in Boston, when the Boston Ballet first did "Road of The Phoebe Snow," Tommy who was playing the "straight" part of the evening, was eager to hear what Herb Pomeroy and Duke Ellington had arranged from Ellington's score.

I remember Tommy at this intermission. He was in his orchestra tails and spouting about Ellington's bag and lead sheets and a lot of other things I didn't quite dig. In this enthusiastic chatter he bumped into a small, neat, quiet man, in a small, tidy double-breasted blazer. Apologies began, then we were introduced all around, with Tommy identifying the man as John Taras of the New York City Ballet up to see the Boston do his piece. And Tommy was off on how nice that was and how hard the kids had worked on it and wasn't it splendid what they were doing and what a nice evening it was for everyone.

Newspaper articles about the unfortunate passing of Harold "Tommy" Thompson

Larrie Londin, Zildjian Day, USC Campus (1983)

my foot on his pedal. I couldn't move it. I couldn't get the pedal to work because my foot wasn't strong enough. I actually had to stand up and try to push the pedal down. I still couldn't push it down. No one in the world had a foot pedal like Larrie. He designed his pedal and tried to put it on the market, but it didn't connect because, I think, he was the only one who could use it."

I also have a story concerning Larrie's pedal. I'm not sure if the pedal he was using at the time was a Premier 252 or his own design. Anyway, when the beater ball was at rest, it was almost resting on the foot board. Like Lennie, I sat down, put my foot on the board and pushed down. The beater ball struck the head but the spring was tensioned so tight it immediately flew back, hitting my ankle with such force I thought it was broken. I got off the stool and limped away. Back to Lennie.

"Now, Larrie, for a big guy, had tremendous finesse around the drumset, and was a great performer and clinician, not to mention a mainstay in the country music recording scene. He knew everyone and everyone knew him. We shared a lot of friends and Larrie introduced me to some major drumming players of that scene, such as Dennis St. James, who had spent many years with Roy Orbison. Another was Ron Tutt, who had spent many years with Elvis.

"Larrie and his wife had a beautiful drum shop in Nashville for many years. Sadly and most surprisingly, he passed away on August 24, 1992 at the young age of forty-eight, while performing a clinic in Texas at NTSU. He had switched from Zildjian to Sabian earlier in his career, and Sabian established a PAS scholarship in his name. I still see his son Sean at the NAMM shows.

"One last story, featuring Joe Morello, Bernard Purdie, and Larrie. At one of the NAMM shows, we put on a clinic with the Ludwig drum company called Drum-A-Rama, and they brought out Joe, who was a strong Zildjian artist at that time. We set up three drumsets in one of the big hospitality rooms, and Joe, Bernard, and Larrie took turns playing and tearing the house apart. Bernard kept calling for me to come up on the stage and play. So I decided to go up and actually duked it out with those guys, and afterward, Bernard said, 'Lennie, what were you doing up there? You should be out on the road. You blew the shit outta those drums. You made me look like a beginner.' Larrie got a big kick out of that. Larrie was a great guy, and we all miss him dearly."

Larrie became known as country music's top studio drummer. His performing and recording credits seem endless—a short list covers 40-plus artists. Although many drummers have said that Buddy Rich was the best, Chet Atkins said Larrie was the greatest. I had the pleasure of working with Larrie when he

Larrie Londin, Bernard Purdie (circa 1985)

endorsed Yamaha drums, and, like Lennie, I had the highest respect for his talents and considered him a good friend.

Anybody for a Bat Snack?

"We all went to see Ozzy Osbourne when he had his rock band and also visit with his drummer, Randy Castillo. The concert was at the Boston Garden, and that was when all the promotion and part of the extravaganza was Ozzy biting the head off a bat. It was really gross, but quite a hit with his audience. I don't know if the bat was alive or dead. Maybe it was a stuffed doll. Randy was a great player, a good friend, and we always enjoyed having him come to the factory. He passed away in 2002."

Larrie Londin, drummer for Elvis Presley, 48

NASHVILLE, Tenn. — Drummer Larrie Londin, who played in Elvis Presley's last concerts and recorded with stars of Motown and country music, has died at age 48.

Mr. Londin died Monday at Baptist Hospital. He had suffered an irregular heartbeat April 24 and lapsed into a coma.

As a recording session drummer in Detroit, he played on hit records by the Supremes, Marvin Gaye and the Temptations.

He moved to Nashville from Detroit in 1969 and toured with various rock 'n' roll and country stars. He played at Presley's last two concerts in 1977.

After that, he began concentrating on studio work. He drummed on pop recordings by Glenn Frey, Journey, the Carpenters and Adrian Belew and on country songs by Randy Travis, Reba McEntire, Vince Gill, George Strait, Dan Seals and others.

Mr. Londin is survived by his wife and two sons. —AP

Larrie Londin

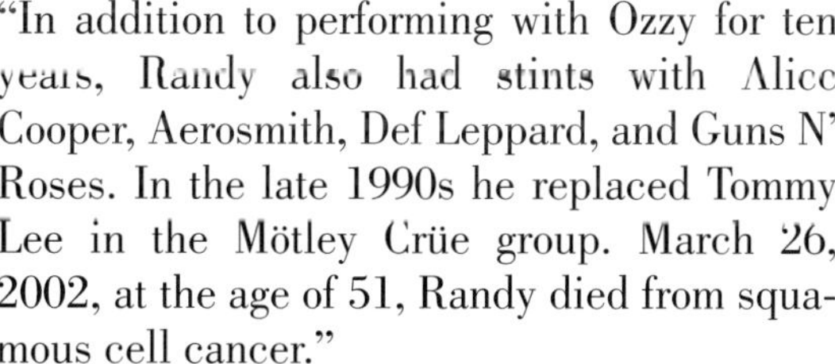

"In addition to performing with Ozzy for ten years, Randy also had stints with Alice Cooper, Aerosmith, Def Leppard, and Guns N' Roses. In the late 1990s he replaced Tommy Lee in the Mötley Crüe group. March 26, 2002, at the age of 51, Randy died from squamous cell cancer."

Drummers Who Also Write

"I gotta mention Joey Stepko, who played with a rock band out of New York called the Turtles. In fact, he spent the biggest part of his career with them. Now, Joey is multi-talented and has spent the past ten years in the publishing business as well as living in New York and playing Broadway shows. As a publisher he worked on the publishing of now famous novelist John Grisham's first book."

Learn to Duck

"Tommy Aldridge was a West Coast drummer and a heavy, heavy rock 'n' roll hitter. When

Tommy Aldridge

Tommy was with Whitesnake, a very popular top rock band maybe 20 years ago, he was noted for his double bass drum playing. In fact, I would say, he was one of the few early rock drummers to master the double bass drums. We were at a Whitesnake concert one night, probably at the Centrum, and we were sitting pretty much down front, when in the middle of the show, it got pretty wild. Someone threw a Coke bottle cap or something and it hit Tommy in the neck area. He was cut around the throat, but he continued to play the show. After a while, he started choking and we could see that he was really hurting—it was not a good thing but he kept playing. But, as you know, those rock concerts can get pretty heavy and all kinds of shit can happen."

Tommy was born August 15, 1950, in Jackson, Mississippi, and taught himself to play drums. After listening to records by artists such as

From left, Simon Phillips, Colin Schofield, Tommy Aldridge, Lennie

Cream, the Beatles, and Jimi Hendrix, and copying their drummer's licks, he got into double bass drums. His first big break came when he joined Black Oak Arkansas, a southern rock band. After leaving the group and experiencing legal problems, which took a year to resolve, he joined the Pat Travers Band. After a few years, he left Pat Travers and spent some time gigging in England, returning to the States and teaming up with Rudy Sarzo to form Whitesnake. Over the years, Tommy's famous double bass drumming led to work with various groups such as Ozzy Osbourne, House of Lords, Thin Lizzy, Ted Nugent, and many others. In recent years, he has been working out of Los Angeles and is still a big-time rock drummer.

L.A. rockers from the '80s

Tommy Richards and Carmine Appice (1980)

Jay Mitthauer of Chase

Bev Bevan of The Electric Light Orchestra

Liberty DeVito (Billy Joel)

Ron Tutt (Elvis Presley)

Chapter 29

Get Me Outta Here, Can't Stop, and a Bald Professor

As you now know, Lennie has many short stories about many drummers, and the next two fit the bill. The first guy to come under the microscope is the great drummer from Boston, Tommy Campbell.

Red Dots and a Tour

"There was a time when Tommy Campbell, a very fine drummer from Boston, played with a lot of groups and taught at Berklee College. I'll never forget the time he was on a concert tour with Sonny Rollins down somewhere, either in Mexico or some South American country. Anyway, before he went on tour, Tommy wasn't feeling well, but he didn't want to miss a big tour with Sonny. The money was probably really good. So he went on the tour, and I think that after he had played a couple of concerts, he got a fever and it started to get much worse. Also, Tommy didn't realize it, but little red dots were starting to break out on his face. It was decided that he would have to go to a hospital because he just couldn't handle it on his own to get better. He got through a concert one night, but the next morning the dots were getting bigger and it looked like he was coming down with the measles.

"Tommy took a cab to a hospital and it wasn't very big. He walked in and spoke to the receptionist, saying that he would like to see a doctor because he had a high fever and all that. Now, the receptionist was smoking a cigarette. She dropped it on the floor and, you know, stepped on it and put it out. Maybe ten or fifteen minutes later, the nurse came out, intending to examine Tommy and she was smoking. She puts the cigarette butt out on the floor. Now, Tommy is trying to get a shot at

Tommy Campbell (1990)

seeing the doctor, and finally, ten or fifteen minutes later, out came the doctor. As he was examining Tommy, he lit up a cigarette, smoking, talking to Tommy, and dropped the butt on the floor, stepped on it, and then said, 'It looks like you got a bad case of the measles coming on. We're going to have to keep you here for a few days.' Tommy said, 'Well, gee, isn't there something you can give me to stop the pain or stop, you know, the fever?' The doctor said, 'Well, not really, you're going to have stay for a couple of days in the hospital.'

Ed Uribe, Victor Mendoza, Joe Hunt, Tommy Campbell

"Now, Tommy was reluctant to stay in that little, you know, meat wagon. The doctor was smoking and butts all over the floor. He goes to the men's room and it was like a real shithole—dirty and everything. That was the clincher. Tommy came out and said to hell with this; I'm getting outta here. He walked out the back door, down the street, caught a cab, and took off. I think he maybe played another concert and then had to break the tour and fly home. Imagine being on the road with measles. Shit happens, baby. That whole trip was a nightmare for Tommy."

Tommy is a very resilient guy, as the next excerpt attests.

Front: John Ramsey, Lennie, Dean Anderson
Standing: Dave Weigert, Jun Saito, Victor Mendoza, Gil Graham, Tommy Campbell, Skip Hadden, Joe Hunt, Ed Uribe, Ed Kaspik

"Before Tommy joined Sonny Rollins, he also played with the Manhattan Transfer for quite awhile. He was a good friend of mine and a teacher at the Berklee School of Music. Tommy stood about six-two—he was very tall and lean and mean. Tommy had a concert with Sonny Rollins this particular evening and in the afternoon had a clinic at Berklee. Being so tall, his favorite sport was basketball, so maybe a day or two before, he broke his foot playing a game. He actually did the clinic with his foot in a small cast, and it was impossible to get another drummer to play the gig with Sonny, so he played it with the cast on. That was pretty unusual, and I was proud to see Tommy doing his thing. Tommy continued teaching and playing, went to Japan, and married a lovely Japanese girl. Today Tommy is living in Japan, still playing and grooving right along."

A brief bio about Tommy Campbell is appropriate here. Growing up outside Philadelphia, he was always surrounded by music—as you can well imagine, since his uncle is the famed organist Jimmy Smith. His father was an organist and singer, and Tommy used to play along when his dad rehearsed with Mickey Roker or when his uncle would bring over a copy of his latest recording. In 1998, Tommy received the Distinguished Alumni Award from Boston-based Berklee School of Music, where for several years he was a drum and percussion

Duffy Jackson, Count Basie Orchestra (1990)

instructor. In addition to his work with Sonny Rollins and the Manhattan Transfer, he's also been in the drum chair for Dizzy Gillespie, Kevin Eubanks, Stanley Jordan, Gary Burton, and many more jazz greats.

How Do We End This Damn Tune?

"Duffy Jackson has been around a long time, is a character, a very funny guy, and a great big-band drummer. He likes to sing and can scat, and is the son of Chubby Jackson, now deceased, who was the famous bass player with Woody Herman. One story about Duffy occurred when he was with the Count Basie band—he was with the band on and off quite a few times. One particular time, when I saw

Jamey Haddad, Berklee educator and percussionist

him, he was playing with the Count and he liked to clown around behind the kit. This time the Count was directing the band, and when they came to a big ending, he would point his finger and the band would end with a big crescendo. Then the Count would point to the drums and Duffy was to take, I don't know, maybe a 20- to 30-second solo to round off the ending. Now, Count would spread his hands for Duffy to end his solo, and Duffy would keep playing. The Count would look up at him, probably wondering what the hell Duffy was doing. Because he was still playing, the Count would bring the band back in, and then Duffy would stop—the band kept playing without the drummer. Then the Count would look at Duffy and then he would start to play again. The Count and Duffy then got this thing going between them—starting and stopping the ending—and they finally brought it to an end. It was a hilarious shtick.

"Another time when I saw the band with Duffy, he took this long solo, accidentally dropped his sticks, started hitting the set with both hands and the hi-hat with his foot—he destroyed the set. It was hilarious. Duffy is a beautiful guy and a real character."

Like Tommy Campbell, Duffy was also surrounded by music; his dad gave him his first drumset when he was quite young. Described as a "jazz wonderkid," at the age of 18, Duffy was touring with Lena Horne, and at the age of 20 he was playing for Sammy Davis Jr. His mentors were Buddy Rich, Gene Krupa, and Louie Bellson, resulting in Duffy's playing in many of the great big bands in addition to the Count, Artie Shaw, Lionel Hampton, and Illinois Jacquet. Duffy is active in IAJE and conducts rhythm section workshops for high schools and colleges, as well as presents master classes for working drummers.

A Bald Drumming Professor

"I gotta say a few words about a great drummer and friend from Pennsylvania, Tony DiNicola. Now, Tony was coined the Yul Brynner of the drumset because he was bald. I first met him when he was playing with Boots Mussilli, a great saxophone player who lived in Worcester, MA, and had his own big band.

Tony hooked up with Boots and was his drummer for many years. He was a Zildjian artist and a great friend of Al Moffitt Sr., and after he got off the road, Tony worked in his brother's music store, ran the drum department, and did a lot of teaching. In fact, he went on to become a teacher in a university. You know, in the old days, you didn't see many bald drummers. I should have sent him one of my rugs.

"Oh, I forgot to mention that Tony not only played with Boots Mussilli, but he was also Harry James's drummer for many years. A 1973 Charlie Ventura session gave Tony some top billing, and now he is a professor of percussion and jazz studies at Trenton State University in New Jersey."

Some Internet research on Tony reveals his being part of the Old Farts Club, a group started by Lew Hoffman, an assistant professor of management at the College of New Jersey. Other members of this elite group include Rick Camber, a professor of philosophy; Karl Gottesman, who plays in a bluegrass band; and Steve Klug, a genetics professor. A rather impressive set of credentials and the club includes a drummer. Tony might be bald, but he sports a great mustache.

Tony DiNicola, Lennie, Al Moffit Sr. Zildjian factory (1970)

Paul Ferrara, with the Pete Fountain Band, New Orleans (1978)

Rocky White, Jazz and Big Band Drummer

Chapter 30

Steve Smith and Some Bats?

Steve Smith with his first drum teacher, Bill Flanagan

This chapter is Lennie's reminiscence of the great drummer Steve Smith. Lennie has known Steve since he was just a young up-and-coming drummer in Boston, and they have shared a lifelong close friendship and a wealth of good times.

"This story starts about 40 years ago, when a gentleman by the name of Bill Flanagan used to come over to the factory. Bill had a little drum department in a section of a music store in Brockton, MA, that was run by one of his sisters. He was a bachelor and lived with his two spinster sisters. Bill would come to the factory to pick up a few of the cymbal seconds that we used to sell to some of the local drum shops. These so-called seconds were good-sounding cymbals, but they had a few pit marks on the surface, or perhaps, maybe, a small dent on the edge. They weren't really that bad and they sold fast in the small shops because they had a good sound and a really good price. Believe it or not, Bill was a good drummer and played with some good big bands during his early career and also played good vibes. He was Steve Smith's first drum teacher, and around that time I really didn't know Steve that well. He was just starting his career playing around Boston."

"Bill used to come over to the factory, wobble in, wanted to hook up with Armand or myself,

Steve Smith

Lennie, Kenny Sherez, Steve Smith, Jackie Santos

pick up some seconds, then talk about his life. We knew he was physically in tough shape, had a big red alcoholic nose like W.C. Fields, and he stuttered so bad he could hardly get the words out, and he had a bad case of the shakes. But we loved him and we had a lot of fun. That went on for a few years and, occasionally, I would bump into Bill in my own hometown area called Green Harbor, and that's where I had just bought an old cottage near the beach. Green Harbor is a small fishing village on the South Shore of Boston on the way to Cape Cod, near Plymouth, MA, where tourists go to see the famous Plymouth Rock.

"The cottage was old, built around 1890, a real antique. It was well built but needed a lot of work. Come to find out, Bill had a cottage in Green Harbor. He lived there in the summertime with his two sisters. Oh, my nerves! We would hook up occasionally, have a few pops, and talk about everything in music. One time, in our discussions, he told me that he had a few bats flying around his house at night. I

Kenny Aronoff, Steve Smith, Lennie

immediately said, 'Hey, Bill, I've got a lot of bats that fly around my house every night, too, and I think they live up in the crawl space in the attic.' I also told him that I had an exterminator come down and take a look at what was happening. He told me to watch where the bats were coming out at night and where they would return in the morning. So for about two weeks I would stay outside the cottage at night and watch the damn bats fly out. Then I'd get up at five o'clock in the morning when the sun came up and watch the bats come back. Well, we finally found the hole and it was up in the eaves. I needed to get a carpenter to get up on the roof and fix it. That took awhile.

"In the meantime, I'm getting ready to throw this wild Fourth of July party. I invited Bill, and he came over, naturally alone—his sisters never went anywhere. Also invited were Leon Chiappini, my buddy from Zildjian, and his wife Gwen. Of course Armand, and my wife and kids were all there. And up until then, I still hadn't met Steve Smith. Anyway, we're sitting down and having some pasta, a few cocktails, when all of a sudden a fucking bat starts flying around the parlor. Leon jumps up and goes berserk, Bill goes berserk, Armand is laughing and, oh, my God, we're all running around like a bunch a crazy people, you know,

Lennie- I appreciate your friendship and all the support you have given me - thank you - Steve Smith

From left to right: Steve Smith, Neal Schon, Ross Valory, Jonathan Cain, Steve Perry

JOURNEY

COLUMBIA 9609

Journey promotional photo that Steve Smith autographed for Lennie

Lennie, Marco Soccoli, Steve Smith, Joey Franco, Manny's Drum Shop, New York City (1990)

and we're trying to hit the bat with a broom. Finally, I got an idea. It so happened that I had a couple of tennis rackets out on the porch, so I ran out and grabbed the rackets, gave one to Bill, one to Leon, and I had the broom, and we were going crazy trying to whack that damn bat. Now, the parlor was a real big room, and we're running around, laughing, falling over each other, hitting each other, and the women and kids were screaming, when finally Leon belts the bat, crushing it up against the wall. Things calmed down, we threw the bat outside, and the party got back to normal. We always talked about that Fourth of July party, and we ended up calling our cottage the Bat House for many years."

If you recall, the tie-in was the fact that Bill Flanagan was Steve Smith's first drum teacher in Brockton. Steve was nine years old in 1963 when he began drum lessons under the tutelage of Bill, and because of Bill's big-band background, Steve's early influences were Gene Krupa, Buddy Rich, Louie Bellson, and Kenny Clarke. He played in his school's bands, some garage bands, and a professional Brockton concert band. In 1972, after graduation, he began studies at Berklee College of Music, working with top teachers like Alan Dawson and Gary Chaffee. Take it away, Lennie.

"Bill continued to come to Zildjian, and I finally bumped into Steve, who was studying at Berklee at the time. Steve came out to the factory and picked out a few cymbals. I got to know him, and he was playing with some of the big bands around Boston. He was starting to get some notoriety because he was playing in Lin Biviano's Big Band, but when he joined violinist Jean Luc Ponty, his reputation really grew. I think that was around 1976. When he got with Ponty, Steve and I really hooked up and I got him a real good cymbal set-up, signed him on as a Zildjian artist, and we became incredible friends.

"After he left Ponty, he joined the popular rock group Journey, went on the road with them, stayed with them for about seven or eight years, made a lot of dough, and became a heavy-duty rock drummer. We became closer

Steve Smith with Buddy's Buddies Big Band

Thèrése DiMuzio and Steve Smith

and closer as the years went on. Steve would come to the factory, and, of course, at that time my chops were in pretty good shape, and I used to do some funky stuff on the hats and cymbals. So when Steve and I got together, I used to show him some things that I had picked up from some of the great players that came by the factory—Lionel Hampton, Buddy Rich, Papa Jo, Gene Krupa, and Sonny Payne. They all played the hi-hats and cymbals differently. Steve and I would work out on the hats and ride cymbals, and we learned a lot of crazy stuff from each other and a lot of new things that could be done. Steve had incredible technique and picked up very fast. So with his ability and passion for learning, he really mastered everything that he went after and took it to the next level. Today we still talk about those years, and he is, without a doubt, one of the finest drummers in the world."

During his last year with Journey, Steve formed a fusion band, Vital Information. His group was a powerful band, which allowed Steve to develop a style that included incredible solos, displaying not only his amazing technique but also his musicality.

"We had Steve do a lot of clinics, and they were always jam-packed. Bill Flanagan eventually passed away. and we all went to the funeral. Steve always refers back to his first teacher, and, of course, when I told him about my knowing Bill for many years down at the Green Harbor area, he loved all that stuff, and especially that story about the bats."

Freddie Gruber, Rob Godfried, Steve Smith, Steve Houghton, Lennie

Steve Smith

Mike Mangini, Steve Smith, Vinnie Colaiuta, Lennie, Tom Coster, Dennis Chambers at Ryle's Jazz Club in Cambridge, Massachusetts

Some of Lennie's drummer friends

Jonathan Moffett performing on the Jackson's tour

Ignacio Berroa, Latin specialist

Andrew Cyrille, New York jazz artist

Sonny Emory, L.A. artist

Nashville's best: Tim Smith, Dick Gay, Lennie, Jimmy Fadden

Lennie with Buddy Williams, New York artist

Chapter 31

From Hush to Rush: Neil Peart

Neil Peart behind his famed double drumset in his early days with Rush

Neil Peart was and is still one of Lennie's favorite drummers. A Canadian, he was born September 12, 1952, and took a journey to England at the age of 18, scratching out a living selling knickknacks to tourists. After leaving a group called Hush, Neil auditioned for Rush in 1974, and although he was carrying his drums in trash cans, he got the gig and has been with Geddy Lee and Alex Lifeson ever since. After Neil became a Zildjian endorser, they did several ads with Neil. However, one time Lennie and crew had a tough time getting some photos.

"Neil is an incredible drummer and has always had a big following and has won many awards, especially in the *Modern Drummer* readers' polls. It is his unique style of drum-

A view from above of Neil Peart behind his famous double drumset

ming that helped make him a big rock star with Rush. Zildjian decided to do a special ad on Neil while Rush was playing in Boston. We all met at the Boston Garden, which was the big venue in those days. We had programmed everything to be there about three or four hours before the concert, to take some live photos of Neil onstage behind his incredible drum set-up. In those days he played a big drumset. In fact, he played two sets of drums—one up front and another in back of him, and he would actually spin around and play both sets of drums during the concert. He also used two octaves of crotales; small tuned cymbals made for him by Zildjian. He asked us to do a favor for him: When we put his cymbal set together, would we take the logos off the top of the cymbals. He didn't mind the logos on the bottom, but he preferred not having them on top. It was just a little quirk that Neil had, and we abided with that. We didn't mind, you know, because when you hit the cymbals, they would go up and down and you would still see the bottom logos. This was cool with us, and I think he just didn't want to look at logos all night long, which really made sense to me.

"Now, we had this set-up at the Boston Garden and we had to get permission from the Garden, believe it or not. What we didn't realize was that the Garden was so unionized at that time that if you wanted to take pictures, you needed an up-front contract with the Boston Garden, which would allow us to be onstage and take photos. So, we were all set up, started shooting, had our own photographer there, and wouldn't you know it, the Garden officials came down on us and stopped us from doing the pictures unless we signed an agreement. We had to pay a fee, and it was somewhere in the vicinity of a couple thousand dollars, and in those days that was a lot of money. They really rolled us over the coals. We had to pay it, or we would not have gotten those pictures taken. The photos ended up in a classic ad of Neil, which later became a big poster that we sent to all the Zildjian dealers. This worked out to be a big campaign for Zildjian and it was well worth the effort and extra money. We always had great relations with Neil."

Neil is still considered to be one of the most popular drummers around, as evidenced by his many number-one awards in the *Modern Drummer* polls. Yet he doesn't rest on his laurels and is always trying to improve his playing. In keeping with this philosophy, Neil took some lessons from the inimitable Freddie Gruber, who is a West Coast drummer and a teaching guru, which resulted in Neil's forsaking his matched grip on some tunes for his newly developed traditional grip.

"I saw Neil around 1996 at the Great Woods venue in Boston," Lennie continues. "He was traveling with the band on a huge tour and had his own personal tour bus, a big super-customized sixteen-wheeler. On the bus he had his own BMW motorcycle, plus one for his daughter and another one for his good friend Brutus, who was also a mechanic and took care of the motorcycles. We met Neil outside,

Lennie, Neil Peart, Larry Allen (Neil's early road tech), Boston Garden (1980)

A dinner for Louie Bellson with (l-r) John King, Louie Bellson, Steve Smith, friends, Neil Peart, Jim Petersczak, friends, Lennie

and he was out there tinkering with his motorcycle. He and his daughter, instead of riding on the band bus along with his band, would go to each venue by motorcycle. This gave Neil the opportunity to continue his writing. He loves to write, he is passionate about it, and has written extensively about his travels and motor cycle journeys.

"Tragedy struck Neil's life when his daughter, Selena was killed in a car accident. His wife died of cancer some 10 months later. These two tragedies understandably sent him into seclusion for quite some time. After a long period of healing, he decided he wanted to get back to playing. The band got back together and Rush went back on the road."

As Lennie stated, Neil's only daughter, Selena, was killed in an auto accident in 1997. The following year, his wife, Jacqueline, died of cancer. Neil has written several nonfiction books about his travels, including *The Masked Rider*, which described his bicycle trip through the African country Cameroon in 1986. After the deaths of his wife and daughter, he wrote *Ghost Rider: Travels on the Healing Road,* which recounts his motorcycle adventures through Canada, Mexico, and the United States. He continues to write, and his most recent book is titled *Traveling Music*. In addition to writing, Neil, along with his Rush colleagues, was awarded the Order of Canada on May 9, 1996.

Lennie and Neil Peart (2003)

A final remembrance from Lennie: "Once my daughter Thèrése and I went to see Neil at the Worcester Centrum. The hospitality suite was beautifully set up and decorated with an Italian decor and featured a big spread of traditional Italian food. Larry Allen, Neil's road tech for many years, was there to welcome us. He explained to us that at every venue they had a different theme of decor and cuisine in the hospitality suite (in case we were wondering why all the Italian stuff). What also knocked me out was that they were also playing Connie Francis records. Can you believe that? So it was like a little Italian feast back in the North End. That made me really feel at home, and whenever I went to see Neil, they always had a big spread backstage and his whole crew always welcomed us on board.

Louie Bellson, Neil Peart, Lennie

"I have always had a great relationship with Neil. He holds a very special place in my heart. He has contributed so much to the drumming world. He is an inspiration, not only as a drummer, writer, lyricist, and photographer, but most of all because, in spite of all his fame and successes, he has remained a very kind and humble soul."

Neil's gold-plated anniversary drum kit made by Drum Workshop (2005)

Neil's drum tech Lorne Wheaton at a clinic presentation (2005)

Chapter 32

Frankfurt, Dobermans, a Fiat—Oh My

Armand and Lennie weren't skipping down a yellow brick road, although they were known to do a Fred Astaire act when things weren't going well. These bizarre stories took place in Germany and Belgium, so at the time, the duo probably wished they were back in Massachusetts or even in Kansas with Dorothy and Toto. While we were writing *Tales*, Lennie claims to have awakened one night laughing like crazy, as he put it, "really laughing my ass off, Jim," and proceeded to tell the following story.

"This happened around 1975, when Bob Zildjian was in charge of the international market. In fact, he was handling the world-wide marketing program. In Germany, the Frankfurt Fair was the biggest international convention for the music products industry. Bob had said that Armand and I should do a series of clinics after the fair was over, especially in Belgium, where Zildjian had a big dealer. Bob put it together for us and made all the arrangements, so Armand and I flew to the fair. It was definitely a trip I'll never forget.

"As usual, after the fair was over for the day, a lot of the dealers and others would like to go out for a little entertainment. In those early days, one place for sightseeing and hanging out was the famous Frankfurt red-light district, a three- or four-city-block area where the girls sat in the windows, and pimps and women on all the street corners—it was all legal and quite a spectacle. They had one place that was called the Super Market, and it was an enormous building. You would walk in to one big major hall with several bars set up, and there were about 100 girls walking around, all aging Hollywood bimbos. So what would happen was a girl would walk up to you and start talking, you would buy her a drink, and if you wanted a little action, she would take you upstairs to a room. [Lennie swears on his mother's eyes that the next part didn't involve any of the Zildjian gang.] One of the guys with us decides to go up to one of the rooms. He was back down in about 15 minutes, really bent out of shape, because they were going to throw him out—there were two big guys ready to bounce him." So this is what went down upstairs:

"Our friend went up to the room and got ready to negotiate with the girl. She took out a little egg timer and said you have 15 minutes and it is going to cost you $100. He said, 'One hundred dollars for 15 minutes? Give me a break! Are you nuts?'And she said, 'That's it.' He said that he needed more time than that, so she replied that she would turn the egg timer over and it would cost another 100 clams. He said, c'mon, and they started to argue for about five minutes, the gal got mad and must have pushed a button somewhere in the room, because within another 10 minutes, our friend could hear some growling outside the door. She went over to the door and told him to make up his mind or get outta there. He kept procrastinating, so she went and opened the door and there were two Doberman Pinschers with a big dude. The Dobermans were flashing their big white fangs, and the big guy said to shit or get off the pot. Our friend said he flew outta the room like a bat outta hell. What a scene that was, and we were laughing like crazy."

Lennie, Armand, Stuff Combe

I'm assuming the rest of the fair was anti-climactic. Now we're off to Belgium and a clinic featuring Armand, Lennie, and Stuff Combe. Things just couldn't get any worse, could they?

"After the fair was over, Armand, Bob's son Billy, and I teamed up with one of our sales reps who lived in Switzerland, a big six-foot-four tall jazz drummer named Stuff Combe. He played all over Europe, a big cat who played his ass off, and he was to help with the clinic. Billy was working at Zildjian at the time in artist relations and manufacturing, playing drums, and had his own little rock 'n' roll band. We hopped a plane to Belgium, and the dealer (I can't remember his name) met us at the airport and drove us to his big drum shop. We walked into the shop and there were about 25 drummers there. I had put together a slide show to show how cymbals were made, the history of cymbals, and ta-da ta-da. The drummers were sitting there, Armand has the remote to start the slides, and I'm loading up the slides in the carousel. The owner introduces us, I plug in the carousel, and Armand starts his spiel. All of a sudden the carousel starts smoking and catches on fire. There was this big fire in the corner and everyone starts jumping around going crazy. I had forgotten to use the A/C converter. Black smoke was coming outta the carousel. The clinic was just about over before it started. We had to wing it without the slides. Stuff Combe played and we all drank vodka.

Billy Zildjian

"By that time it was late in the day, and we went back to the hotel to get a bite to eat. Stuff takes us downtown, and by the time we get there, there aren't many good restaurants open. We're walking around and they've got these outdoor vendors selling bratwurst and knockwurst, and then we spy a pizza parlor. So we four went in, sat down, and ordered a couple of pizzas. When the pizzas came out, they were absolutely disgusting. I've never seen a pizza like that before in my life. I mean, the pizzas were yellow and swimming in some weird looking sauce they were using—they were gross. So we sat there, what the hell could we do, there was nothing left open that time of night, so we just swilled those goddamn pizzas down. Eventually, I had to go to the bathroom, so I asked the waiter where it was. He pointed and said to just go up those flight of stairs. I went over to the stairs and the corridor was probably about three feet wide, and instead of railing they had ropes. Can you believe it, ropes. It was like being on a ship. I grabbed the ropes and started going up the stairs, got up one flight—no bathroom. So I climb up to the next flight and there's a door. I open the door and I'm on the goddamn roof. The bathroom was the roof. Guys are standing there taking a leak on the roof—I'm telling ya. I said what the hell is going on? It was hilarious. I go back down and I'm telling Armand and the guys what I found on the roof, and Stuff is saying, 'Don't you know they don't have plumbing over here?' It was crazy. We left the pizza parlor and there was a bratwurst stand outside, so we all had about two or three 'brats' with the hot mustard that almost tore our insides out. We finally went back to the hotel

Stuff Combe

Stuff Combe, Armand Zildjian taking a lesson from Alan Dawson

and went to bed. We should have never eaten those brats. You know what I mean...chili today, hot tamale."

Well, wasn't that an interesting day. I'm still pondering the bathroom on the roof, wondering about where the women go, and what if one has to, uh—sorry, I won't go there, lost my sense of propriety for a moment. Onward. Believe it or not, there is more to come, and this is a killer. The next morning our intrepid foursome waited at the hotel for their ride to the airport. Who should show up to drive them but the drum shop owner's wife, behind the wheel of a black four-door "tiny" Fiat. It seems the owner was busy, so he sent his wife. The color of the car was appropriate, as you will soon learn.

"Now, you wouldn't believe what this woman looked like. She was an older lady all dressed in black. She had black high-buttoned shoes on, a black coat, black gloves, a black hat, black everything, plus the black car, but she was as white as a ghost. She reminded us of a character out of one of those old black and white Count Dracula movies, something out of the 18th century. The owner and husband was short and chubby, and bald-headed, and wore a dapper suit. He and his wife made for a very interesting, if not humorous, couple.

"Picture the following: 20 miles to the airport, a very small car, and the challenge of getting us four plus the wife in the Fiat, what with six-foot-four Stuff, Billy, and me in the back seat and Armand in the front. We finally managed to stuff ourselves into the back seat, with Billy and me crunched up on either side and Stuff draped across us. There was no room to move, yet we were all laughing and wondering why they didn't rent something a little bigger? Off we went.

"About halfway there, and due to the awful food we had eaten the night before—that goddamn awful pizza and bratwurst—nature took over. A 'barking spider' was heard, causing Armand to crack his window with a funny look on his face, and he starts to laugh. Then there were more 'barking spiders,' the car is steaming up, all the windows are down, it's still wintertime, with the poor wife trying to keep her dignity, sitting up very stiff, both hands on the wheel and urging the little Fiat to go faster.

"The longer we went, the more cushion creepers seeped out and the funnier it got, but thank God we finally got to the airport. Billy, Stuff, and I could barely get outta the car. I made a beeline for the bathroom while Armand, trying to keep a straight face, was thanking the poor ol' wife. That whole trip was certainly no trip to Hawaii. We went to more Frankfurt Fairs, but that one took the cake. When we got back, we told Bob Zildjian that everything was just wonderful, that we put on a great clinic, had a great time, and that the food was wonderful in Belgium. You think Bob really believed us?"

Dear reader, as you can see, things don't always go as planned. It's still amazing to me that the dynamic duo of Armand and Lennie came out of most of these escapades in good shape while things were crashing down around them. Sort of keeping their cool while Rome burns. Back to cymbals.

NAMM Show Parade with Industry friends, Lennie, Brook Ludwig Crowden, Armand Zildjian, Fred Sanford (circa 1995)

Armand and Lennie discussing cymbals (circa 1968)

Chapter 33

Things That Go Crash in the Night

After the craziness of the last chapter, Lennie and I decided it was time to have a little cymbal-making history lesson. Cymbals are some of the earliest instruments known to man and have been an integral part of many cultures and religions, as well as warfare. Turkish armies marched to the beat of drums and the clashing of cymbals and gongs. Psalm 150-5 says, "Praise him upon the loud cymbals: Praise him upon the high sounding cymbals." In Japanese Buddhist temples, huge bells are struck by very large, suspended logs. Armies incorporated cymbals accompanied by large, heavy timpani sounding the charge. In more modern times, the English film company J. Arthur Rank introduced each movie with a hefty chap striking a huge gong.

There is a general consensus that cymbals have been in existence in the Middle East and Asia since 1000 B.C. as tiny finger cymbals. An early alchemist, Avedis, a Turkish Armenian, in 1623 developed a special processing technique for making an alloy of copper, tin, and silver, creating cymbals that were superior. He was given the name Zildjian (cymbal smith) by his fellow guild members. Turkish cymbals became popular early in the 1800s and were being shipped all over the world. For many years the traditional way of making cymbals continued, including casting, hammering, and lathing. In fact, some cymbals are still made in the traditional way, but for the most part modern technology has taken over.

"Cymbal making always reminded me of when I used to watch my wife make cookies. She would mix up a special batter, her own recipe, and she would have a cookie sheet. After mixing her special batter, she would pour it into the cookie sheet, which had these little individual pockets in it. Next, she would put the sheet in the oven and cook for about an hour, take the sheet out, let the cookies cool off, then flip the sheet over and—bingo—all of the cookies would fall out on the table.

"When you look at it, the beginning of the Zildjian process was very similar to Peg's making cookies. First of all, they go out and buy the raw metal in 100-pound ingots of copper and tin. They would store the ingots in a special room that was like a nuclear research center, with ovens and a lot of melting equipment. Now they are ready to make some cymbals. The copper and tin are cut up into small pieces, put into an enormous vat, melted, and blended together. After the mixture is melted down to a certain temperature, it would be poured into a series of small crucibles that would be on a pedestal on the floor, which could be tipped over by a handle. So, okay, each one of these crucibles would contain a certain amount of metal, similar to the cookies on a cookie sheet, and when they cooled off, these crucibles are flipped over and individual small castings fall out. They are like little pies, little thick pies, and when they cool off, they become, naturally, hard, solid discs. Now, we are talking about individual castings, and each casting is going to make a cymbal.

"The castings are stored in big bins according to thickness and size. When the workers get a work order to make certain sized cymbals, they know exactly what size castings they are going to need. Now starts the heating and stretching process. The castings are put into a very large oven, similar to a pizza oven, with a door in it so the men can take the castings out when they are red-hot and have reached a desired temperature. They would reach inside these ovens, with what they called a rake—about a six-foot-long metal rod with a flat shovel on the end. They would pick up those castings, put them on a conveyor belt that would take them to the rolling mills. The castings would be put through the rolling mill and stretched out. This would be done nine or ten times during the course of the day to get the cymbal to the desired size to meet the order requirement—you know, like an 18, a 20, or 22. Once they get the cymbal to the right size, the process is stopped and it is allowed to cool off.

"After the cymbal has cooled, perhaps the next day, they have to locate the center of the cymbal. Next it is put on a shearing/trimming machine, which shears off the outer edge of the cymbal as it spins around, taking the excess metal off the outer edge and making a perfect round and right-sized cymbal. The cymbal is then reheated, sent through a cupping press, and that's when they put the different-sized cups in the cymbals.

"The next process uses what we call a drop hammer. The cymbal is put on a die, then the drop hammer drops down and squeezes the cymbal in between this 50-ton press, giving the cymbal the beginning of its shape. It shapes the cup, the bow, and the curvature of the cymbal. Now you have a piece of metal that looks very close to a cymbal.

"After it is pressed with the big drop hammer, the cymbal has to go through another hammering process. That's when they take the cymbal to a machine with a smaller hammer, which adds the bumps and knocks in the cymbal on both sides, and even further shapes the cymbal a little bit. This hammering machine is a specially designed machine just for cymbal hammering, and that gets all of those little hammer marks on the top and bottom of the cymbal. It is not a true hand-hammered cymbal, since its not being done by a person by hand, but these machines are controlled by the worker, so it is a very close approximation.

"After the cymbal is hammered, it then goes to the lathing room. This process puts the striations and the so-called tonal grooves on the cymbal. These are cut into the surface by using a very sharp tempered steel cutting tool attached to a long, sturdy handle and is done by hand. After this process, the cymbal looks like a finished cymbal and now has a tone. Finally, the last step is putting the cymbal on an edging machine that puts the final edge on the cymbal. This machine also smoothes out the center hole, as well as the edge, so both are round and smooth.

"Although there have been many changes in the making of cymbals, the basic materials of copper and tin haven't changed much over the years and probably never will. But the manufacturing process has been modernized in many ways. Some companies still hand-hammer their cymbals, but machines have been designed that give the workers the opportunity to control the hammering by computers. Generally, truly hand-hammered cymbals have a dark, lower sound, while cymbals hammered by a machine tend to be brighter and higher in pitch.

"The lathing process hasn't changed that much, although the lathe itself has had enormous development. In fact, some cymbal lathes are now automated. If you look at a modern cymbal, a lot of them are not fully lathed. A lot of the cups are not lathed, and the cymbals are left in their raw state to give them their particular sound. Or they will only lathe half of the cymbal—there are all kinds of variety and processes taking place today. I've already mentioned some of those cymbals in previous chapters.

"One last thing: cast cymbals and non-cast cymbals. I've already talked about cast cymbals; now I want to mention non-cast. For non-cast cymbals the alloy is different and starts out as a sheet, and the cymbals are stamped out. Because of this process, the cymbals are more similar in sound and have less spread, a tighter feel, a faster decay, and a more compressed frequency range. I have noticed that younger drummers like the sheet metal cymbals as they are half the price and sound pretty good. However, the jazz and orchestral players choose the cast cymbals because they are the top of the line. It's all a matter of the drummer's taste."

Lennie is well-known for his expertise in selecting cymbals and now shares some of what he learned over the many years with Zildjian and working with a variety of artists.

"Over the years I developed a knack for picking out cymbals and creating sets for all the great drummers by matching and blending various cymbals together. It took a lot of time to put these sets together, but now, after testing cymbals for the last 30 to 40 years, I can tell if a cymbal is a good one without even striking it with a stick or mallet. Cymbals have their own personality, their own texture, their own response. After handling thousands of cymbals, I can almost 'feel' and hear the sound just by seeing and touching the texture of the metal. Even striking it with my thumb on the outer edge, I could hear the fundamental pitch, the overtone series, and pick up on all the variations.

"Occasionally, when putting together sets of cymbals, I would put together two sets at a time. I had a routine that would work for me. I would work for about an hour, then stop, get a cup of coffee, and take about a short break to get my ear readjusted, because after a while, the cymbals all started to sound alike and the sounds start running into one another. And when that happens, you can't pinpoint the cymbal's true identification.

"I've always made it a point to know the type of music the cymbal is being selected for—rock, jazz, funk, blues, orchestral, marching band, whatever. You have to sort that out first and then choose the cymbal that falls into those categories. The first thing to consider is the pitch, the fundamental pitch—whether it speaks in a high voice or a low voice. I would tap the cymbal and play it on the bell and the bow to get the dominant pitch. Then I want to see how the cymbal responds—how fast the cymbal reaches its full vibration and maximum sound. This, of course, is predetermined by the weight of the cymbal and the diameter. The weight also determines the response. A thinner cymbal will react faster, and a heavier cymbal will react slower and sustain the sound much longer. With a crash cymbal, you want to have a faster response, while a ride cymbal needs to have a certain weight in order to maintain the ride rhythm. Also, with a ride cymbal, I look for a more pinpoint definition and a combination of overtones.

"As I said, once I knew what a particular drummer's style and groove was, then I could go ahead and develop a nice set-up. It might be for a big band, a rock set-up, or an all-around set-up for a beginner or for a university percussion ensemble.

"Here is a helpful hint in picking out crash cymbals. Pick up the cymbal and put your middle finger through the center hole while holding the cymbal up close to your ear. Strike the cymbal with your opposite hand or finger on the outer edge of the cymbal; you will hear the dominant pitch of the cymbal as it starts to vibrate. If the cymbal does not vibrate freely and quickly, you should discard it—more than likely it's too flat and will not respond fast enough. Orchestral players will do this with a mallet; I use this method in blending in two or three crash cymbals to form a musical triad rather than strike it with a stick. You will also hear and see the amount of vibrations that are needed to activate the cymbal."

One last story to close out this chapter—about the development of some unique cymbals.

"There was a time when Zildjian sold a Chinese cymbal with turned-up edges, and we called them China Boys. And we had a 'China Boy' stamp. But a funny thing happened because the name was evidently an insult to both the Chinese and the Japanese, whoever we were selling to at that time—must have been Yamaha—anyway, they wouldn't buy them. So, although we decided to enlarge the line, make about two or three other sizes, and

Zildjian Day at Dick DiCenso's Drum Shop (1991).
Left to right: Dick DiCenso, John DeChristopher, Dave DiCenso, Bill Morgan

redesign the cymbals and make them a little different, we first had to change the name. We needed a new logo, one that would be accepted by the Chinese and the Japanese.

"Now, in those days, I was also known as 'Doctor Poo Poo' to a lot of cats, mainly because I knew every Chinese joint in Boston and Boston's South Shore. Late evening's after hanging, I would always end up in a certain Chinese restaurant in Quincy. My good friend Dick DiCenso had a drum shop in Quincy, and he and I would always check out the bands together, especially Louie Bellson. Dick had a great rapport with Louie, so maybe a couple a times a year we would catch Louie and then stop by the Chinese restaurant. They got to know me really well because we were there quite often. It was called the Chinese Bowl, but I had another name. I called it the Toilet Bowl—the food was gross, but it was the only place opened until two or three in the morning. We used to go there and get whatever was left on the menu. The place was so bad that the cockroaches were jumping from one table to another and I used to snap the roaches over to other tables. It was pretty funny.

Lennie and Dick DiCenso

Dick DiCenso

"Anyway, I got to know the owner and his sons, so I took the new China cymbals there and told them that I needed a symbol that suggested power. Because the cymbals were going to be funky and loud, they drew a logo with bright red Chinese lettering that meant power. You would have to know Chinese to understand it, but everyone felt it looked cool. We used that logo on the cymbals and it worked—we sold a lot of those cymbals to Yamaha, and they became very popular."

Chapter 34

The Cream of the Crop, and Two Big E's

Ginger Baker

In every musical genre there are a handful of unique individuals who innovate and help define the style. In the rock world many of these individuals were known for what many might consider somewhat eccentric behavior both on and off the stage, but all were unquestionably known for forging new drumming boundaries. One such individual is red-haired dynamo Ginger Baker.

"During this period there were a few bands at the forefront of the rock explosion and each had a very talented and innovative drummer. Drummers and bands such as Charlie Watts and the Rolling Stones, John Bonham and Led Zeppelin, Keith Moon and the Who, along with Ginger Baker and Cream come to mind. It was sometime in the early '60s when I got a call at the factory that Ginger Baker wanted to get hooked up with Zildjian. I knew that this cat was big-time and one of the leaders of rock 'n' roll. He was with the rock band Cream, and in those days he was truly a classic piece of work. Ginger flew into Boston. I sent a limo to pick him up and had him driven to the old factory in Quincy. He got out of the car, very thin, flaming red hair and beard, wearing a bright blue toreador outfit and looking like something out of the Civil War. What a commotion he caused—everyone in the factory was checking him out, and he took the Zildjian Company by storm. He stayed with us for two or three hours; we set him up with a

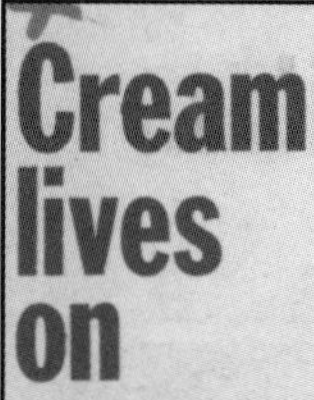

Cream lives on

BACK in the bad old days, drummers and guitarists were heard but not seen, or even understood by your average pop fan.

If a hit record came up that miraculously featured an instrumentalist, then the merry musician might gain a foothold in the scheme of things.

Gradually a change has come about, and now the MM Pop Poll is dominated by the great players.

In 1970 Eric Clapton is top of the poll, in the guitar section, and all due credit to Hank Marvin that ten years later he still gains a significant amount of votes (tenth).

Eric deserves his placing because he has become practically a father figure on the rock guitar scene and remains a fine player.

However much other guitraists freak-out, somehow Eric retains his mastery, and it is pleasing for all his fans that with Derek and the Dominoes, he has rewarded their trust in him by working harder than ever.

Jack Bruce, his buddy from Cream days has scored as top bassist, and one recalls the days when he was practically unknown, except among fellow musicians, with the original Graham Bond Organisation.

Bruce is probably one of the first British players to give inventive credence to the use of an instrument once damned as poor relation of the double bass.

The final member of Cream, Ginger Baker scored a resounding success in the drum category, closely followed by his old replacement with the Graham Bond Organisation, and now a titan of Colosseum — Jon Hiseman.

Like Gene Krupa in an earlier age, he is a People's Drummer, and there is nothing he enjoys more than pleasing people with his exciting, pace-setting solos. The "Baker climax" oft copied, is still rarely equalled for excitement, by today's more sophisticated rock players.

Ian Anderson, the man who introduced the solid-flute, is probably the finest one-legged dancer in Britain today.

To be serious for one instant, his victory under the heading "Miscellaneous Instrumentalist," is not unexpected.

Anderson, often referred to as "Jethro Tull" is not merely a fine flute player, he has the rare gift of comedy and the essential capabilities of the good band leader.

It doesn't matter if he has been influenced by Roland Kirk, in the same way it doesn't matter if Joe Cocker has been influenced by Ray Charles.

Ian has a genius of his own which communicates and produces a Pan like allure. So it's down the Pan with Jethro Tull!

GINGER BAKER: people's drummer

Ginger Baker newspaper clip

Ginger Baker and Eric Clapton

special set of cymbals and signed him up as a Zildjian artist. Afterward, we took him to lunch—what a spectacle, he was someone like from another planet."

Cream was one of the '60's hottest rock bands, with guitarist Eric Clapton, bassist Jack Bruce, and of course Ginger on drums. He was born Peter Edward Baker in south London in 1939. He had a wide range of interests that included playing the trumpet. As a teenager he was also an avid cyclist, with his sights set on becoming a professional in that sport. But drums caught his imagination, and the first time he sat behind a set of drums, he got a job in a band. Some of his earliest influences were Baby Dodds and Alton Red, but it was Max Roach who set him on his drumming path. After spending a year on the road with an English trad band, Ginger built his own drum kit using a form of plastic, bending the shells and shaping them over a gas stove. He used that kit until he purchased a Ludwig drumset in 1966. Before Cream, which was formed in 1963, Ginger played with many jazz groups, wanting to become part of London's jazz scene, but his boisterous style of drumming didn't always fit the jazz style. After getting into R&B, he still used many jazz licks in his playing and could probably be considered one of the first jazz fusion drummers. He always thought himself to be a jazzer rather than a rock 'n' roller. Lennie continues.

"After he left Cream, he moved from England to Italy and started to raise olives. In addition to the olives, Ginger opened a drum school and started to do some teaching, and stayed in Italy for quite awhile. He used to call me quite often, and we became very good friends. [laughing] Ginger always sent me bottles of his olive oil. You know, later on in his life, he got into playing polo—he loved horses. After he came back to the States, he moved to the West Coast, put a band together, and started to do other things besides music. We had Ginger do a few clinics for us and took him to the *Modern Drummer* show, where he put on a master clinic. After the show, *Modern Drummer* always put on a gala party for all the artists, and this was one I'll never forget. Ginger and I were sitting at the same table and he picked up a pair of spoons and started playing. He didn't know that I was a pretty good spoon player (a skill left over from my vaudeville days). I picked up a pair of spoons and we had a battle of the spoons right there at the table. All the drummers came by, Joe Morello, Jim Chapin, Freddie Gruber, all laughing. I think I scared him with my technique. We had a lot of fun, and the drummers got a big kick out of it.

"While we're on the subject of a great rock drummer, I want to again acknowledge some of the guys who left a huge mark in the rock world and set the standard for so many rock drummers for the last 40 to 50 years. John Bonham of Led Zeppelin is sadly no longer with us, but he was a powerhouse drummer whose style and sound has been imitated by countless drummers. Keith Moon of The Who is also sadly gone. He was another powerhouse who, like Ginger, was one of the early adopters of the double bass drums and the huge drum kit. He was an incredibly energetic drummer, kind of wild and crazy, both on and off the drumset. Charlie Watts of the Rolling Stones is the drummer for the oldest rock band still in existence, the Rolling Stones. He is still out there with the Stones touring the world for hundreds of thousand of fans, as they have done for decades. Finally, no book about drums or drumming would be complete without acknowledging Ringo Starr. He is probably the most well known name in drums in history because there is likely no one who

Rock legend John Bonham of Led Zeppelin (1975)

does not know The Beatles. Now, I never really worked with these guys the way I worked with other artists. Some played Zildjians at one point or another, but I did not hand-pick their cymbals or make any special selections for them. These acts were so big that their equipment needs, and pretty much everything else, was always handled by their management companies, and that's how they got their drums and cymbals. Regardless, I know them and felt I must acknowledge them for the tremendous mark they have made in the drumming world."

We now change genres from a rock 'n' roller who wanted to be a jazzer, to another legend, the first Big E—Elvin Jones—a jazzer for sure, and one who was an influence on a new generation of drummers. Elvin, born in 1927 in Pontiac, Michigan, was raised in a musical family. His brothers were pianist Hank and trumpeter and bandleader Thad. All legends. Elvin started on the drums at the age of 13, listening to influences Kenny Clarke, Max Roach, and Papa Jo Jones. After leaving the Army in 1949, he first went to Detroit, where he got to play with Charlie Parker, Sonny Stitt, Wardell Gray, and Miles Davis. A move to New York got him hooked up with Miles after a few stints with the likes of Bud Powell, Art Farmer, and J. J. Johnson, plus some recording gigs, but the biggest move of all came in 1960 after he left Miles. For the next six years, Elvin was the driving force behind John Coltrane. After leaving Coltrane in 1966, he was involved with many innovative piano-less groups with Joe Farrell and bassist Charlie Haden. Elvin had more than 500 recordings to his credit, including those whose compositions and arrangements were written by his wife, Keiko.

The legendary Charlie Watts of the Rolling Stones, circa 1970

Rock legend Keith Moon of The Who (1970)

Elvin had always been a powerful drummer, but even he was no match for Lennie and Armand.

"Armand and I were attending one of the trade shows in Chicago and we were hanging pretty tough for about three days. Working the show during the day, partying at night with the dealers, and hanging with the cats. Elvin was playing at the Jazz Cellar with his own group, so we decided that we were definitely going to see

Spoon battle with Ginger Baker and Lennie at a Modern Drummer *festival with Freddie Gruber, standing behind Lennie*

him play before the week was out. But by the time we got to see Elvin, it was the last night of the show, a Saturday, and that was also Elvin's last night. We went to dinner with a bunch a dealers and finally made it to the club at the group's intermission. Naturally, we got a seat right up front directly in front of Elvin's drums. He was playing Gretsch drums and was very much into the old K Zildjian vintage type of cymbals. These were the cymbals that originally came from Istanbul and were very popular among a lot of contemporary jazz players like Tony Williams, Art Blakey, and Philly Joe.

"While we were waiting for Elvin to come back onstage, Armand and I were sitting together and he began dozing off. By the time Elvin got behind his drums, Armand was out

Terry Bozzio, Dennis Chambers, Adam Nussbaum, Louie Bellson, Ginger Baker

cold, blowing z's, and snoring. Frankly, I could barely keep my eyes open. But it got pretty funny, because when Elvin got onstage, he was pretty much focused on Armand and me because we were right in front of him. Well, Elvin started the set with a drum solo—once in awhile he would do that. While he was doing his thing, he was watching Armand out of one eye and started kicking the shit out of the drums. That solo went on for at least five minutes. Then Pat LaBarbera, the sax player, started blowing the head of the tune, grooving right along. Armand was still sleeping. He slept through Elvin's solo, through Pat's solo, and then Elvin started hitting the cymbals and drums harder and louder, trying to wake Armand up. It didn't work. Now Elvin was making horrific faces at Armand; I was laughing my butt off along with the band. All the

Jim Chapin, Joe Morello, Ginger Baker

cats thought it was pretty funny. After Armand slept through the first tune, I finally had to nudge him, wake him up, saying, 'Armand, c'mon, get yourself together.' After the show, we explained everything to Elvin and he realized that it was a convention 'hang' and everyone was beat. He was okay with it because he's been there."

Elvin was no pussycat. He had a temper and used it on many occasions. There always seems to be a guy in the audience when a group is trading fours who counts to see if the improvisation comes out right on the first beat of the fifth measure. One time, as the story goes, there was a guy like that listening to Elvin and the group and he went up to Elvin at the break, resulting in the following great response. The guy was lucky this happened

Lennie with Elvin Jones

after Elvin had mellowed out, because in the olden days, this guy would have ended up with his teeth in his hands. Elvin got off the bandstand, and the guy went up and said, "Mr. Jones, I couldn't help but notice that some of the fours didn't come out right on the beat of the fifth measure." Elvin looked at him and said, "Well, some fours just take longer than others." End of conversation.

The following Elvin story occurred much more recently. A jazz club in Fullerton, California, called Steamers has jazz seven nights a week. My wife Kathy and I were there Saturday, May 8, 2004, enjoying the great sounds from the Jeff Hamilton Trio, with Tamir Hendelman on

Early autographed Elvin Jones promotional picture

piano, Christoph Luty on bass, and, of course, Jeff on drums. During a break, Jeff came over to say hi while we were talking, and the subject of Elvin Jones and his failing health came up. I asked Jeff if he had heard that Barney Kessel, the great guitarist, had passed away the previous Thursday. Jeff had not and he said he had a great story about Barney and Elvin. I had just told the other people at the table the "trading fours" story before Jeff arrived, so his story was apropos.

"I had joined Monty Alexander's Trio in 1975, and we were playing at Paul's Mall club in Boston. Barney was the trio's special guest artist," Jeff began his story. "Barney was dressed in a sport coat, a striped shirt, and a bow tie. He would never be featured in a fashion magazine. After rehearsal, John Clayton,

Elvin Jones in his early days with Slingerland

Barney, and I went out to lunch, and Barney asked if we knew Elvin Jones. I told him that I hadn't met him, but knew that he was a legend. Barney said that he and Elvin were doing a recording and trading fours, and it seemed that Elvin's fours were longer than four measures." [At this point, we all thought Jeff was going to tell my trading fours joke.] Jeff continued: "Barney said that he had told Elvin that 'even though I'm tapping my foot trying to follow the fours, I always come out wrong. Is there any way you can help me follow them?' Elvin said flatly to Barney, 'Well, you get to play, and when you're finished, it's my turn.' "

We all started laughing and then I told Jeff the other Elvin "fours" story.

Johnny Lee Lane, Marvin "Smitty" Smith, Louie Bellson, Elvin Jones, Richard Walker, Lennie

Lennie continues with this special Elvin remembrance.

"One of my most memorable occasions was when several of us from Zildjian went down to New York City to attend Elvin's 75th birthday party. It was held at the Blue Note Jazz Club and was one of the most exciting and fun-loving parties I have ever been to and I will never forget that night."

Elvin Jones and Howard Kurham at the Jazz Bakery in Los Angeles, CA

Today—Tuesday, May 18, 2004—while writing this chapter, I received the terribly sad news that Elvin, at the age of 76, passed away in New York. The drumming family and the music world have lost a giant. I knew that Elvin was very ill, but I still hoped I wouldn't have to write of his death.

Now, for the second of the Big E's—Peter Erskine—another drumming child prodigy. Peter was born June 1954 and started playing the drums when he was four. At the age of 18, he joined the Stan Kenton Orchestra, left after three years to attend Indiana University, and studied with famed professor, George Gaber. In 1976 he joined Maynard Ferguson's band, which led to Weather Report in 1978. Peter's credentials read like a who's who and include Steps Ahead, Steely Dan, Chick Corea, Boz Scaggs, and many more. He is a composer, has published several method books and videos, and has won the *Modern Drummer* Readers' Poll several times in the Mainstream Jazz Drummer category. Lennie has a lot of memories of Peter.

"The first time I saw Peter with the Stan Kenton Orchestra was in the summer of 1972 in Boston. He was really young; I think he was 18 at that time. Armand and I would catch the band when they came to town, and the wild thing about Peter's cymbal set-up was the size. Stan wanted large cymbals to be heard over his loud band. Check out these sizes—they are unbelievable. His main ride cymbal was 27 inches, and he had two crash cymbals that were 24- and a 22-inch swish. I remember that

Paul's Mall Jazz Club: Left to right: Margaret, Cecilia and Lucy DiMuzio; Peter Erskine; Peter's father. Seated: Lennie with daughter Thèrése (circa 1973)

the 27 ride cracked and we replaced it with a 26. We always tried to have Peter play cymbals that met Stan's requirements.

"One of the best times seeing Peter with the Stan Kenton Band was his last night with the

Captain Armand Zildjian, Elvin "the Dude" Jones, Rabbi DiMuzio

Peter Erskine (October 1983)

band in the spring of 1975. It was a Sunday afternoon and I, my wife, and kids went to hear the band at the Jazz Workshop in Boston. Peter's dad was there and also Vinnie Colaiuta, who was a student at Berklee. It was a treat for my kids to hear Peter play, and we all had a great time.

Peter Erskine in action

"I just thought of another time at the Jazz Workshop when Peter was with the Kenton Orchestra. Armand and I were there and we stayed after the second set and the other people had left. The waiters and waitresses were cleaning up when all of a sudden Armand wanted to replay a certain moment from a Boston Celtic's basketball game. He was trying to act like Larry Bird making a lay-up using a loaf of bread, and I was trying to stop him. Things got a little wild, some tables and chairs got knocked over, but finally Armand made an incredible lay-up. It was hysterical, and Peter and the guys in the band were cheering and applauding.

Lennie with Peter Erskine

"The next time I saw Peter was during a NAMM show at a club in Chicago, and it was his first night on the Maynard Ferguson Band. Armand and I and a lot of the cats from Slingerland and, of course, Zildjian were there to hear Peter and the band. I think that Peter got the call to join Maynard only a week before the gig and didn't have a chance to rehearse with the band. But he picked up a bunch of albums and listened to them during that week. When he joined the band, he quickly memorized some of the charts and sight-read the rest of the book. Peter was a fine drummer, well schooled, and could read like a hawk. He played great that night and everybody loved him."

I have to add the following story about Peter and Louie Bellson at the 1983 PASIC in Lexington, Kentucky. Peter and Louie were performing Louie's "Concerto for Two Drumsets and Orchestra," Vic Firth was in the orchestra's percussion section on timpani.

Armand Zildjian, Peter Erskine, Lennie

They held a rehearsal where Louie had mapped out what he wanted during the various sections, including a soft roll at the end of the cadenza, and then the orchestra would come in and the piece would be over. (We learned this after the concert.)

The concert that night was a huge success. Both Peter and Louie were spectacular, their solos were great, and then came the soft roll from Louie at the end of the cadenza. Louie proceeded to play one of the softest rolls known to mankind. We three JEWOPs (Lloyd, Lennie, and I) were straining to hear the roll, and Louie was looking at Peter as if to say, "Start your soft roll." It looked to us as if Peter was shaking his head no. We started to laugh because it was apparent that something was happening between Louie and Peter. Peter finally started a roll, considerably louder than Louie's because we could hear it. The orchestra came in and they wrapped up the piece.

Peter Erskine and family

We got with Peter afterward and asked him what in hell had gone on at the end of the piece. He first told us about the rehearsal and then about the performance. As I remember, his response went something like this: "At the rehearsal, Louie played a soft roll at the end, but it wasn't the volume he played at the concert—the proverbial mouse-pissing-on-cotton dynamic level. Man, my hands were shaking and I finally sputtered my way into an awful-sounding roll. That roll proved that Louie and Buddy possessed the greatest hands in the history of drumming." As I said, we all thought the concert was great and had to sympathize with Peter for the trick Louie played, literally, on him.

Peter Erskine with his special winter hat

Ginger Baker, Elvin Jones, and Peter Erskine, three drummers from very different worlds that have all made an incredible and lasting mark in both the drumming community and the music world at large.

Louie Bellson in concert

Peter Erskine and Lennie in the vault selecting new cymbals for Peter (circa 1977)

Bernard Purdie, Max Roach, Ginger Baker, writer Chip Stern (seated)

Chico Hamilton and Joe Corsello at the Berkshire Jazz Festival

Chapter 35

Tales and Snippets: #1

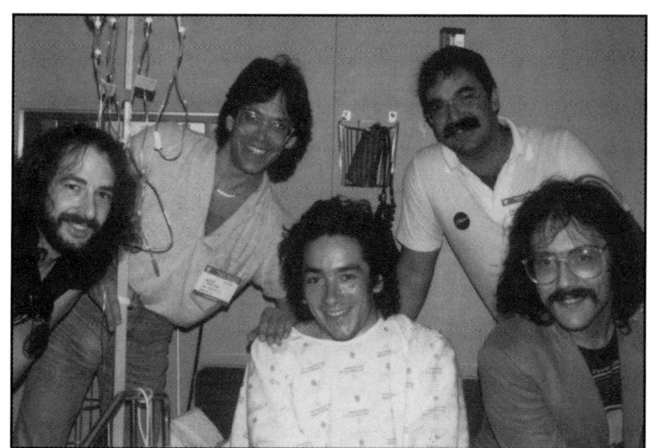

Alan Cornett visited in the hospital by Steve Smith, Jeff Porcaro, Peter Erskine, Vinnie Colaiuta

According to the Oxford English Dictionary, a snippet is "a small piece or brief extract." In the myriad of tapes Lennie sent me, he mentioned many people who were very important to him and should be recognized. The following snippets are extracts from Lennie's narratives. We begin with a drummer whose drum stool is a wheelchair.

Lennie with Alan Cornett at a NAMM show

"This is beautiful, warm-hearted story about a good friend of mine who I think every drummer and musician should know about. When I think about determination, faith, and passion for drumming and music, I think of Alan Cornett. Alan was very deeply connected with the music business and drumming, and he would often visit the NAMM shows with his dad, Ed, who worked for Yamaha for several years. Following a near-fatal accident, Alan was paralyzed from the waist down. Knowing that he may never walk again, he went through many years of therapy hoping to return to the one thing he loved so much, his drumset.

After many years of struggling with the paralysis, and living in a wheelchair, with the help of his wonderful family and friends, Alan designed his own drumset that he could play from his wheelchair.

Alan Cornett behind his specially designed drum set

He writes to me often and is out performing with his group. His brother, who is the bass player, takes him to the gigs and helps him set up the drumset.

Rick Allen of Def Leppard with Alan Cornett

Dave Yost at 19 years old

Alan is a great inspiration to us all. He never gave up and I hope we can all learn a lesson from his perseverance and his incredible journey to continue on with his passion for drumming and music.

Next, a story of a drumming photographer.

"David Yost was really cool and took a lot of great photographs over the years I knew him. He passed away about five years ago. David was also a good friend of fellow JEWOP Lloyd McCausland, and we would see him at most of the shows: NAMM, PAS, and educational shows. He worked for the National Association of College Book Stores and was a big wheel in that organization. He was also a Gene Krupa–Buddy Rich freak and quite a drummer himself. Naturally, we had a nice relationship with him, and he liked to hang out with Lloyd and me. David would often send me beautiful drummer photos, and once he sent a great picture of Buddy and Gene standing together looking at Buddy's drumset, along with several other historical photos. He also sent me a very nice letter telling me that he wanted me to have all of these pictures. The picture of Buddy and Gene has been blown up and hangs behind Buddy's drumset in the drummers' lounge at the Zildjian factory. The picture was also used in many ads.

*Freddy Gruber, David Yost,
Roy Haynes, Anaheim, CA (January 1995)*

"Armand and I loved to see Shelly Manne when he came to Boston to perform, especially when he had time to come to the factory to pick out a few cymbals. In the early days, he played mostly on ride cymbals and perhaps one small crash. As I remember,

Shelly Manne at Zildjian (circa 1963)

Shelly was the type of drummer who liked to swipe at his ride cymbals, sort of a sideways motion, and then maybe cut them on the edge to get sort of a light crash sound as he was riding along. Because of his style, he didn't really need that many crash cymbals, but he always had a kind of a combination of crash and crash-ride cymbals.

"For years, Shelly's basic set-up was a pair of 14-inch medium-weight hi-hats, nothing too heavy or light, but a good balance between the top and bottom cymbals. He also had a 19-inch medium-thin ride, a crash ride, and a 22-inch medium ride. Occasionally he might use a 20-inch ride, but he preferred the larger rides. On his right-hand side he had a swish cymbal, and you'll notice in the photo (on the next page) it had 20 rivets. It was one of those old funky swish cymbals with a lot of chatter. And he had a 16-inch crash to his left. Shelly used that set-up for years.

"Like I said, Shelly liked to pick out his ride cymbals. He had an incredible ride beat, one of the best I've ever seen. Now Armand also had a great left-handed ride beat. I was playing quite a bit in those days, so I wasn't too shabby either, so we used to try to keep up with Shelly while testing the cymbals. We would be matching ride beats to one another, and it got to be a lot of fun. But Shelly burned us pretty bad—we couldn't keep up with him—but we always had a great time duking it out with him. But the highlight was always going to see Shelly playing with his group. He was such a great player."

Shelley Manne (circa 1970)

Shelly Manne, born June 11, 1920, in New York City, grew up surrounded by music as his father, a percussionist, became involved with music theater and other aspects of the New York scene. Fortunately for the drumming world, after only a few lessons on the saxophone, Shelly got to take drumset lessons from the great Billy Gladstone. At age 19, after only three months of lessons, Shelly got a gig on a cruise ship between New York and Le Havre, France, and his career began. Soon it was obvious to all who heard him play that Shelly was going to become one of the greatest jazz drummers of all time. The list of bands, small groups, singers, studio dates, and tours he played on is staggering. His first recording date was in 1940 with the Bobby Byrne band, and then he played with artists such as the Andrew Sisters, Will Bradley, Coleman Hawkins, and Boyd Raeburn. In 1946 his on-again/off-again gig as Stan Kenton's drummer

John Ramsay

commenced, followed by Charlie Ventura and Woody Herman. He joined the Lighthouse All-Stars in 1951, and out of that came Shorty Rogers, Andre Previn, Shelly Manne and His Men, June Christy, and Stan Getz. Shelly got into the club business with the Manne-Hole in 1960. Then came the LA Four, tours, and studio dates. He finally stated that he was getting worn out in 1982. I had joined Yamaha drums, based in Grand Rapids, but I got to the West Coast a lot. On September 24, 1984, Shelly, Emil Richards, Joe Porcaro, and Larry Bunker had a three-day gig in the studio, taping the music for a Disney movie, ***Baby***. Emil and Joe invited me to the taping on Wednesday the 26th because they knew Shelly was my favorite drummer. When I got to the session, no Shelly—he had passed away the night before at the age of 64. A giant was gone.

Now more stories about special drummers.

"Art Blakey was a legend. He didn't come to the factory too often, but I used to send him

John Ramsay, Art Blakey, pianist Donald Brown, and saxophonist Billy Pierce

cymbals. Art liked the old Ks, you know; he was from that vintage, and liked to play big cymbals. Usually 20s, 22s, sometimes a 24 ride. I would venture to say that his style of drumming, which was bebop, never really 'constituted' a lot of crash cymbals. Art mostly relied on his two or three ride cymbals, although one of them might have been a crash ride—he never overloaded his cymbal set-up with a lot of small stuff. I'll never forget the time that Armand and I met him outside the Blue Note, and this was probably four or five years before he passed away. [Art died in

Rudy Collins

1990.] We were outside having a cigarette and Art was telling us all about his family. I'm not sure how many kids he had, but he had us in stitches. He was a great player and influenced a lot of young players on all instruments, especially those who worked with him on his band, the Jazz Messengers. I have to mention John Ramsay, who was Art's road tech for quite awhile. He does a great imitation of Art and has written a great book about him, *Art Blakey's Jazz Messages*. John is a good friend of mine, head of the percussion department at Berklee, and one of Boston's finest jazz drummers."

Lennie also wants to acknowledge the following bunch of guys.

"An old friend of mine from way back was Rudy Collins, a very good jazz drummer. There were times when there wasn't much work around the Big Apple, so Rudy got connected with some Broadway shows and ended up doing a lot of work in the theater. Another New York jazz drummer was Freddie Waits, who used to come to the factory for some special cymbals. He played with some of the great beboppers and was a top call for a lot of the hip bands."

This snippet begins in New York and ends up in LA and, as usual, has some very interesting turns along the way.

"Sol Gubin was a great New York drummer, also played many Broadway shows, and could play anything. Now, Sol was a very close friend of Buddy Rich, and he was one of the few drummers that Buddy would let sub for him.

"Eventually Sol moved to LA and made his 'stand' out there doing a lot of work, including a lot of going-on-the-road jobs. He'd come to the NAMM shows; we'd hook up and go out to dinner together. One memorable time, Buddy was playing out in LA, so we all went to see the band. At that time, Buddy had a big RV with couches in it, a full kitchen, and a couple of bedrooms. Buddy and Steve Peck would stay in the RV while the band stayed on the bus. Now, after the show was over, Sol invited Armand, me, and Bobby Nelson to his house in the Valley. Bobby was working for Zildjian at the time and he had rented a car, so we followed Buddy's RV to Sol's house. We didn't

Sol Gubin

leave the venue till after one o'clock, and Sol lived way out in the Valley. He had a lovely home, and when we got there, we had some food, hung out, played some sides, and had a few pops. About four in the morning, we decided to go back to LA. We jumped in Bobby's car and we didn't know where in hell

Ted Reed, Lennie

we were, and got lost out there in the Valley. We drove around and finally pulled over and fell asleep. When the sun came up, we got our bearings together, tried to figure out where we were, and it took us two to three hours to get back to the hotel. It was a fun evening, and getting lost was a real nightmare."

The next story is about the man who wrote what is now a must-have book in every percussion student's repertoire, *Progressive Steps to Syncopation.*

"Ted Reed: one of the great teachers. I used to see him at many of the trade shows. His book *Progressive Steps* is one of the best, and he loved to talk about all the great players and all the different types of drumsets. Ted was a collector of vintage snare drums. In his collection he had some beautiful rare classic Billy Gladstone snare drums, and I think that some of them he had gold-plated and would display them at various shows. They must have been very valuable because, what I heard, Mr. Gladstone made only 50 snare drums in his lifetime and they became collectors' items."

One of the best father-and-son teams follows.

"Joe Porcaro is one of LA's top studio percussionists and has played in every drumming area from jazz to opera as well as Hollywood film scores. He's also into education, because along with Ralph Humphrey he does the drum gig at the LA Music Academy. I've known Joe for many years and used to see him at all of the NAMM shows—he's an incredible musician. His son Jeff was one of the hottest rock drummers going, and his group Toto was one of the most successful rock bands. Unfortunately, Jeff died from heart failure at a very young age. It was a terrible loss for everyone." [Jeff passed away in August 1992 at the age of 38.]

We continue in LA with some drumset players and studio percussionists.

"The first time I met Steve Schaeffer, a West Coast drummer and studio player, had to be 25, 30 years ago. Armand and I were in New York and went to one of the big venues where Sarah Vaughan was appearing. Steve was her drummer and he played his butt off. I think he continued with Sarah for at least four or five years. Then he went on to play with some other great artists as well as played on many movie tracks. I still see Steve quite often, and he is one of the top studio players in LA. He will always be a good friend of mine.

Steve Schaeffer on drums with Al Cohn and Zoot Sims (1966)

"Emil Richards: one of the all-time great studio percussionists, mallet player, and collector of percussion instruments from around the world. I must have met him at least 35 years ago, and we became good friends. We would always see each other at NAMM shows and he was always interested in all types of percussion sounds. In fact, he's recorded percussion sounds from around the world. In addition to all of his performances, Emil has a tremendous rental business, using all of his vintage collectibles that are incredible and unusual instruments. Now, he was also the

The Burma Bell that Emil Richards helped Zildjian design

Walfredo De Los Reyes, Emil Richards

person who helped me develop the Zildjian Burma Bell, a little bell that is suspended and struck with a mallet. He had various sizes of those bells that he had collected and found in India, and he gave me one and allowed us to reproduce it. Zildjian put the Burma Bell on the market, and it is a beautiful-sounding instrument. Emil was also interested in helping us develop other instruments like sound plates and things like that. He is a wonderful person and musician."

Don Lamond

Sadly we continue to lose the great ones.

"One of the great Woody Herman drummers, Don Lamond, who lived in Florida, passed away on December 23, 2003. Every time I went to Orlando, and a few times with Armand when we were attending a show, we would drop in to see Don. We'd hang out, have dinner, and check out the show. Don had played in one of the big hotels in Disneyland for many years. I loved his playing, and he was a good friend."

Far be it for Lennie to be a name dropper, but he was involved with so many drummers over the years that often those associations led to hanging out with other musicians, especially singers.

"You know, in 1970 I had dinner with Dean Martin, Armand, and a bunch of golf pros at the Sands in Vegas. Also, I used to spend a lot of time in Nashville and got to know and become friends with some country singers, such as Kenny Rogers, Reba McEntire, Clint

Reba McEntire

Black, and Charlie Daniels. Fun times."

Before closing this chapter, we include a story that doesn't include drummers, but people in the industry. What makes this tale interesting is that, once again, Lennie is involved due to company circumstances beyond his control but then manages to create an hysterical event. This one is off-the-wall and requires its own title.

The New England Clam Chowder Caper

"This next story took place about 20 years ago. It was in the summertime, and both Jerry Donegan, Zildjian's international sales manager, and Colin Schofield, marketing manager, were on vacation. One of our foreign distributors had sent over two of his representatives to come by the factory, check out everything, go over the cymbal selection, and stuff like that there. So I had to replace Jerry and Colin. I worked with the reps all day, and after the day was over, I took them to Bella's Italian restaurant, my favorite watering hole and just around the corner from the factory. The reps were nice fellas—one was tall and the other was short and chubby. When we got to Bella's, it was packed, so it must have been a Friday night. We were telling jokes—they liked to tell jokes, and, of course, they didn't know they were dealing with one of the world's greatest joke- and storytellers, Lennie D.

"So I started laying some funny stories on them and we were cutting up and having a ball. The waitress came over and asked what we would like to have for dinner. I said, 'Fellas, when in Rome, do what the Romans do and start off with a bowl of New England clam chowder.' So I ordered three bowls and we kept telling jokes. The chowder gets delivered and I'm in the process of telling one of my favorite jokes about Charlie Callas, the great comedian. The short, chubby fella was getting a big kick out of the story, laughing his ass off—and laughing so hard he was kinda bouncing back and forth, bobbing and weaving, and all of a sudden his head came forward and he fell right into the bowl of clam chowder. It splashed all over me. His head was in the fucking bowl, bubbles were coming up, and it was steaming-hot, and his face stayed in the bowl. I looked at his buddy and said, 'Man, that joke really killed him, and he said, 'Yes, it did.'

"His face was still in the bowl—he hadn't taken his face out. Finally, I grabbed him by his hair and pulled his face outta the bowl. His eyes were rolling around in the back of his head, his face was beet red, he didn't say a word, and he looked like he was dying. Believe it or not, he was as limp as a piece of spaghetti, fell off the chair, hit the goddamn floor, and was out like a light. Pandemonium broke out, Jim. God, everyone in the place was yelling to get a doctor, get a doctor, and I'm between laughing and crying—I didn't know what to do. I thought he had died, maybe from a heart attack. (I really didn't think my joke was that bad!) We called the EMTs and within ten minutes they were there with all of their equipment, and they started working on him and revived him, got him sitting up, put him on a stretcher, and took him to the hospital. Well, the dinner was over, and we didn't know what the hell was going on—the poor soul.

"He stayed in the hospital overnight. When he got back to the hotel, I called them. Apparently, he had had a diabetic allergic attack. He had been on the road for a couple of weeks, was exhausted, and having some wine and clam chowder did him in. What a nightmare."

Dennis Chambers preparing for a clinic

Now we come back to the "sane" world of drumming, and Lennie has a few words to say about another outstanding artist.

"One of the world-renowned funk/jazz drummers, Dennis Chambers, came on board the Zildjian Company when he was with the groups Parliament and Funkadelic—I think the time frame was around 1985. That band was out there. In fact, they would come on stage and do a bit while dressed in diapers. Really funny. He is one of the hottest and top drummers today. He's come a long way from the diaper band.

"Now, Dennis is really into his art. He is a collector of vintage equipment and is also a computer whiz. Over the years, Dennis has been a great source of information, especially in developing new products for Zildjian. He actually designed a big seller for the company called the Crash of Doom, a very esoteric and unusual type of crash cymbal that is completely opposite of the bright, high-pitched cymbals that are on the market today. The first size was a 20-inch, and the company is still selling it today. It's a very loud cymbal that calls your attention to that sound immediately after being struck. I guess you could call it his signature cymbal sound."

Dennis Chambers during a performance demonstration

Dennis truly is a great funk drummer, but his jazz chops are even better. Dennis is another of those amazing drumming prodigies who began playing at age four and was playing in night clubs at the age of six. Amazing! He joined Parliament and Funkadelic right out of high school, and after leaving them, he began session work in New York. His list of playing credits includes David Sanborn, John Scofield, Mike Stern/Bob Berg, the Brecker Brothers, Bill Evans, Stanley Clark, Steve Khan, and John McLaughlin. Viewing that list, I would say Dennis has the genres of funk and jazz pretty well covered.

A good portion of *Tales* centers on Lennie's position as Zildjian's artist relations manager. This next snippet is about another very special AR guy, who passed away much too young.

"I want to mention a good friend of ours, in fact he worked for you, Jim, at Yamaha: Steve Ettleson. He was a really good drummer and a friend to many around the world. I first met Steve when he was playing at the Playboy Club in Chicago, around the late '60s. Later he was the drummer for *Hair* in LA as well as the TV show "Name That Tune." If I remember correctly, he also backed up singers like Pearl Bailey and Perry Como.

"Steve did a great job with Paiste Cymbals, Drum Workshop, and then Yamaha. He followed those gigs with Remo and Evans and was just going to start work with Mapex when, tragically, he was struck by a car and killed on

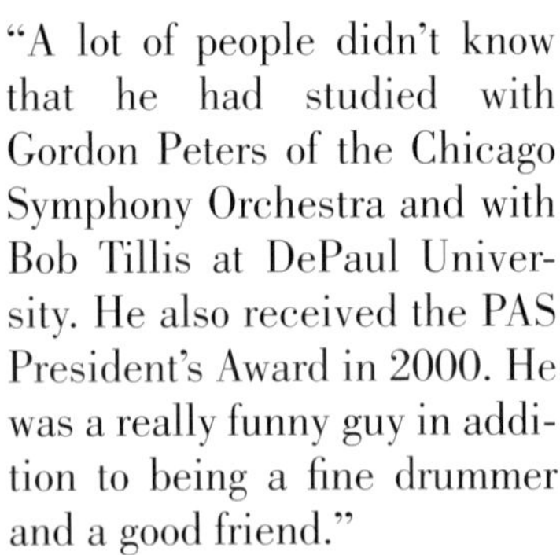

Ventura Boulevard in Studio City, California, May 31, 2001.

"A lot of people didn't know that he had studied with Gordon Peters of the Chicago Symphony Orchestra and with Bob Tillis at DePaul University. He also received the PAS President's Award in 2000. He was a really funny guy in addition to being a fine drummer and a good friend."

Steve Ettleson

As I said at Steve's memorial and was repeated in a PAS

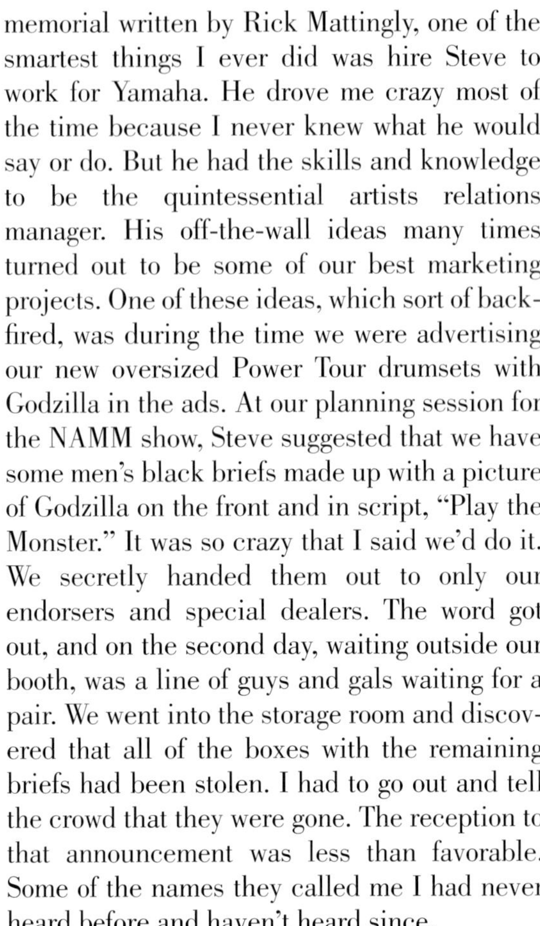

memorial written by Rick Mattingly, one of the smartest things I ever did was hire Steve to work for Yamaha. He drove me crazy most of the time because I never knew what he would say or do. But he had the skills and knowledge to be the quintessential artists relations manager. His off-the-wall ideas many times turned out to be some of our best marketing projects. One of these ideas, which sort of backfired, was during the time we were advertising our new oversized Power Tour drumsets with Godzilla in the ads. At our planning session for the NAMM show, Steve suggested that we have some men's black briefs made up with a picture of Godzilla on the front and in script, "Play the Monster." It was so crazy that I said we'd do it. We secretly handed them out to only our endorsers and special dealers. The word got out, and on the second day, waiting outside our booth, was a line of guys and gals waiting for a pair. We went into the storage room and discovered that all of the boxes with the remaining briefs had been stolen. I had to go out and tell the crowd that they were gone. The reception to that announcement was less than favorable. Some of the names they called me I had never heard before and haven't heard since.

In keeping with that same Godzilla project, we usually made a video for our Yamaha salesmen to instruct them on our new products. Steve was to introduce the new hardware that went with the oversized drums. I was working on something and not watching Steve's presentation when this huge laugh went up. I looked up and there was Steve—he had kneeled down and put his shoes under his knees. He was under a cymbal stand, peering out beneath the cymbal and saying, "Our new cymbal stands are really tall." It was hysterical. Lennie and I discussed how good Steve was with the artists and product development and felt that we should mention others who have excelled as artist relations managers: Johnny DeChristopher (Zildjian), Joe Testa (Yamaha), Joe Hibbs (Tama), Marco Socolli (Vic Firth), Jim Catalano (Ludwig), Ken Austin (Pearl), and Ray Brych. There are more, but the above readily came to mind.

"Another New York jazz drummer that used to come to the factory quite often was Horacee

Lennie with Dennis Chambers

Arnold. In those days he was really a hot player and did a lot of work in New York. Horacee is still active but has become quite a painter. He always was very artistic and on the deep side, and painting is another goal that he has been pursuing, and a showing of his paintings is in the works.

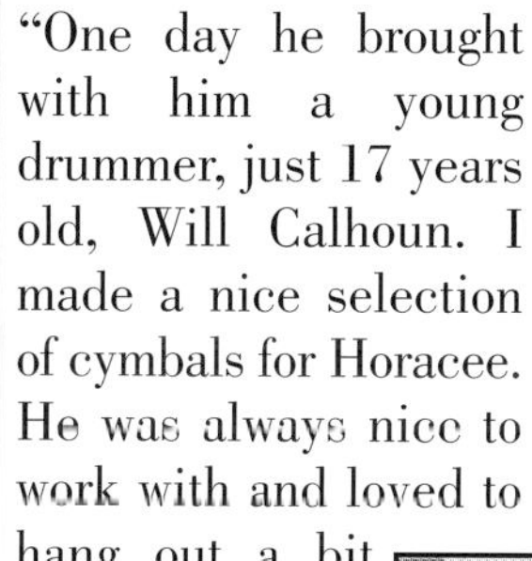

Horacee Arnold during a clinic

"One day he brought with him a young drummer, just 17 years old, Will Calhoun. I made a nice selection of cymbals for Horacee. He was always nice to work with and loved to hang out a bit and tell some stories. When they were leaving, Will said, 'Mr. DiMuzio, someday I would love to be a cymbal endorser. How do I become an endorser for the company?' I said there is really no magic formula; you just gotta be a good player, you gotta have a good job with a good band, and perhaps, maybe, a possibility of a record contract—that's generally what is really necessary.

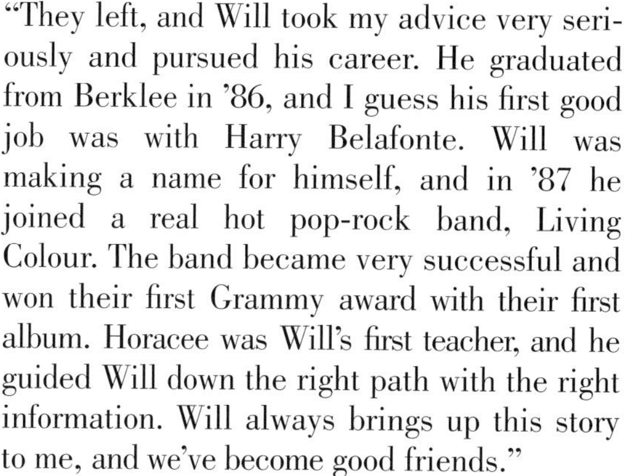

"They left, and Will took my advice very seriously and pursued his career. He graduated from Berklee in '86, and I guess his first good job was with Harry Belafonte. Will was making a name for himself, and in '87 he joined a real hot pop-rock band, Living Colour. The band became very successful and won their first Grammy award with their first album. Horacee was Will's first teacher, and he guided Will down the right path with the right information. Will always brings up this story to me, and we've become good friends."

Will Calhoun in clinic

I must add another word about Horacee. Both he and Ed Soph were Yamaha artists, and in 1984 in conjunction with DCI Music Videos and Quasi Prodution Limited, Yamaha produced one of the first drumset videos, *The Drum Set: A Musical Approach.* A trio made up of Bob Quaranta on piano, Tom Barney on bass, and John Scofield on guitar, provided the musical accompaniment for Ed and Horacee to demonstrate the various genres.

Lennie with Will Calhoun, John Blackwell, John DeChristopher, Berklee College faculty Dean Anderson, John Ramsay, and Skip Hadden, with Berklee students

Some of Lennie's Drummer Friends

LA drummer John Guerin and family

Denzel Warren Benbow, New York artist

Keith Knudsen and Chet McCracken (Doobie Brothers)

Aynsley Dunbar

Jaimo Johansen of the Allman Bros. Band

Nashville recording artist Eddie Bayers Jr.

Lennie, Jeff Porcaro, Louis Bellson, John Guerin, and Robbie the Robot at NAMM 1977

Chapter 36

An Apple for the Teacher—Plus a Cymbal

Lennie with Frank Epstein introducing Zildjian's new line of orchestral cymbals that Frank helped develop

This chapter was difficult to keep on a continuum due to all of the contributing voices. Even so, it demonstrates how a company can develop many branches from one trunk of an idea.

Tom Hannum and Lennie during their presentation of the Zildjian Achievement Award to Tom

Although a formal educational committee wasn't established until 1989, in the early '60s Lennie became involved with the educational side because of two books. As with other similar situations, Lennie wasn't seeking the education market. It found him.

Former Chicago Symphony Orchestra cymbalist Sam Denov

"Sam Denov, the cymbalist with the Chicago Symphony, wrote a book, *The Art of Playing the Cymbals*," Lennie states. "It was published by Henry Adler in 1963 and was a bestseller for many years. It was the first of its kind and was not only for orchestral cymbals but also concert and marching bands, as well as drum corps. There was not much written on hand cymbals, and we all used Sam's book as a reference. Eventually it went out of print,

Fred Sanford

but now it has been reprinted and is distributed by Warner Bros. Publications. Even in those early years I had a nice relationship with Sam.

"Then in 1964, Henry Adler published Roy Burns' book, *The Selection, Care, and Use of Cymbals in Stage and Dance Bands*. It was also a very good book, another one-of-a-kind, and we sold a lot of copies. Now, those two books were partially responsible for getting me involved with people who were in education, even though at that time I was Manager of Sales and special Cymbal Selections.

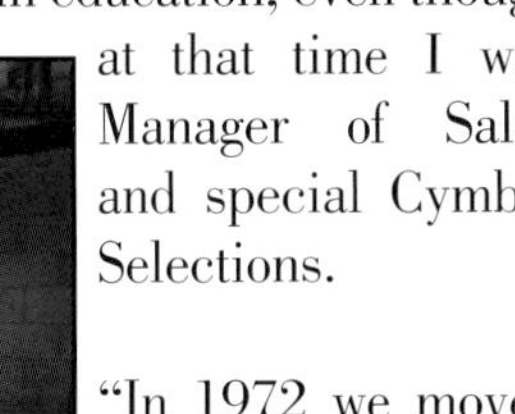

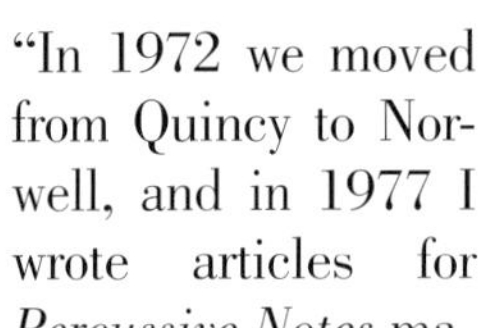

John Beck

"In 1972 we moved from Quincy to Norwell, and in 1977 I wrote articles for *Percussive Notes* magazine. The first member of an ad hoc education committee was Frank Epstein, who came on board around 1980. After Tommy Thompson died, Frank became the cymbalist with the Boston Symphony Orchestra and purchased all of Tommy's cymbals from his estate. Frank gave those cymbals to the Zildjian archives, keeping three or four pairs that he fell in love with. Those special pairs are part of his personal selection, and he is still using them today. At that time, Frank and I became close friends, and he was a frequent visitor to the factory. Due to his position with the BSO Frank became well known all over the world and he was often asked to make special selections of cymbals by some of his colleagues around the globe. Sam and Roy were not only great writers and players, but two of the finest clinicians and educators ever.

Armand Zildjian, Jim Petersczak, Lennie

George Tuthill

"After Frank, the next member was Fred Sanford, followed by Thom Hannum. At the time there was not yet an official budget at Zildjian for these meetings, but we would have informal get-togethers at PASIC, MENC, trade shows, and other venues. We decided that our first really big thrust was to be in the drum corps market, and that's why we hired Fred and Thom as consultants. In 1987 we developed and introduced ZMAC—Zildjian Multiple Application Cymbals—a line of hand cymbals designed primarily for the drum corp but also for the growing education market.

Johnny Lee Lane

"As Frank, Fred, and Thom slowly developed into an educational team, we added Steve Houghton, then a teacher at the Percussion Institute of Technology-(PIT) in LA. He became another of Zildjian's artists, and a consultant. He was

Jay Wanamaker

Left to right: Johnny Lee Lane, Fred Sanford, Steve Houghton, and Thom Hannum at a Chicago Midwest Band Clinic

not only a great player and teacher, but also a conductor and author of many percussion method books."

Thom Hannum, Jim Campbell, Fred Sanford

Thom Hannum, who is now teaching at the University of Massachusetts, offers the following recollections: "I got involved with Zildjian in 1982, due to meeting Rab Zildjian and Dave Deranian, advertising manager for Zildjian, at the DCI Championships in Montreal. They were at that contest doing some fact-finding concerning drum corps. I was working with the Philadelphia Crossmen at the time. Over the course of the summer, we had cracked a few pairs of cymbals, so Rab gave us two pairs of cymbals to use. I was astounded that a company would do that. I thanked him and asked if there was anything I could do to help the company. Rab replied that maybe I could do some R&D and to give him a call when I returned home to Massachusetts, where I was attending U-Mass. I really don't think he expected me to respond, but I did, and my association with Zildjian began.

Steve Houghton, Lennie, Gary Chaffee

"I was working on my master's at U-Mass, and after becoming involved with Zildjian, I switched my thesis topic to cymbals. At that time, Zildjian catalogued heavy cymbals for drum corps, medium weight for marching band, and lightweight for concert band. I had come to the conclusion that the cymbals were cracking because of how they were being played, not because they needed to be thicker or heavier. So I took a lighter pair of concert band cymbals back to school.

Jay Wanamaker, Jim Coffin, Fred Sanford

"By this time, I was working with the Garfield Cadets, from Garfield New Jersey, and began experimenting with pairing up different Zildjian models. For example, K medium and K dark and a variety of orchestral models. At one time, I even used two China Boy cymbals with straps as hand cymbals. After four years of experimenting, we came to the conclusion that for most band directors, having to choose

The Avedis Zildjian Company brought together an unprecedented line-up of outstanding percussionists to conduct clinics, free to the public, for Zildjian Day in LA, hosted by the University of Southern California. Pictured (left to right): Phil Ehart, Larrie Londin, Carmine Appice, Ralph MacDonald, Steve Gadd, Lennie, Tony Williams, and Rab Zildjian. Alex Acuña also participated, but missed the photo shoot (February 1983)

Swedish drummer Bert Dahlander with jazz historian Harold (Donald) Meade

Top row, left to right: Chris Noblet, friend, Armand Zildjian, Greg Bissonette, Lennie, friend, Jerry Donegan. Bottom row, left to right: Bill Morgan, Leon Chiappini, Colin Schofield, Mike Morse, Steve Tirpak

from so many types wasn't practical—we needed to create something different. The result was the ZMAC line. We could recommend a certain size and weight for a particular need. Since the typical band budget was limited, this new line helped the directors select cymbals that could be used in a variety of settings. After some sustained success with the ZMAC line, it was time to design a higher-end cymbal for the drum corps and marching bands. This idea of multi-application resulted in designing the Stadium Series, based on Frank Epstein's successful Orchestral Series; Instead of one standard-weight cymbal, Zildjian offered three weights for each size. In addition, I was always trying to specify my

Armand Zildjian, Kenny Aronoff, Ralph MacDonald, Steve Gadd, Rab Zildjian (in front kneeling), Steve Smith, Larry Londin, Lennie DiMuzio (in front kneeling), Bernard Purdie, Alejo Povada, Geraldo de Oliveira

Zildjian Day, Dallas, TX (left to right): Armand Zildjian, Louie Bellson, Vinny Colaiuta, David Deranian (kneeling), Tony Williams, Roli Garcia Jr., Simon Phillips, Tommy Aldridge, Lennie

cymbal selections based on pitch. Setting up ten cymbals in a row, I sorted within a pitch range and, emulating Frank's idea, established two weights in each size class."

Steve Houghton recalls the early days of Zildjian's inroads into the educational market: "I guess this all started in the late '80s and was the direct result of Jim Roberts, the CEO, leaving the company—he and others always kept education in the closet. For many years, Lennie and I had discussed the undeveloped potential of education activities, and he always dreamed of a full-fledged department. At that point, Armand had asked his daughter

Left to right: Bob Morrison, Casey Scheuerell, Colin Schofield (kneeling), Scott Miller, Gregg Bissonette, friend, Dennis Chambers, John King, friend, Lennie

Craigie to look after education temporarily, which she did. We had the first education summit meeting in Norwell, and in attendance were Fred Sanford, Thom Hannum, Johnny

Left to right: friend, Marvin Sparks, Armand Zildjian, Johnny Lee Lane, friends, Ed Thigpen

Alabama Day of Percussion, April 18, 1996, Tom Hannum, Casey Scheuerell, attending students

Lee Lane, Casey Scheuerell, Lennie, and me. We outlined some plans for the department and also took a photo for the first Zildjian Educator ad. That evening we had a typical Zildjian dinner with Lennie at the helm. Not surprisingly, We were sore from laughing."

"Once the message got out of Zildjian's strong interest in school education," Lennie continues, "especially through our association with the Percussive Arts Society and other organizations, many percussionists gravitated toward Zildjian to help support the cause. My view was to develop a team of percussion specialists who would present clinics at special events. In addition to the percussionists Steve

Jim Campbell, Lennie

mentioned, we added John H. Beck (Eastman), Jay Wanamaker (USC), George Tuthill (drum corps), Bob Breithaupt (Capital University), Jim Petersczak (Crane), and Jim Campbell (University of Kentucky.) We not only had meetings at Norwell, but also we would get together during PASIC and the Mid-West Band Clinic. The results from all the artists' input were overwhelming. I need to add that Johnny Lee Lane—I always called him the Mayor of Chicago because he was a real natty dresser—was responsible for bring-

At a recent Berklee percussion faculty visit to the Zildjian factory we (left to right) jazz legend Louie Bellson; Armand Zildjian (president Avedis Zildjian Company); Rick Drumm (vice president/marketing, Ren U.S.A.); Dean Anderson (chairman, Berklee percussion department); ar Lennie DiMuzio (director of education and artist relations, Avedis Zil jian Company).

Left to right: Louie Bellson, Armand Zildjian, Rick Drumm, Dean Anderson, Lennie

Lennie, Armand and the Berklee School of Music percussion faculty

ing a lot of African-American educators and drummers into the Zildjian camp."

Jim Petersczak, also a member of Zildjian's educational team, had this observation: "Lennie set the standard for artist relations people in the music industry and began a definition of that career, paving the way for the many who are artist relations managers today. In addition he was a big supporter of PAS, and he and you, Jim, were at the first PASIC in Rochester, helping me lay the foundation for those annual conventions. Lennie was also the driving force behind the *Armand Zildjian Tribute to Buddy Rich* audio tape. It was presented on National Public Radio with Wally Siegel as host and executive producer and me as the coordinator."

Left to right: Lennie, friend, Simon Phillips, John DeChristopher, Dave Deranian, Rab Zildjian

Lennie inserted the following as he thought about the development of the education market: "While we were working on the education side, other things were happening at Zildjian. Although the company continued selling through distributors, they decided to develop their own sales force of three sales representatives. The three were David Deranian in the East, Ron Stevenson in the Midwest, and Steve Tirpak on the West Coast. In 1983 we came up with the idea of the famous Zildjian Day, the big spectacular drum event with all of the top artists performing. All of this happened before the Zildjian Educational Showcases. The format for Zildjian

Left to right: Freddy Gruber, Rob "The Drummer," Steve Smith, Steve Houghton, Lennie

1982 NAMM Show, Atlanta, GA, (left to right): Jerry Ricci (in front), Dave Deranian, Lennie, Tim McCormick, Dom Famularo

Days was that it would be like a big clinic, a big drum event, with five or six artists, each

Left to right: Peter Erskine, John Beck, Armand Zildjian, Steve Gadd, Lennie

having about 45 minutes to an hour to perform. The first one was in LA at the Bovard Auditorium on the USC campus, with Jay Wanamaker as host and organized by Rab Zildjian, Steve Tirpak, Jim Petersczak, and me. The artists were Phil Ehart, Steve Gadd, Ralph MacDonald, Larrie Londin, Carmine Appice, Tony Williams, and Alex Acuña. Chicago was the second venue, and the artists

Fred Sanford

NAMM Show Parade with Lennie and Fred Sanford on drums

were Steve Gadd, Ralph MacDonald, Steve Smith, Larrie Londin, Bernard Purdie, Alejo Poveda, and Tommy Aldridge. Unfortunately, Tommy had to cancel, as his wife presented him with twins. Kenny Aronoff, who was living in Chicago and playing with John Mellencamp, replaced Tommy on the bill. That show was a tremendous success. The third show took place in Boston, and we considered it the grand finale for the year. The artists were Vinnie Colaiuta, Peter Erskine, Steve Gadd, Ralph Mac-Donald, Larrie Londin, Steve Smith, and Louie Bellson. This was the biggest show of all because we combined it with the 360th Zildjian anniversary party held at the factory in Norwell. It was a full weekend of festivities. Zildjian Day took place at the Berklee Performance Center, and a lot of people stayed over for the party. It was after that party that the JEWOPs had a meeting on Nantucket Island. Zildjian Days actually set a precedent and a program that became the industry standard and a classic promotional event for all of the percussion manufacturers around the world. As we fine-tuned each of these events, Zildjian Days got bigger and better, and we included more artists and sponsors—like different drum companies."

Modern Drummer Show (1988)

During the 1980s Zildjian and Yamaha worked closely together on many events, because both companies had the same advertising agency—two New Yorkers, Steven Ross and Robbie Clyne. They were very active in developing ad campaigns and being involved with the artists and shows like Zildjian Days and Zildjian Educational Showcases.

Lennie with Los Angeles drummer and teacher Jerry Steinholtz

Colin Schofield joined Zildjian in 1984 in the U.K. and was transferred to LA as West Coast artist relations manager. "I was sent to LA essentially to better position Zildjian to compete with the California-based Paiste Cymbals, a company that was kicking our butts due to the efforts of their artist relations manager, Steve Ettleson. Steve Tirpak and I were initially in the same office, but he was sales support and I dealt with the artists.

"Lennie remained in charge of artists relations, along with his education duties, until Johnny De-Christopher joined the company in 1989."

Steve Houghton, Bob Breithaupt, Casey Scheuerell

Steve Houghton, Lamar Burkhalter, Lissa Wales

Colin continues, "Lennie alone ran the education program from 1989 until 1997, when Richard Walker was hired to assist him. Ri-chard left Zild-jian in 1999, at which point John King, supervised by Lennie, took over the position of education manager. During this period Lennie had also begun work on development of the orchestral cymbal program."

Lennie jumps in: "I must interject that Colin was transferred from the West Coast office to Norwell in February 1986. He was involved with all facets of marketing, advertising, product development, and sales. After Colin was transferred, Steve Tirpak continued to run the West Coast office until he was joined by Mike Morris, who eventually took over that office. Mike, with the help of Johnny D. and myself, resumed a series of Zildjian Days that took place over the next two years. We did another in LA, one in San Francisco, New York, and again in Boston. Mike did a good job organizing the Zildjian Days while continuing to work with the West Coast artists."

As stated, in 1989 Lennie became the manager of the newly created education pro-gram department that was established to foster "Zildjian's support of all aspects of the percussive arts." One of the results from the formation of this department was the publishing of *The Educator*. Steve Houghton remembers: "*The Educator*, an educational newsletter, was a nice addition to the program. Lennie would contribute a good article to each issue, and I think we called it 'A Letter from Lennie.' Around the same time, we came up with a concept called a Zildjian Performance Showcase.

Chicago Symphony cymbalist Sam Denov, Lennie, A.J. Pero of Twisted Sister

Lennie with Frank Epstein of the Boston Symphony Orchestra, Tanglewood (1995)

Our first one, I think, was in Arizona around 1992, and little did we know that over the next few years we would produce about 14 events all over the country, with the showcase concept becoming a signature Zildjian program."

Lennie, Airto Moreira

"As Steve said," Lennie continues, "we decided, based upon the success of the Zildjian Days, to create the Zildjian Performance Showcases, geared toward the top universities, and to use only the finest clinicians available. We extended the showcases over a weekend, which allowed us to cover all aspects of percussion—from Latin to big band, combos, drum corps and marching bands, and orchestral performances. This was a great opportunity for students everywhere to see and hear the finest of teachers, as well as

Lennie with drummer Bill Reichenbach Sr.
Lennie says, "One of the fastest ride beats I've seen or heard."

percussion music. And, of course, it was all free to the students.

"We always had a headliner at the Showcases to draw a crowd. Drumset artists like Louie Bellson, Gregg Bissonette, Peter Erskine, Steve Gadd, Alex Acuña, and Tom Brechtlein; orchestral percussionists Neil Grover, Tony Cirone, and Frank Epstein; top university drummers and educators such as Bob Breithaupt, Ed Soph, and Jimmy Campbell; and, of course, from the marching side we had Fred Sanford and Thom Hannum. Steve Houghton was al-ways there, per-forming with an orchestra or band, conducting, or playing multiple percussion performances."

Tom Float, Chuck Morris, Gregg Bissonette, Steve Houghton

"Lennie loved the showcases," Steve Houghton says, picking up on Lennie's statements. "In fact, he loved any event that had education, music, and the 'hang.' Armand started to attend these events, and they became important moments for the company. These were different from Zildjian Days, because the showcases had clinics and performances with wind ensembles, orchestras, big bands, percussion ensembles, combos, and so forth. I can remember a showcase in Toronto when they announced Armand's name and the crowd went nuts—like he was a rock star. That night, Armand and Lennie told stories until the wee hours of the morning. Each showcase had different memories, but Lennie was right in the middle of all of them, holding court and taking care of the guys effortlessly. Of course, Lennie had to work at these shows, and I remember him playing hand cymbals at many of the sessions. He had a gorgeous sound, but I must admit he didn't look like an orchestral player.

Henry Adler, famous teacher and author, with Lennie at a NAMM show

"His dream of an education department never really came to fruition because he was moved to the orchestral area."

Recalling those early education days, Bob Breithaupt has some interesting observations, especially about Lennie and PAS: "During those days, Lennie was clearly a one-man show, if there ever was one. His support of PAS activities was legendary. An example: The drumset master classes, a brainchild of Ed Soph, Steve Houghton, Ed Thigpen, myself, and others, needed support, and Lennie was right there—without worrying about 'balance' between companies and all of the other political posturing that made organizing things difficult in the mid-'80s. Also, the facilities for holding the master classes were

Amy James (percussion specialist) with Lennie

insufficient, since they were usually small meeting rooms. On one occasion, '88 or '89 I believe, PAS was unwilling or unable to find other rooms, so Lennie arranged for an additional room to be underwritten for holding master classes. By the mid-'90s, the master classes had become a fixture of the convention, one of its most beneficial components, and has evolved into settings for all facets of the convention, not just drumset.

Rob Wallis and Paul Siegel of Hudson Music

"As the host of the 1993 PASIC in Columbus, I was under a great deal of pressure to make the event a success. Some of the previous PASICs had not been successful, with slightly more than 2,000 attendees. In addition to that, an undefined group with an unclear mission, the National Drum Association, had formed and was claiming 3,000 members, all sending money to participate in an organization that seemed to do little more than announce where upcoming clinics were to take place, and how drummers could unite, for an unspecified purpose, under their banner. In any event, this group was receiving growing corporate support and was making the leadership of PAS very nervous. PASIC '93 had to do well to ensure the future of PAS. In December of 1992, I met Lennie at the Mid-West Band Clinic and again when I flew to Norwell in the winter of 1993, both meetings to outline plans for the convention. At that time, the PASIC host was responsible for the planning, administration, and negotiation of most of the convention details. Lennie was a dream colleague, committing as much support that Zildjian could muster and, in addition, providing much of the underpinning of a new model for the convention as a world-class event, including negotiating with and sponsoring an appearance of Airto Moreira and Flora Purim and their band. This effort created one of the most unforgettable moments of a PASIC convention—the final Saturday night performance where the crowd was transfixed on Airto. That was completely arranged by Lennie, as I had no previous connection with Airto. In the years since, it has become evident that Lennie must have worked under the philosophy that 'It is easier to ask forgiveness than permission.' Certainly the participation of Zildjian in raising the profile of the PAS events would bear that out. I can only imagine the conversations with Armand when the accounting was reported!"

Zildjian Days and the educational showcases were all very successful, and when I was with Yamaha, we were always willing to support all our artists who appeared at those events.

Chris Noblet (former Zildjian vice president of international sales and marketing) and Lennie

I try to end each chapter on an upbeat note, but this one will be different because one of the giants of the marching percussion world, Fred Sanford, passed away in January 2000. Fred was an icon in the marching world, a pathfinder, and a joy to work with.

While growing up in Casper, Wyoming, he became a drummer in the Casper Troopers at the age of 12, remaining with that group until he was 21.

In the drum corps world they call that "aging out." While a student at California State University Fullerton, he worked with the Anaheim Kingsmen. Then he moved to San Jose State, where he studied with Tony Cirone. Fred used his drumming and writing talents to take the Santa Clara Vanguard drum line to five national titles from 1973 to 1979. Graduating from San Jose in 1970, he moved to New Jersey, where he taught high school music but kept his ties with the Vanguard.

Former Zildjian vice-president Colin Schofield, currently vice-president of Premier Drum Company, and Lennie

His manufacturing career took off in the '70s, when he became a design consultant with the Slingerland Drum Company, which resulted in the famous TDR snare, Cut-a-way toms, and Tonal bass drums. The '80s found him working for the Ludwig Drum Company as product development manager and staff clinician. During the '70s and '80s, he found time to work with the Madison Scouts, serve as the percussion coordinator for the 1984 Olympic Games in LA, and assist the McDonald's All-American Band. He was inducted into the Drum Corps Hall of Fame in 1991.

Lennie with Ian Croft, former Zildjian employee and current editor of Drum *magazine*

Fred was instrumental in developing Zildjian's drum corps and marching cymbal line. During that time, he was also a consultant for Yamaha and helped us become a factor in the drum corps and marching band field. He made my life much easier during my early Yamaha days. When I watch the Rose Parade every

New Year's Day and see all of the Yamaha marching percussion, I recall Fred and the great fun-filled times we had together.

At the 1999 PASIC in Columbus, Ohio, many of us were hanging out at the end of the day when someone made a phone call to Fred. When I took my turn, he sounded upbeat, and we laughed together as we recalled some of our adventures. Little did any of us know that cancer would claim him January 23, 2000. Both Lennie and I have many fond memories of our friend Fred Sanford. In his honor, we toast him with his favorite drink, a brandy Manhattan, and say thanks for all he contributed to students, to our companies, and to our lives.

Drum Corp International finals, Gillette Stadium, Foxboro, MA

World-renowned conga drummer Giovanni Hidalgo

Chapter 37

Tales and Snippets: #2

Louie Bellson, Steve Gadd, Gregg Bissonette, Vinnie Colaiuta, Dennis Chambers, Dave Weckl at Zildjian Day

As promised, here's another chapter about Lennie's friends whom he wants to acknowledge and recognize. We're going to begin with one of the most interesting, talented, and exciting of today's top drummers.

Lennie gives us one of his behind-the-scenes looks at Vinnie Colaiuta.

"It was 1983, and after the success of the Chicago Zildjian Day, we decided to do Boston and hold it at the Berklee School of Music. Now, Vinnie was one of the hottest cats on the West Coast and a top contemporary jazz artist. Incidentally, when he attended Berklee, he studied with Alan Dawson and Gary Chaffee, two of Boston's top teachers. Gary, who I see quite often, told me that Vinnie was probably his best contemporary student. Vinnie could read like a hawk and was a 'head' drummer, into the heavy stuff, avant-garde. We had all the drummers staying at the Sheraton Hotel behind the school. I picked up Vinnie and we walked over to the school.

Bernard Purdie, Steve Smith, Vinnie Colaiuta

Modern Drummer Festival gathering, left to right: Dave Weckl, Ian Wallace, Tris Imboden, Lennie (standing), Kenny Aronoff, Steve Smith

"We went backstage and Vinnie was really nervous—he had never done anything like this type of performance, this heavy magnitude. And it really showed. Anyone who knows Vinnie would know what I'm saying. His eyes were twitching, he was talking like a banshee, saying over and over again, 'Hey,

Steve Gadd at a clinic performance for Zildjian

Lennie, what am I gonna do?' So I just said, 'Vinnie, for God's sake, don't say a goddamn thing—just go out and play drums. That's what the kids are here for. They aren't here to talk to ya; they want to see you play.'

"Now it was Vinnie's turn up to bat. He walked out on stage, and you wouldn't believe it, the first thing that came out of his mouth was, 'You know something? I'd rather be standing bare-assed on the Santa Monica Freeway than being here and doing this.' The crowd broke into pandemonium, laughing, and it was the funniest thing. It is amazing how he broke the ice. After he said that and everyone was laughing and clapping, it was just Vinnie being himself, being real. Then he said, 'Let me play the drums for a while and then I'll feel better and we can talk about some things afterward.' It's an understatement, but he just tore the goddamn house down. He must have played his solo for 15, 20 minutes non-stop. He showed off all his shit, some awesome technique. He was an incredible technician, and a mind player—he went over big time."

Lennie, Steve Gadd, Kenny Sherez, Dave Deranian

Vinnie's playing is always amazing, but you never know what you are going to hear. Some nights it is in the stratosphere, other nights a music lesson, but always entertaining. Once I had to write an article for *Percussive Notes* concerning his clinic appearance at PASIC. I couldn't get him to answer my calls, so I phoned his mom. He called me within the hour. It was nice to know that Vinnie still listened to his mother.

Diane Schuur, Jim Rupp

We have it on good authority that drummers for many years have put their cymbal decisions in Lennie's hands.

"Jimmy Rupp was, and still is, a great player, from Columbus, Ohio, and still today is playing with the Woody Herman Signature Band. He is also the proud owner of the drum shop known as Columbus Pro Percussion. Every time I see Jim, he reminds me of the first time he got the call to go on the road with Woody's band. I think the year was 1982, and this was the first one of his big gigs. At that time, the Herman Herd was one of the best and hottest jazz bands around. Jim called me at Zildjian, and this was the first time I had spoken to him. He told me about the new gig and that he really needed a special ride cymbal to boot the band. I recommended a solid 24-inch ride cymbal, to push the band, something that everyone on the bandstand could hear and on which he could lay down a strong beat. He thought a 24 was rather large, but I said, 'No, Jim, for a big band like that, you are going to need something that will carry the whole weight of the band.' He used that cymbal with the band and continued to use it and use it and absolutely fell in love with that big 24-inch mutha. And still today he is playing that same ride cymbal. I sent him a few more cymbals over the years, but he always reverts back to the old one. He says it has got such a great timbre, just mellowed-out, just a great cymbal that he loves."

Steve Gadd, Stix Hooper, Jonathan Moffett, Lennie

Steve Gadd and Ralph MacDonald performing at a Zildjian Day

I contacted Jim Rupp to get the date he joined Woody's Band and received his first cymbals from Lennie. According to Jim, "Lennie first

Steve Gadd and Luis Conte at a PAS show

picked out a cymbal for me when I was in high school. I played at a high school jazz festival, and Kent State was the guest college band. The band director, Bob Chmel, who had been the drummer on the Glenn Miller Band, was a great swinging drummer, and I heard his 22-inch Swish Knocker. I talked to Bob and he said to have my local store call Zil-djian and have a guy named Lennie pick it out for me."

Steve Gadd

There's more to Jim Rupp's story. He had heard Danny D'Imperio play with Woody Herman's band in 1978 and heard what he says was a "killing pair of hi-hats," made by Zildjian, and that Lennie had picked the pair out for him. At that time Jim was in Maynard's band, and they played the North Shore Music Theater in Boston. And who was in the audience? Armand and Lennie.

Roli Garcia, Jr. at 10 years old.

"Man, I was scared to death of Armand and the Zildjian guys being there," Jim continues. "But they were very gracious, and Armand told Lennie to take me to the factory and help me pick out some cymbals. I will always be grateful for their support and encouragement and for the great cymbals. I first went on Woody's band in 1982, and I've been on and off with the band ever since. It's such a great big band book, and the musical standards are so high. I feel honored to still work with the band and occasionally hang with Lennie."

Lennie relays another Jim Rupp snippet:

"Over the years Jim, while growing his drumshop with his partner, Bob Breithaupt, had gotten deeply into all facets of percussion education—orchestral, jazz, rock, marching, what have you. And they put on one of the biggest drum show extravaganzas every year in Columbus. Jim and I just want to say thank you to Jim and Bob for contributing so much to the kids and the drum world."

Steve Gadd was first mentioned in the chapter concerning the K line of cymbals, but if anyone deserves more press, it's Steve. It is safe to say he is the most imitated drummer in the world. Chick Corea was quoted as saying "Every drummer wants to play like Steve because he plays perfect." He is also one of our favorites.

"Steve Gadd is an incredible drummer and considered one of the best around today. All his life, you know, he has played with some of the greatest, cats like Chuck Mangione, Chick Corea, Paul Simon, and Art Garfunkel. And he has been the drummer on many of the greatest albums ever recorded.

"One time that I really remember was when he performed at North Texas, the university where they have that great jazz program. I picked up Steve in Boston and we flew to Texas together, and I got him tucked into a place on campus. He was to have a rehearsal because he was going to perform with the great One O'Clock Lab Band, directed by Neil Slater. Anyway, I had to take Steve over to the hall, and on the way we kept bumping into students, and Steve, being such a beautiful person, had to stop and talk to them. They were asking all kinds a questions and things like that there, and I didn't really want to bug Steve about the rehearsal time slot. The crowd was getting bigger and bigger, and every time I

Ed Soph

tried to move Steve along, you know, more kids kept showing up. I'm telling you, it was like he was the president of the country and needed bodyguards. By the time I got him to the rehearsal hall, the band was getting ready to pack it in—there was no time left to rehearse. Neil had to get outta the hall because another group was coming in. So they would have to run down the charts an hour before the show. That was going to be the best that they could do, and Steve was going to have to do some sight-reading. We had a few hours before the show, so we got a little bite to eat, Steve took a short nap, and I picked him up a couple of hours before the show. This time I used the car so we could avoid the kids. We got to the hall and went backstage. Neil was there. Steve wanted some coffee—he was a coffee freak in those days—so I had to run out and get some Dunkin' Donuts coffee. I get back to the hall and Neil has all the drum charts laid out, and he and Steve went through the music. After about an hour, it was showtime and the hall was packed, the kids were out there screaming, and all that. It was time for the band to go onstage. Steve got behind the drums and had his music on a little stand about three or four feet away from him. I mean, it wasn't really an enormous stage, things were kinda tight. The real theme of the story is that Steve sight-read all the charts. I've never witnessed anything like that before in my life. You want to talk about a performance—wow—his ability was tremendous; he nailed every tune. It was an overwhelming success—he lived up to his reputation. When Steve and I parted, we never said goodbye or I'll see you later. Steve always said, 'Hey man, don't forget to practice your road rudiments. You know, five against one.' I would reply, 'You got it, baby. Jump back.'"

I have another snippet about Steve. He has played Yamaha drums for many years, and when he performed at his first PASIC in Dallas, I was in charge of getting him to a variety of venues, including a rehearsal with a local Dallas big band. There were a few problems, time-wise, but we did get that accomplished. It was bizarre—the students followed him everywhere, even into the restroom. Like Lennie said, Steve needed some bodyguards. We started fairly early in the morning, and by 4:00 in the afternoon, I was almost out on my feet. I got a hold of Lennie and asked him to take over for me while I took a cold shower to get my energy back. After a couple of hours, I took over again and got Steve to the evening concert. Once again, he was magnificent.

(That Dallas PASIC was the time that Armand decided to practice his drumming on the metal shade that was on a hanging lamp in the Zildjian hospitality room.)

One last tidbit concerning Steve's amazing ability, especially his time feel. On October 14, 1989, a Buddy Rich Memorial Scholarship Concert was performed at the Wiltern Theater

Ed Soph

in LA. The band played Buddy's charts, and the following drummers were featured: Louie Bellson, Gregg Bissonette, Dennis Chambers, Dave Weckl, and Steve. It was an amazing concert, and each drummer put his stamp on the charts. However, the following attests to Steve's amazing ability to handle any musical genre. After the concert was over, I was in the green room, where there was a reception for the band and the drummers. Bobby Shew, a great trumpet player and friend, took me aside and said, "Jim, of all the great drummers who played tonight with the band, there was only one who we felt really comfortable with—Steve Gadd." That show was released on video by DCI/Warner Bros. Publications. Armand, Lennie, and I were at that sold-out concert.

Marvin "Smitty" Smith, Thèrése DiMuzio, Kenwood Dennard

You've already read about some Zildjian Days, but this was a special one where they programmed a drum battle between a very young player and a drumset icon.

"In 1985 in Dallas, Zildjian put on an incredible Zildjian Day featuring Kenwood Dennard, Louie Bellson, Vinnie Colaiuta, Simon Phillips, Tommy Aldridge, Tony Williams, and a ten-year-old, Roli Garcia. Roli was from southern Texas, and his dad used to take him to the NAMM show, where he would play at the various drum companies' booths. We got to know his dad and Roli, and he was the greatest young performer around at that time—this kid was amazing. So we decided to have him at the show in Dallas. It was a spectacular show because of the great players, and we had Roli do a drum battle with Louie Bellson. This was a funny scene because Louie had never seen Roli play. We had two drumsets on the stage, and the two of them had a little drum battle. Roli, even though he was only ten years old, had a lot of avant-garde and contemporary things happening. Well, Louie was always a straight-ahead big-band, super jazz drummer, and I'm telling ya, it was pretty funny, because Louie played, and then Roli played, Lou would look over, and he was absolutely amazed. His eyes would light up, he would look over at me, and shake his head. After they got done playing, Louie grabbed ahold of me and said, 'Hey, Lennie, what the hell you doing to me? You didn't tell me that kid could play that good—he blew me off the stage.' The crowd loved it.

"A quick note about Kenwood Dennard and his appearance at that Dallas Zildjian Day. He was at the peak of his career and was doing a series of clinics while in Texas. He had decided to drive from Boston in his van with all of his equipment. Not only did he play his drums, but he also had a MIDI set-up and would surround himself with all of his equipment and crawl inside and sit in the middle. It was something to see. Now, he played the drums with his right hand and with his left hand played a synthesizer, which was tucked in right alongside the hi-hat. He also had a pipe that went up to his mouth and acted like a trigger. Kenwood played the drums, the synthesizer, and sang. It was one-of-a-kind—no one else was doing anything like that. He did all different types of music—scat singing and doing tunes—it was a beautiful thing. It was exciting."

Many of the drummers Lennie worked with played in Woody Herman's Band. You've already met Jim Rupp and Steve Houghton.

The following four snippets are in the order the guys joined the band, beginning with the incomparable Jake Hanna.

Jake Hanna (1931–2010)

"Probably one of the funniest drummers I ever worked with was Jake Hanna. His one-liners were priceless and he was also a great story-teller. I met Jake in '58 or '59. He's was a hometown boy, born in Roxbury, Massachusetts, and grew up in Quincy, MA. I saw him with Woody's band and he played his butt off, and he did some funny stuff in those days behind the drums, especially his animated comedy routines. It was a killer. He remained a top notch and highly regarded player throughout his career. He eventually settled in Los Angeles and I always looked forward to seeing him at the NAMM shows in LA. Unfortunately he passed away on February 12, 2010. I will miss him very much and so will the entire music community."

All of the drummers loved to see Jake, and at the NAMM shows they were always looking for him. One year folks couldn't find him so there were buttons passed out asking "Have you seen Jake?" Jake's beautiful sound graced not only Woody Herman's band, but the bands of Maynard Ferguson, Ted Weems, Duke Ellington, Harry James, and Herb Pomeroy. While in New York, Jake was also in Merv Griffin's TV studio band and moved with the show to California. As Lennie stated, the guys loved to hang with him at the NAMM shows and whenever you got around Jake you heard a lot of laughter.

It seems many of the drummers Lennie likes to talk about have a great sense of humor. Here are some of Lennie's recollections, followed by some interesting accounts from the drummers themselves.

"I first met Ed Soph when I saw him perform with the One O'Clock Lab Band at North Texas just before he graduated, and he knocked me out," Lennie continues. "After that, he immediately went out on the road with the Woody Herman Band. You know, Ed is one of the best drummers around, a great teacher, and he's written a whole bunch of drum method books. He's a funny guy, a practical joker, and known by all as the 'barking spider' king. Ed is one of the drumming world's top clinicians."

Now we get Ed's version. It is a winner.

"Lennie and I first met at Geronimo's Bath and Beauty Club, an alternative-lifestyle establishment on Beacon Hill. Lennie played drums in the house band and did a remarkable impersonation of Mae West. Evidently, back in the halcyon days of the company, this was where most endorsement deals were consummated. I was a naive college grad with stars in my eyes."

Knowing Lennie, I think that could have been the truth, but Ed was just bullshitting us. Here's the real story.

"Okay, Lennie and I actually met at Lennie's on the Turnpike in the summer of 1968, before North Texas. Woody's band was playing there, and Lennie, Armand, and Bob Z. came out to

Jeff Hamilton

catch the band. They told me my cymbals were dead and that I should come out to the plant, then in Quincy, to get some new ones. I did, and I also had lunch with Mr. Avedis Z. at the local Howard Johnson's. That was the beginning of my relationship with the Zildjians and Lennie."

Ed is also one of Yamaha's leading education clinicians and has presented master classes in the United States, Canada, Europe, the Middle East, and Asia, Australia, and New Zealand. In addition to being the drummer on Woody's band, Ed has also performed and recorded with many top artists, such as Stan Kenton, Clark Terry, Bill Watrous, Randy Brecker, Marvin Stamm, Pat LaBarbera, Bill Evans, and Bill Mays. Both Lennie and I have had some great times with Ed, and he continues to spread the drumset gospel in his own articulate style.

Now another Woody Herman alumnus.

"Jeff Hamilton is one of the great West Coast drummers and a great drumset teacher. I've known Jeff for many years and saw him play with the incredible Oscar Peterson. Of course, Oscar is a great jazz pianist and he would play tempos that were absolutely unbelievable. To see Jeff play brushes at that breakneck speed was awesome. What a brush man. I really can't describe it—you have to see him play. He is probably the best brush player going today, and if you happen to look at Jeff while he is playing, he'll look back at ya and break into a big fat smile. Jeff has an incredible history of playing with nothing but the best artists in the business. He likes to use light cymbals, nothing too heavy. His ride cymbals are mid-range to lower in pitch and have a lot of shimmer and bounce. Nothing high or pinging or loud. Jeff is definitely unique."

To back up Lennie's comments about Jeff's playing history: Jeff left his studies at Indiana University in 1974 to play on the Tommy Dorsey ghost band, followed by a two-year stint with Monty Alexander's Trio that commenced in '75. In '77 he joined Woody's band. Other artists include the L.A. Four, Ella Fitzgerald, Count Basie, and Rosemary Clooney. In the '90s he toured with Ray Brown and Oscar Peterson, as mentioned by Lennie. Now he has his own trio plus the Clayton-Hamilton Orchestra.

Here's another Woody Herman drummer to round out the foursome.

"Joe LaBarbera, another West Coast drummer, and I became good friends many years ago when he was backing one of my favorite singers, Tony Bennett. I not only loved his playing, but he introduced me to Tony one night and that was the big balls. I got to know Joe's brother Pat, who was playing lead tenor on Buddy Rich's band, and his brother John, an arranger and composer who now is the jazz instructor at the University of Louisville. Joe likes to use light ride cymbals, mainly because of the small group, you know, with Tony. Perhaps a 20-inch K light ride, along with an 18- or 19-inch ride and a pair of K hi-hats. He didn't really use too many cymbals, but he might have added a 15- or 16-inch dark crash."

Joe LaBarbera

Joe's professional career really got started with Woody's

Freddie Sargent. Joe LaBarbera

Lennie demonstrating orchestral cymbal technique

band, followed by the Chuck Mangione Quartet. After locating in New York, Joe worked with some of the best, including Phil Woods, Art Farmer, Gary Burton, Art Pepper, Jim Hall, and Bob Brookmeyer. In 1978, he joined (along with bassist Marc Johnson) the great pianist Bill Evans to form yet another historic Evans trio. After Bill died in 1982, Joe worked with the great Tony Bennett for several years. Joe is still in LA performing not only with his own group, but with many top West Coast artists such as Bud Shank, Bill Perkins, and Lanny Morgan.

"Maynard Ferguson also featured a lot of great drummers over the years, some we've already talked about, but here are a few I want to mention. One of the early guys was Tony Inzalarco, followed by Peter Erskine, Jimmy Rupp, Gregg Bissonette, Ray Brinker, Dave Tull, Jason Harnel, and Marco Marcinko. There were many more, and forgive me for not listing them all, as I don't have all of their names."

Lennie now reminisces about a Boston friend and drummer who had a great gig.

"I met Freddie Buda in the late 1970s. He was clearly one of the up-and-coming cool jazz drummers in Boston and was destined for an incredible career. I was gigging around town playing in some of the show bands, and occasionally I would have to send a sub. I had only heard of Freddie then and had yet to meet him, but someone told me to give him a call. I did, and he started to sub for me on some gigs. We soon became good friends, and he developed a great reputation. Over the years this led to many, many gigs, the greatest of which is getting chosen to be the drumset artist for the Boston Symphony and the Boston Pops. Can you imagine trying to hold 150 musicians together, and with a conductor on top of it. Well, Freddie handled that job great, and he has been a first-call drummer for at least 25 years. He recently retired from the orchestra, but he is still playing, doing some contracting, and chilling out."

Fred and I first met when I was with Premier. In 1976, for the Boston Pops 200-year anniversary celebration concert, I had Premier make a red, white, and blue drumset for their TV show. Because of that kit, Fred sent me an autographed sketch of the Pops legendary conductor Arthur Fiedler, thanking me for my cooperation. In the '80s I switched Fred to Yamaha. I always enjoyed watching Fred play with the Pops because he had a unique style—that right elbow up in the air in preparation for a solid hit.

Fred Buda, Boston Pops Orchestra

Frank DeVito

We mention Roy Burns many times in *Tales*. However, Lennie wants to describe a very special clinic and some of Roy's great solos.

"As you know, I met Roy when he was a young dude. Roy was always one of my favorite drummers, and when he peaked in those early days, his playing was awesome: incredible technique, creativity, and energy. He always came up with some new shit and let the lumber fly.

Victor Mendoza, Lennie, Horacio Hernandez

At the Mid-West Band Clinic in Chicago in 1965, Roy played with the Vandercook College Band and played a long and incredible drum solo. I said to myself, 'Whoa, jump back, Buddy. Make room for Roy—he's coming up fast.' After a standing ovation, I helped him off the drum stool and we went to get a cup of coffee. Roy was drained and still so humble, and I remember him saying, 'I still got to do some more wood-shedding.'

"Roy played with so many bands, did clinics all over the world, and, that not being enough, still explored other goals. He never seemed to be satisfied and finally went into the business side of music and founded his own company, Aquarian Drumheads. His business continues to grow and today is a strong competitor in the drumhead business. Roy always told me, 'You know, Len, I might not be number one in the drumhead business, but I'm really number one in my life. I'm married, have children, got a great business, and I can still play my ass off.'

Frank DeVito, Baja Marimba Band

"The book would not be complete unless I mentioned a few more of my good friends who made such a big impact on Latin music, and bridging that genre with American contemporary jazz. All you have to do is mention the names Horacio 'El Negro' Hernandez and Giovanni Hidalgo, and drummers almost, kinda, bow to their talents. 'El Negro' and Giovanni have taken technique to another level of perfection and have recorded and performed together all over the world. With his awesome ambidextrous style of playing and maintaining the clave beat with his left foot, 'El Negro' lays down all those complex rhythms with both hands around the drumset. Giovanni is considered one of the greatest conga players

Jim Petersczak, Ed Soph, Lennie

on the scene today, and both of these cats are incredible musicians and percussionists. Horacio joined Carlos Santana's band in, I think, 1997 for a world tour. He had worked with a lot of groups before Santana, mostly in Cuba, Rome, and finally in New York. When those two players perform, you have to hang on to your seat. They are the best." Lennie then begins to reminisce about another drummer friend who many people do not realize what a great career he had—Frank DeVito.

"Frank and I have been friends for many years, and what a lot of people don't realize is that Frank worked on many of the great bands. He was born in Utica, New York, and developed his chops by drumming with Charlie Parker, Dizzy Gillespie, and Bud Powell as a sub for Roy Haynes. Later on, he was on Hal McIntyre's band. After Frank started living in California, he got a lot of studio work. I think one of his last great gigs was with the Baja Marimba Band. Of course, now Frank is known for his percussion accessories company, Danmar. I always look forward to seeing Frank at the various shows, and I want to recognize him in our book."

"Even though we mentioned Ed Shaughnessy in an earlier chapter, Jim, I want to say a few more words about this great drummer. Most people associate Ed with big bands because of the 29 years he spent playing on the NBC Tonight Show Orchestra led by Doc Severinsen. What they don't realize is that Ed has played with many small groups and some of the greatest jazz musicians. A few that I remember are Gary Burton, Stan Getz, Charlie Ventura, and Benny Goodman. The list goes on. He still goes all over, giving clinics; Doc usually has a tour; and during the summer, Ed teaches in band camps. Along with all of his drumming talent, he is a very funny guy with a great laugh. He and I have been friends for a long time. In 2004, Ed was inducted into the PAS Hall of Fame. He has been a seven-time Best Big Band Drummer winner in *Modern Drummer* magazine."

Now it's time to change gears and move to another, completely different chapter in Lennie's life—orchestral cymbals.

Ed Shaughnessy

Jazz artist Ronnie Bedford

Chapter 38

Special Cymbals for the Cymbalists

Lennie with cymbalist Anthony Cirone, formerly of the San Francisco Symphony

If you recall, Lennie's working with the late Tommy Thompson and then with Frank Epstein of the BSO finally resulted in his working on the orchestral side of cymbal making. It is an interesting tale, since most folks would not associate the good doctor with the sophisticated world of orchestral players.

Paul Francis, the Chicago Symphony Orchestra percussion section, and Lennie, during a CSO visit to Zildjian

"As the educational department was growing year by year, one of my next objectives, my goal, was to organize and develop a strong orchestral department. When Bob Zildjian left Zildjian on January 1, 1982, he formed the Sabian Company in Canada and started manufacturing cymbals. One of his main goals was to develop a comprehensive and competitive line of orchestral cymbals. Around the early '90s, Frank Epstein, cymbalist with the BSO and a consultant for the Zildjian Company, wanted to develop a more complete and

Lennie with Angela Zator Nelson of the Philadelphia Orchestra

unique line of orchestral cymbals. He and I discussed the situation many times and realized that we needed more orchestral cymbals that would meet the demands of symphony orchestras all around the world. After discussing it with Armand, he agreed and gave us carte blanche to form an R&D team and go for it. So that's exactly what we did. Our first R&D team consisted of Frank, myself,

Lennie and Michelle Humphreys, cymbalist, Baltimore Symphony Orchestra

and three of my fellow workers at the factory: Paul Francis, Al Gloubin, and Leon Chiappini.

"Paul was unique, a good drummer, and a fine cymbal maker. He knew every aspect of making cymbals, from start to finish. Al also knew every aspect of making cymbals, and Leon was a great cymbal tester. We started making prototypes and sending them out to some serious percussionists around the country—players like Tony Cirone, the San Francisco Symphony, Tom Stubbs, the St. Louis Symphony, and others—all friends of Frank. After a year of research and feedback from the artists, we had to critique all of the idiosyncrasies that the players would look for in an orchestral cymbal. We were able to narrow it down to what we thought would be a good classical cymbal line.

"Classical orchestral cymbals are a lot different from the regular drumset cymbals. The demands of the orchestral player are a lot more complicated, because they are looking for other aspects of the cymbal sound than what the drumset player would be looking for. For example, the drumset player would not be as concerned about the outer edge, the hole, the overall shape, and the way the cymbal responds. If the cymbal is slightly warped, it will not crash properly. Both cymbals have to be perfectly round in order to respond properly and open up. They cannot be uneven. The hole must be finished, smooth, and round so as not to wear out the cymbal straps. If the cymbals have a high bowl configuration, they will choke up. If they are too flat, they will bottom out and lose projection. These are some of the idiosyncrasies that orchestral players will be concerned about. As we know, drumset players usually play with sticks, hit the cymbals in a different manner, and listen to a different response, whereas the cymbalists always play the cymbals in pairs, unless they use a suspended cymbal and strike it with mallets. The cymbalist needs a great volume range, from very soft to very loud.

Jim Campbell, Armand Zildjian, Tom Stubbs, Lennie, Steve Houghton

"Drumset players like to use a lot of cymbals for variety—splash, crash, ride, and special effects. The orchestral percussionist also needs a variety of cymbals, many different hand cymbals from small to very large. They need this multiplicity of choice in order to cover the extreme amount of literature, from orchestral to percussion ensembles and wind ensembles.

U.S. Military band members selecting cymbals at Zildjian with Lennie

"After a few years of development and critiquing all the unique and finer aspects of the line, and with the approval of the Zildjian Company, we introduced the new A line of classical orchestral cymbals around 1993. After introduction, we immediately began to contact some of the finest percussionists from around the world. Frank Epstein was very helpful and instrumental in helping me contact some of these artists, as well as

Lennie with cymbalist Muryelle Légaré of the Quebec Symphony Orchestra

coming to the factory once or twice a month to further critique the line—making sure that everything was being done properly.

"Also, I set up and organized a whole new orchestral department with the assistance of Frank and my assistant, Annette Macamaux, who worked with me for many years in contacting the heavy-hitters in the drumset world as well as helping me fine-tune the educational department. She also worked for Colin Schofield, who at that time was the marketing VP, and she is still working for the current Zildjian marketing VP.

Lennie's executive assistant at Zildjian, Annette Macamaux, and president Armand Zildjian's personal assistant, Pam Smey

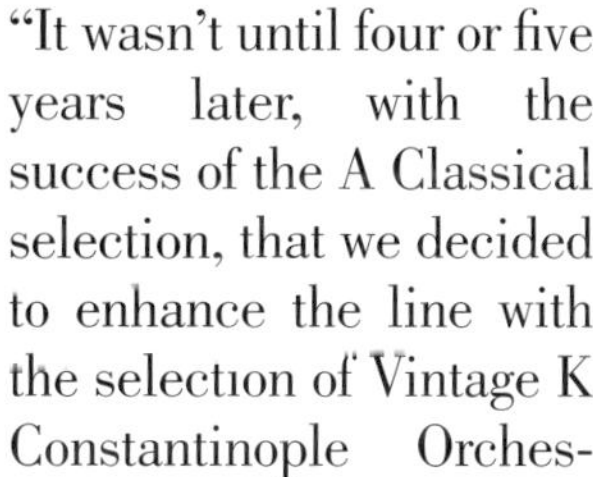

"It wasn't until four or five years later, with the success of the A Classical selection, that we decided to enhance the line with the selection of Vintage K Constantinople Orchestral cymbals. Once again we brought the R&D team together and set forth to develop this line. Returning to the drawing board and repeating the same strategy as we did with the A line, prototypes were produced and sent out to the special cymbalists who were truly captivated by the sound of these old Ks. These players were from the older generation and they always looked for the classic sound. A lot of them still have some of the older K Zildjian cymbals that were hand made anywhere from 50 to 100 years ago in Istanbul. Some of the great orchestras like the Vienna, Berlin, Munich, and others still use those old cymbals, which are passed down from one generation to another, and those cymbals stay with the orchestras.

British orchestral percussionists visit Zildjian (circa 1975)

Peter G. C. Chrippes, cymbalist, London Symphony Orchestra

Marlene Hartley, who was executive assistant to Zildjian's vice president of international sales

"Word spread very quickly throughout the orchestral world, and with the relentless support of Frank Epstein, we made contacts with all the major orchestras in the world. We pursued more clinic appearances with the orchestral artists and geared up production. Once we felt comfortable with the line and had completed our R&D, we officially introduced the new line."

Percussion section of the National Symphony Orchestra of Ireland with Lennie during a visit to the Zildjian factory

To close out this chapter, we list some of the percussionists and famous orchestras Lennie worked with:

Andy Barclay, London Philharmonic; Paul Berns, Indianapolis Symphony; Alon Bor, Israel Philharmonic; Stephen Bruns, Norway Symphony; Tony Cirone, San Francisco Symphony; Manuel Garcia, Puerto Rico Symphony; Patsy Dash, Chicago Symphony; Steve Fitch, Phoenix Symphony; Kurt Hans Goedicke, London Philharmonic; Victor Viktorkanatru, St. Petersburg Philharmonic; Peter Kates, Bergen Filharmoniske Orkester; Jacque Lavelle, Montreal Symphony; Jan Pustjens, the Royale Concertebaun Symphony, Amsterdam; William Platt, Cincinnati Symphony; Andrew Reamer, Pittsburgh Symphony; David Searcy, La Scalla Opera House; Tom Stubbs, St. Louis Symphony; Sam Tundo, Detroit Symphony; Fred Mueller, Berlin Philharmonic; Arnold F. Riedhammer, Munich Philharmonic Orchestra; Jiri Svoboda, Czech Philharmonic; David Hockings, London BBC Orchestra; Mikhail Peskov, Kairov Russian Opera; Lung Heung-Wing, Hong Kong Philharmonic; and Richard Weiner, of the Cleveland Symphony.

Just imagine what the conversations must have been like with the European percussionists. I can almost hear Lennie saying "Jump back, baby" in his Russian be-bop slang.

Peter Kates and members of the Bergen Filharmoniske Orkester

Former Zildjian educational manager Richard Walker

Jim Coffin, Lennie, Armand Zildjian (1990)—wonderful memories

others thought it was a mistake and was harming the company. He and his lovely wife, Andy (Andra), took me to one of their favorite restaurants in Boston for dinner, at which I expressed my reservations about his new hire. In no uncertain terms he told me to butt out. He was correct, I had overstepped my bounds, but I did it because I felt strongly about Zildjian. One other time the problem was between Zildjian and Yamaha and had to do with our purchasing of cymbals and the discount we believed we deserved. We were at a stalemate, and things had not been resolved by the winter NAMM show in Anaheim. When we displayed our drumsets at the show, we always used Zildjian cymbals exclusively. I was upset, so at that show we had not only Zildjian cymbals on the stand but also Sabian and Paiste (this was before the insurgence of so many other cymbal companies). I was at the display and in walked Armand, not smiling. He wanted to know what was going on, and I told him I was upset about the discount problem. We talked it through and arrived at a compromise, but I didn't remove the non-Zildjian cymbals. It was really a non-issue since many of our Yamaha artists used Sabian and Paiste, but it put a little wedge between our companies. That didn't last long, though.

One time when I was visiting Zildjian, Lennie and I were going to go hear a drummer (neither one of us can remember who it was) and would be out late. For some unfathomable reason, Armand and Andy said we could stay at their house in Hingham since they would be gone. We got to their place around 3:00 a.m., Chinese food in hand. In the kitchen was a huge wooden table; we ate our food there and probably had some more pops, and then it was time for bed. What I hadn't realized until it was time to retire was that their home was full of priceless antiques. Everywhere we looked, there was some incredible object. There was just enough room to walk to the bedrooms. I was afraid I would hit some object, knock it over, break it, and have to take out a second mortgage on my house. We ended up getting a few hours of sleep as well as leaving their beautiful home intact. I know I held my breath as I walked toward the door, and breathed a sigh of relief when I got outside.

The last few years of his life, Armand and Andy lived in Scottsdale, Arizona, where he got to play golf with his friends, *Downbeat* owner Jack Maher and then-NAMM CEO Larry Linkin. Surviving Armand in his immediate family are Andy and their four children, Wendy Mets, Craigie, Debbie, and Rab. Rab has been at several percussion shows recently, and talking to him is like hearing Armand—the same gravelly voice and laughter.

I always felt honored to be a part of their family and treated as a friend. There were many happy times and a lot of fun. I would give anything to hear once again "Beautiful, baby!"

Armand Zildjian at the wheel of his classic Bentley (circa 1987)
This is one of my favorite photos of Armand. I think some of the happiest moments in Armand's life were when he was driving his classic antique Bentley touring convertible. For many years Armand would tour with the Bentley Touring Club through the Berkshire's rolling hills, stopping at his favorite antique shops and restaurants. Armand loved his antiques and his music, and, of course, more than anything, his family and his friends; and everyone loved Armand.

Lennie and Armand enjoying an afternoon at
Fibes Drum Company owner Bobby Grasso's home in PA. (circa 1975)

Chapter 40

Tales and Snippets: #3

Lennie gets roasted and then toasted

Jim Coffin, Lennie, and Lloyd McCausland at the start of Lennie's surprise "roast party" at the 1997 PASIC show

The following snippet is a bit off-the-wall and required some thoughtful editing. But the occasion was so funny that to ignore it would be criminal. The year was 1997, the event was PASIC, and as previously mentioned, Lennie received the PAS President's Industry Award that year. Unbeknownst to Lennie, the Zildjian guys had set up a roast following the banquet. It was the roast to end all roasts, and Lennie was really taken by surprise as he was led into the room and saw all of the people laughing and cheering.

Colin Schofield

With great difficulty, the master of ceremonies, Colin Schofield, who stated that after the evening's entertainment he will probably have to start handing out his resumé, managed to get the crowd somewhat under control. The

Sandy Feldstein takes to the microphone to share his special memories of Lennie for the roast

first speaker was Sandy Feldstein, who first strode to the mike wearing The Nose, which immediately set the tone for the evening. He

Lloyd McCausland

Neil Grover

John Beck

Bob Breithaupt

spoke about Lennie's early career, when he was known as a great drummer, and then he added, "but we all know him as Lennie The Nose." After each example about Lennie's career, Sandy would finish saying, "but we all know him as…" You get the idea.

Sandy was followed by JEWOP Lloyd McCausland, who closed out his narrative with the time he and Lennie were at an MENC conference in Colorado Springs. According to Lloyd, they were doing the "hang" in the bar that night, working for their companies, and there was a young lass who was attempting to stand vertical. At the close of the evening, Lennie assisted the nice young lady, who continued to have trouble staying upright. They left the bar. It had been snowing, the gal slipped and fell into a snow bank, and Lennie ended up falling on top of her. Lennie extracted himself and hailed a cab, which turned out to be a police car. The officer wanted to know what was going on, and Lennie responded, "I'm trying to get this young lady home." The tale ended at that point.

Next was a poem by Neil Grover, a Boston Pops percussionist and owner of Grover Pro Percussion. He began by saying Lennie had shown some interest in the Boston Ballet, and for a percussionist it was gratifying to look out into the audience and see Lennie snoring in

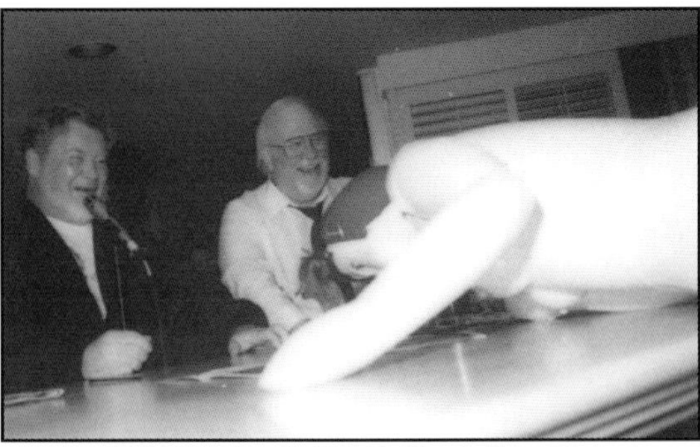
Lloyd McCausland, Jim Coffin, inflatable guest

Lloyd McCausland, Jim Coffin, and the inflatable guest, Cassandra

the third row. There was so much noise and laughter that the following transcription might not be quite accurate:

Ode to Lennie

Lennie DiMuzio,
here's to you, from
your admiring
cymbal-loving New
York Jew.

Certainly it's overdue,
this party, a roast, to

Lennie eyeing the development of things

The crowd goes wild

thousands of players, to whom you're the most.

Now let us retell, the story—a tale, for all who love cymbals, you're the cat who can wail.

Groovy, baby, far out, I hear you say, wait a minute, that lingo from this day and age?

Our parley is genuine, true to the heart, but don't stand behind him, lest he should fart.

The crowd was going wild!

When the glorious history of Zildjian is told, there must be a footnote, a name listed in bold.

Like a fifth Beatle, your praises unsung, when it comes to cymbals, man, Lennie's well hung.

Jim Coffin

Neil left to thunderous applause.

Next was Bob Breithaupt, and he recounted a summer workshop in Columbus, Ohio, that featured Steve Houghton and Ed Soph. The group had discussed what to do for some of the evening's entertainment. Bob told Steve of a Wednesday night jam session at 333 Third St., and they thought that was a good idea. That evening, Steve and Guy Remonko, another workshop clinician, got in one car, and Bob and Ed got into Bob's car—with video camera in tow. Steve was wearing a black tank top that had *Le Batterie* printed on it and was carrying his green leather stick bag. They went upstairs and had arrived at the hippest gay bar in Columbus. Steve saw two guys dancing and another two guys making out at the bar. He realized the joke was on him and he bolted right out of there.

Next on the podium was John Beck, the venerable Eastman professor, who began by stating he had entered the fray a little later, but that he knew the JEWOPs, and that Lennie was a special teacher. "Just watching Lennie, your life changes," John said. "I want to tell you how Lennie changed my life. I learned that five o'clock is not the end of the day, but the beginning. A pop is not a balloon breaking, and 'Jump back, baby' means prepare for action. 'Hang' is not a lynching, and to be truly successful, you must be able to play the banjo."

Then Armand was introduced. He also came to the mike quite ready to roast Lennie and proceeded to recount numerous stories from their years together. He mentioned that Lennie went by three last names (aliases)—DiMuzio, Portanova, Cooper, and others—as mentioned in Chapters 1 and 2. Next came the story also found in Chapter 2 about Lennie's first drumset, but one of the best stories Armand told was about the time Lennie had a bat in his house during a Fourth of July party. The full story is in Chapter 30. Of course, Armand embellished the bit about using tennis

It was a memorable evening full of incredible stories and jokes

Entertainment Break

A*dam Nussbaum*, one of Zildjian's world-renowned Jazz Artists, performed Friday, September 19, in ***Norwell***, in a very different and special Master Class. Adam, who has been involved in the development of ***Zildjian's*** new ***Professional Brushes***, spoke about the history and technique of using brushes in Jazz.

For the ***Grand Finale***, Zildjian's own ***Lennie DiMuzio*** joined Adam on stage to display his ***secret talents – spoon and banjo playing.*** **Adam's** innovative style and fantastic brush solos combined with **Lennie's** lost art of spoon playing provided more than enough excitement for a Friday afternoon.

News clipping about Adam Nussbaum and Lennie's duet performance at the Zildjian Company

rackets to hit the bat. Armand's remaining narratives are best left to the imagination, as they were in keeping with classic comedy roast vernacular, but they also clearly spoke of his affection for his lifelong friend and the great times they had shared.

After Armand, my turn came. I believe it was Judy McCausland who called out, "Tell about the doll." I didn't know that tale, so Lloyd took over. He recounted when they were at a meeting in Texas and Rick Drumm, then with Vic Firth Sticks, had them over for dinner. Just before they were going to leave, Rick gave Lennie an inflatable doll that Lloyd said, "Rick didn't need anymore." While Lloyd was telling the rest of the story, the doll was carried in. Now, the appearance of the doll had as much impact on the audience as the most popular guest. One might have thought the doll was going to roast Lennie as well. As the doll was introduced we learned that Lennie had named the doll Cassandra. We also heard that earlier that day there was more to the Cassandra story. Lloyd had not yet checked into the hotel, and had stuck his luggage in Rick's car. When they got to the hotel to unload, Lloyd commandeered a dolly, put his luggage on it, laid Cassandra on top, and covered her body, but left her head out. They wheeled it into the hotel themselves because the bellhop wouldn't have anything to do with it. Lennie says, "It was funny as hell. Lloyd was in the wrappers, we were jiving around in the lobby, and all the people in the lobby and behind the counter were breaking up." We finally deflated Cassandra and tucked her away for posterity."

After the doll was put away, I stated that Lennie had been a big influence on my career. Because of my being associated with him, I lost my job, my house, my car, and my retirement money, and at the mention of his name, my dog would bite me. After I closed out my portion, the audience was treated to a video produced by Rob Wallis and Paul Siegel titled *The Man, the Myth, the Smell.* They had several clips featuring Lennie, the first being Lennie telling the Zildjian story a la Gabby Hayes. One of the highlights was with Adam Nussbaum behind the drumset and Lennie playing the spoons. Adam was whistling "Sweet Georgia Brown," and they traded fours before taking it out. That was followed by Adam using brushes on a big pad while Lennie played his banjo.

The evening's festivities closed with Lennie expressing his deepest gratitude to his colleagues at Zildjian and to the Zildjian family, and his love for the business and all of his friends. He added that the roast was overwhelming and gave kudos to Johnny D. and his acting skills, for getting him to the roast unknowingly, telling Lennie he was taking him to a special product demo. It was a spectacular event—never to be duplicated.

Now for some more snippets about drummers. Lennie opens with one of the greats.

"A lot of New York drummers attended Roy Haynes' 60th birthday party at Tavern On the Green. I took my daughter Cecilia with me. The place was beautiful. Bill Cosby was the

Roy Haynes, 60th birthday party

Bill Cosby hosting Roy Haynes' birthday party

emcee, and it turned out to be a roast with a lot of Roy's friends getting up to speak. Cosby also roasted Max Roach at the party. Roy and I have been friends for many years, and he is still playing—he never seems to age. He was a great influence on Terri Lyne Carrington."

Roy not only influenced Terri Lyne, but also he has been influencing drummers and the jazz world for more than 62 years. At the age of 16, he began playing with guitarist Tom Brown, bandleader Sabby Lewis, and saxophonist Pete Brown. His career really took off when he joined the legendary bandleader Luis Russell, and now at the age of 78, he is still roaring. Heavyweights such as Lester Young,

Max Roach, Roy Haynes, Lennie, and guests at Roy's 60th birthday party

Bud Powell, Miles Davis, Charlie Parker, Eric Dolphy, and Stan Getz all swung to Roy's powerful playing. It was an honor for me to present Roy his PAS Hall of Fame plaque.

Max Roach

Now to another side of the drumset spectrum. You'll "believe it or not."

"Jim, I became a friend of a Boo Macafee, but I always called him Boo Boo just for kicks, because he had a good sense of humor and was a fun guy. This story took place back in 1981 when he was playing in Nashville with a lot of good country groups.

"One day he decided he was going to break the world's drum solo record and get into the *Guinness Book of World Records*. He began to prepare himself and would call me quite often at the factory concerning the contest and that it would be televised. The show finally took place and it was held at Winkler's Drum Shop in Nashville. Boo Boo would have to prepare himself physically and mentally for a week prior to the show. He also had to get acclimated to not eating much and get checked out by his doctor. The Guinness management set up rules that said he could take short breaks during the competition to go to the men's room

GUINNESS SUPERLATIVES LIMITED

RECORD CERTIFICATE

This is to certify that Boo Boo McAfee

of Nashville, Tennessee, USA did break the

Drumming record this

13th day of August 19 81

738 hours - 13th July to 13th August, 1981 Details.

Norris McWhirter Editor, Guinness Book of Records, London

Guinness Book "longest drum solo" awar d to Boo Boo Macafee

Dean Anderson, Dave Weckl, Lennie

or to get something to eat. However, he had to keep one stick in his hand, either twirling it or tapping it on something to keep the solo going. He also had them put a telephone aside of the drumset so he could call me and update how the solo was going. He planned on playing for a month, and although that sounds unbelievable, the show took place. Boo Boo did call me in the middle of the solos while playing with one hand and with the other holding the phone. To make a long story short, Boo Boo played for 738 hours, which comes out to one month and eighteen hours. The photo of Boo Boo shows him on the 17th day of his solo, in the hospital due to his feet swelling badly, continuing playing on his snare drum with brushes. He gave me a copy of the *Guinness Book of World Records* certificate, certifying that he did break the drumming record on August 13, 1981.

Land Richards of Gladys Knight and the Pips

Boo Boo Macafee

"Boo Boo is still living in Nashville and actively playing. A few years ago he and his partner devised an electronic device to measure the actual speed of a drummer's hands. I saw Boo at the NAMM show in 2004, sitting behind the unit. It looked like a digital recording machine. He was monitoring all the young drummers who came by, trying to see how fast they could play a single stroke roll or a paradiddle. Leave it to Boo Boo to come up with this. He's quite a guy and loves any challenge having to do with drumming and the drums."

Matt Sorum, Kenny Aronoff, Lennie

I'm still wondering how Boo Boo was able to keep one stick in motion while going to the bathroom.

As mentioned in Snippets #2, Lennie always seemed to hang with drummers who had a great sense of humor. You met this next drummer earlier in the book, but Lennie has a few more words to add.

"Another great and really funny drummer is Gregg Bissonette. He is a trip-and-a-half, and going out to dinner and hanging with Gregg

Kenny Aronoff

would take you down laughing. He could be a great stand-up comedian, and he does very funny imitations of both Charlie Callas and Sid Caesar. He is an all-around great drummer, can play all styles, and is performing a lot of clinics for Mapex drums. Gregg also has a great relationship with his dad, Bud. Bud retired quite awhile ago and took on the responsibility of being Gregg's road tech as well as his business manager."

The Bissonettes are a Detroit musical family. Gregg's dad was a bandleader, and his brother Matt is a great bass player. Both Gregg and Matt were in Maynard Ferguson's band during the same period. Then Gregg moved to LA in the '80s, where he became one of the best session players, recording and playing with artists such as Carlos Santana, Hans Zimmer, Gino Vannelli, Brian Wilson, Linda Ronstadt, Enrique Iglesias, David Lee Roth, and Celine Dion. Gregg is establishing a solo career while continuing to display his great drumming skills with the Ringo Starr Band.

Johnny Sciarrino, Drummer for Wayne Newton

Time to change direction once again, for Lennie to recount a story about an unusual guy who is a friend to many in the business world.

"Whenever Armand, Colin Schofield, John DeChristopher, and I went to New York to visit dealers, we always stopped by Manny's Drum Shop to see all the cats and to check out the cymbal

John "J.R." Robinson in clinic performance

situation in town with Marco Soccoli, who at that time was running the drum department there. Once you met Marco, you would never forget him. What a great guy. Between the conversations and the laughs, and the 100 proof grappa he used to slip us now and then, we always had a ball. Marco is so Italian you could smell the garlic sauce on him and see the spaghetti coming outta his ears. He spoke fluent Italian. In fact I think he speaks several languages, and he would let you know it, believe me. Well, Marco came from a big family, and I think that his grandmother lived in the Bronx, and he used to rave about her cooking and the sauce that she made that you would die for. Whenever I saw him, he would always say, 'Lennie, the next time you come to

Percussionist and educator Norm Goldberg

Lennie, Steve Gadd, Bill Crowden (circa 1970)

New York, we've got to see Grandma and I'll tell her to make up some sauce and meatballs, and we're going to sit down and have a lot of wine and eat hearty.' That went on for four or five years, and Marco was insistent that we visit his grandmother. Unfortunately, before that happened, she passed away. So we never got to eat her great Italian cooking and sauce.

Marco is now working for the Vic Firth drumstick company as artist relations manager. He said that being an artist relations guy was the job he always wanted, and he learned everything about the job from 'the cat,' Lennie.

Bill Ludwig III, owner of Not So Modern Drummer Publications; daughter Maggie; wife Lisa

Marco is a unique individual. He is very bright, and very entertaining. He has an explosive manner and always talks at the top of his voice; and when he is talking with you, his head is always moving, always checking out the scene. He truly is funny and a joy to be around.

Now to one of the stars who seriously explores the drumset, always breaking new ground, and constantly expanding its horizons.

"I met Dave Weckl when he was living in the Big Apple and starting to play with all the hip jazz cats. It was in the early 1980s when I brought him on board with Zildjian. His career was going up by leaps and bounds. He has always been very serious about his goals, and he has become one of the top drummers and recording artists of modern times. Man, his work with both of Chick Corea's bands—the Electric and the Akoustic—was amazing. Those bands were outta sight. I think he was with Chick for six or seven years. Dave is also an incredible educator and author of a lot of very popular educational books and videos. He's also a top clinician, plus tours with his own fusion band. What a player."

Chicago drummers
Alejo Poveda and Ruben Alvarez

Dave Weckl, Lennie

Jackie Santos, Alan Dawson, Rudy Collins

Dave's tenure with Chick Corea propelled him into the upper echelon of the drumset world. A St. Louis native, he left the University of Bridgeport (CT) after two years and got involved in the New York scene, becoming one of the top session players and working with artists such as the Brecker Brothers, Eliane Elias, George Benson, Diana Ross, Madonna, and Robert Plant. After Corea, he moved to LA and did his own thing plus played with the GRP All-Star Big Band and recorded and toured with guitarist Mike Stern. Now, in addition to doing more instructional videos, he is recording and touring with the Dave Weckl Band. He is also a frequent clinician at the PAS and NAMM conventions.

"There is one guy I want to mention who has really made it in the drum business world. I first met Rick Drumm about 25 years ago when he was playing in the Barnum & Bailey Circus band. He came out to the factory and I picked out some cymbals for him and then went to the show. I think this was around 1978, somewhere in there. After the circus, he joined Remo and stayed there for over ten years. Rick always said that at Remo, JEWOP Lloyd took him under his wing, and he wished Lloyd would have worn deodorant. Rick's a funny guy. Anyway, after Remo, Rick became the CEO of Midco International for a few years and then ended up as president of the Vic Firth drumstick company for many years. Rick has now moved on from Vic Firth and made further career advancements in other top music industry businesses.

Alejo Poveda

"I don't see how Rick finds the time to play with all of his many business duties and traveling, but he still keeps his chops up and plays with good bands wherever he is. And with all this he' s also raised a wonderful family."

This next top drummer, although well known, had to jump into the Zildjian Day frying pan because of a set of twins.

"There is quite a story about Kenny Aronoff. I had signed him up as an endorser while he was playing on John Mellencamp's band. This happened when he was living near Chicago, and that is where we were going to put on the second Zildjian Day. Tommy Aldridge was scheduled to be one of the artists, but he had to cancel because his wife was having twins. Kenny had given me a call asking for some tickets to the show, and I told him he didn't have to buy any tickets and he could stay in the Zildjian suite. We decided to have Kenny take Tommy's place and lead off the show. When I told him we wanted him to take Tommy's place because of the birth of the twins, he said, 'Wow, I am a twin.' Anyway, he was really nervous, and he had to lead off the show, but all of the drummers told him not to worry. Man, he was really nervous, but we got him through it and he did a great job.

"Now, Kenny had a great educational background. He studied with some of the BSO percussionists and was actually offered a job as a timpanist with several symphony orchestras. His career really took off when he joined the John Mellencamp band. But when we get together, we always talk about that Zildjian Day in Chicago."

Kenny studied at the University of Massachusetts and the University of Indiana, where he was awarded the school's Performer's Certificate. In the summers he performed at the Aspen and Tanglewood music festivals. After leaving the Mellencamp band, he played on major tours with the likes of Smashing Pumpkins, Bob Seger, Melissa Etheridge, Joe Cocker, Jon Bon Jovi, Mick Jagger, Alice Cooper, and the Rolling Stones. His drumming style has led to a successful career as a studio musician as well as the title of #1 Pop/Rock Drummer and the #1 Studio Drummer for five consecutive years in *Modern Drummer* magazine reader's poll.

"Every time I was at the NAMM show in Anaheim, our good friend John Robinson used to come by and tell us what he had been doing. I was always amazed at the list of stars that he had recorded and toured with, and when he told me that he was with Barbra Streisand, you just don't get any better than that. I saw her when she first came on the scene on the Johnny Carson show, and she has become one of the greatest female singers of all times. Now, J.R. had a ball playing with Barbra and made a lotta dough on that gig. He tells the story of when John DeChristopher and I attended his wedding in 1994. J.R. didn't know that the ride from the airport to his home with Johnny D. driving was like a late-night 'chill-o-rama.' Talk about buying your driving license at Sears. Johnny drove like he had just escaped from Alcatraz and was running from the police. White knuckles all the way—pedal to the metal, baby. Even when we used to go to Boston to see some of the artists, I would tell him that I would meet him there. Johnny D. is doing a great job as Zildjian's artist relations manager."

John Robinson and I are also longtime friends, and we were both born in Iowa. I came into this world a little sooner than he did—23 years earlier, to be exact. He told me when we first met that he considered driving up to the University of Northern Iowa, where I was teaching, to take some drum lessons but decided against it because he lived in southwest Iowa and UNI was in the northeast. Though I was flattered, I told him that his not going was probably the wisest decision he ever made, because I might have goofed him up. Anyway, J.R. began playing drums at the age of eight and started his first band at ten. What a career he has had and is having. His first big break came when Rufus and Chaka Khan heard him play and invited him to finish their tour. John moved to LA and next came Quincy Jones. His studio career took off. He has been with Quincy since 1979 and Barbra Streisand since 1993, and as of this writing, he has 30 motion pictures to his credit, including *My Cousin Vinny, The Bodyguard, Free Willy, South Park, The Waterboy,* and *Rush Hour*

"Chicago, Chicago, that toddling town," Lennie begins, "I always loved going to Chicago. A great town, hitting Rush Street with all the great clubs and incredible food. We always made it a point to hook up with the late Maury Lishon, his wife Jan, and his sons. Maury owned Frank's Drum Shop, probably

Jonathan Mover, Marco Socolli

Lennie with Shinichi Usuda (a major Japanese dealer), Mike Baker, Mrs. Baker, and the new Baker baby, NAMM (1991)

one of the best, maybe *the* best drumshop in the country. There was always something happening there. Maurie was truly a character, a small man who carried a big stick. He smoked cigars, and believe it or not, I can still smell 'em. We always had a great time with the Lishons. Later, Maury sold his shop to another great guy, Bill Crowden, who was married to Brook Ludwig, daughter of Bill Ludwig II, a beautiful woman and lots of fun. Bill eventually changed the name to Drums Limited, had lots of clinics with great players like Steve Gadd, and carried on the tradition of Frank's. I also got to know Bill Ludwig III (Junior) and his wife Lisa. There was never a dull moment happening with them, and both Bill and Bill Junior knew all the cats in town and hooked me up with all the heavy hitters. Bill Junior and Lisa still live in Chicago and they will always be my first contacts when I hit town.

"There were two other guys in Chicago that I must mention—Alejo Poveda and Ruben Alvarez. Alejo and Ruben were two of Chicago's top Latin percussionists. Man, they were hot. I first met Alejo in a hot Latin club playing with his own band, Chevere—that had to be at least 25 years ago. Later, Ruben joined the band, and he usually played the congas while Alejo played the full percussion rack. Alejo has a sextet now and is cooking in Chicago, with both he and Ruben playing a lot of sessions and teaching in the schools. Alejo could have been a stand-up comedian because he had jokes up the ying-yang, lots of one-liners. We all liked to chow down and do the hang scene."

Alejo is also very special to me, because I had him on Premier drums and later switched him to Yamaha. When he first got his Yamahas, he phoned me and said, "Jeem, I love my Jamahas." I never could get him to say Yamaha. He is a great drummer, and his groups covered the jazz genre as well as Brazilian bossa novas.

"I have a few more drummers who I want to recognize, especially for their great talent, friendship, and passion for music. As I mentioned in Chapter 3, I met Alan Dawson when I got drafted in 1957 and auditioned for the Army Band. He was the percussion instructor at Camp Killmer in New Jersey. Alan grew up in the Boston area and lived about ten miles from the old Zildjian factory. I would often see him at the factory, but I saw him mostly downtown playing with either his band or backing up a top artist who was on tour. Alan was a gentleman, a very humble soul, and a family man. I always felt that because of his family ties, he didn't like to be on the road too long, and that might have been one of the reasons why he never received the worldwide recognition he deserved. Alan taught at the Berklee School of Music and later opened his own drum studio. Believe me, he always had a waiting list. I am sure that all of the great players and his students and family were devastated when he passed away."

Lennie, Adam Shendal (drummer for Wayne Newton), Newton band member, Thèrése DiMuzio, Walfredo Reyes, Lennie's wife Peggie

The list of Alan's performance credits is very long, including Oscar Peterson, George Shearing, Woody Shaw, Dexter Gordon, Phil Wilson, and Terry Gibbs. The list of famous drummers who studied with Alan is equally impressive: Jake Hanna, Tony Williams, Terri Lyne Carrington, Steve Smith, J.R. Robinson, Harvey Mason, and Vinnie Colaiuta are but a few of the many drummers that sought Alan's teachings. Sadly, Alan Dawson passed away February 23, 1996, of leukemia at the age of 66.

"Although we've already mentioned Mo Mahoney, I must mention that he was responsible for introducing me to a young hot cat, Adam Shendal, another one of Wayne Newton's drummers. Adam grew up in Vegas and without a doubt is one of the finest self-taught drummers I have ever met. He could have left Vegas and traveled with any of the top artists and bands, but his mom and dad live there and he was making *mucho dinero* with all the stuff that he was into. He is still grooving and is one of the top drummers in Vegas, producing and recording and going strong as ever."

Alan Dawson at home in his teaching studio

As Lennie and I discussed who else should be mentioned in *Tales,* we both realized that in the early days, the few drum shops around the country were the driving force behind the percussion world and clinics by the artists.

Lennie recalls New York City's premier drum shop: "Frank Ippolito's Professional Drum Shop was the place to go to see the top players. Papa Jo Jones also gave lessons there in a studio provided by Frank. One of the other major East Coast drum shops was in Bethesda, Maryland, and was run by Mickey Toperzer. Mickey was also a great drummer and always spoke the truth—our kind of people." [In one of the early chapters in *Tales*, Lennie told us a lot about Boston's Jack's Drum Shop.]

Of course, the place to go in Chicago was Frank's Drum Shop, owned by Maury Lishon. I would take my University of Northern Iowa percussion students on field trips, and one of the major stops was at Frank's. Roy Knapp, the venerable teacher, had a studio at the

Maury Lishon, wife Janice, percussionist Charlie Botteril
Frank's Drum Shop, Chicago (1980)

shop. Maurie and Jan Lishon were friends with both Lennie and me for many years, and when I left teaching to enter the business world, Maurie was my mentor. I was so pleased when Jan, who ran the print music side of the shop, asked me to sign my first method book and then placed it on display in a special rack by the door near the elevator.

West to Minneapolis, there was Marv Dahlgren's Drum Shop. Besides having the drum shop, Marv performed with the Minneapolis Symphony and also did some teaching at his shop.

Whenever our business took us to Las Vegas, we had to stop in and see Mo Mahoney. He ran the main Vegas drum shop in those days and also kept a very active playing schedule.

We've already mentioned Bob Yeager and his Hollywood Pro Drum Shop, but there were other drum shops, such as Drum City, run by Roy Harte. Remo Belli was a partner, and in the back of the shop, they began experimenting with plastic heads, which eventually led to the birth of the Remo drum head business.

There are many great drum shops doing business today all around the country, especially the Five-Star Drum Shops. Most are run by

Phil Ehart of the band Kansas

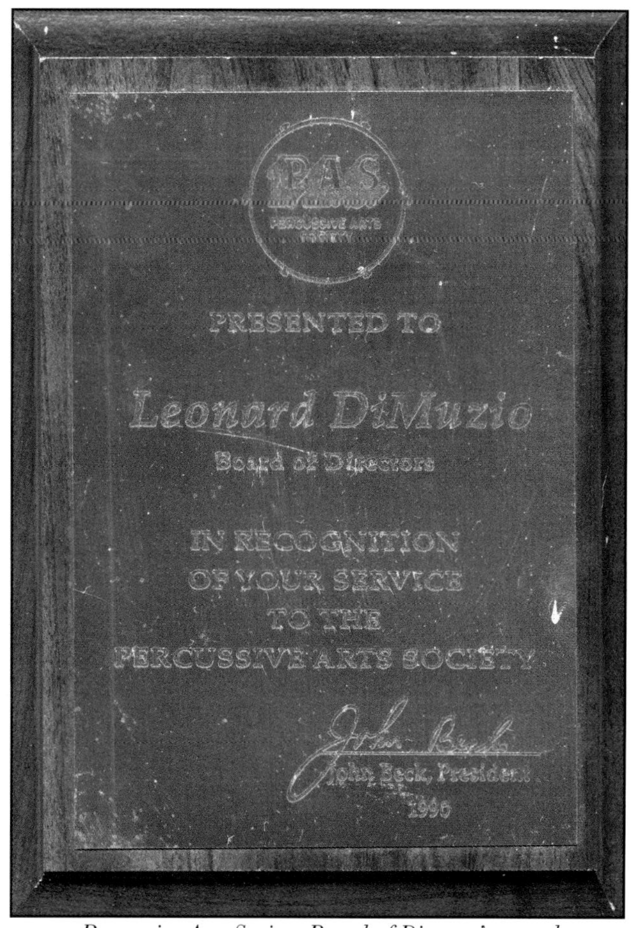

Percussive Arts Society Board of Director's award
presented to Lennie in 1990

drummers and continue the legacy set by the early owners, who not only knew drums, but also kept up an active playing career. Ellis Toland of Philadelphia Music City comes to mind. There are many great drum shops with great drummers as owners; far too many to list.

The drum industry continues to grow, but, sadly, many music stores that sell percussion do not specialize in percussion, and only sell it in addition to other instruments and products. Consequently, many do not have very knowledgeable salespeople. Whatever is hot, they sell, but it's only about selling something, anything, and not about the right choices for the individual, or about the best percussion instruments, or caring service. I remember Maurie Lishon telling a young drummer he didn't need an expensive drumset and that he should start with a basic kit and then, as he got better, come back and trade in his beginning set for a better one. Those early shops kept the drum business alive in the best of ways.

This ends our "Snippets" chapters. We now move on to show what some other folks have written about Lennie.

Rabbi Lennie, Armand Zildjian's favorite Lennie makeover

Chapter 41

Have You Heard This One?

A lot of drummers and industry people have their favorite Lennie stories. They usually begin, "Have I ever told you about the time..." Most are funny, but many were about the serious side of Lennie. That's what this chapter is mostly about—Lennie's serious side—and it is appropriate that it is near the end of the book.

When I was young and just starting attending trade shows, my father would say to me, "Stay away from the Zildjian suite. Lennie DiMuzio is up there and I want you to stay away from him." Naturally, as soon as my father went to bed, I went right up to the Zildjian suite and hung out with Lennie. I found out my dad was right.

—Carol Calato

I have a clean Lennie story for you. It is indicative of his amazing ear rather than his other well-known attributes. I was visiting the plant and was trying cymbals in the warehouse room, not the fancy display area. He was on the far side of the room talking to Bob Breithaupt. I found a really nice ride and called to Lennie, who was out of sight, asking what he thought. He simply replied, "What are you doing with the orchestral cymbals, Ed?" And that's just what I had pulled out.

—Ed Soph

In 1976 I graduated from Berklee College of Music and joined the famous jazz guitarist Pat Martino. Bob, the manager, said to me that I was in the big time with Pat, and therefore he got me a Zildjian cymbal endorsement. So I took a long trip from my NYC hometown, and when I got to Norwell, MA I got on a pay phone to connect with Zildjian and get started with them. I called the people at Zildjian and said, "Okay, I'm here! I'm ready to get started." The rest of the conversation went something like this:

"Who's calling?"
"Kenwood."
"Kenwood who?"
"Kenwood Dennard."
"Who are you with?"
"Pat Martino."
"Pat who?"
"Martino."
"Sorry, I haven't heard of you."
"But Bob said he got me an endorsement with you."
"Bob?"
"Yes."
"Bob who?"
"He manages Pat."
"Sorry, we can't help you at this time."
"Wait! Listen! Something must have gone

Kenwood Dennard

Carol Cohen and Steve Ross

wrong. But I sincerely feel I'm going to be an influential drummer someday. My name is Kenwood. Please give me a chance to play for you guys."

Well, the person said okay, and it was Lennie. He invited me to the factory and showed me around. What a gentlemen he was. In 1977, I went back to the factory while I was with Brand X (I took over Phil Collins' chair in the group). I went back repeatedly to the factory and got to meet many of the testers and the friendly and excellent cymbal-smiths. In 1978, I went back for cymbals to use with Pharaoh Saunders.

But it wasn't until 1979, when Dizzy Gillespie accompanied me to the factory to help me pick out his signature 24-inch swish cymbal that he insisted all of his drummers use, that Lennie finally facilitated my getting an official endorsement.

That is a golden memory for me, and I tell it often to inspire sincere effort and self-responsibility in my students. Little did I know that in Lennie's case, my sincere efforts would pay off way better than I could have imagined. We developed a long and incredibly warm association that has lasted for some 26 years.

—*Kenwood Dennard*

Jim Petersczak and Lennie at a PAS show

Back in the '70s, I sent a message for Lennie to be sure to watch the Carson show that night. I had the stage crew bake a great-looking

Marco Marcinko, Lennie

cymbal out of resin for Buddy Rich's appearance. We did-n't substitute it till after the rehearsal, and when Buddy wailed it on the show, it exploded into a zillion pieces. Lennie loved that gag. Buddy's line to me was: "You did that, you son of a bitch."

—*Ed Shaughnessy*

Dave Throckmorton, Thèrése DiMuzio, Lennie, Armand Zildjian

I dug out my 1988 diary and looked up the account of a post-gig that was so Lennie. It was June of 1988, and I was with Maynard Ferguson at the Blue Note in New York City for a week. The first night of the run was billed as Maynard's 60th Birthday Celebration. Many former Maynard players came down along with other notables, including Chuck Mangione, whose band I joined in 2000 just in time for his 60th birthday.

Lennie came down from Boston and made the gig. It was exciting to have him there, and he really seemed to love the band. Always great to see Maynard. After the second show, Lennie took me and percussionist Billy Hulting, along with a waitress Billy had snared, out in a cab. We drove around Manhattan for an hour trying to find a suitable restaurant open late on a Tuesday night. It took a few tries with Lennie

Maynard Ferguson, Maynard's sax player, Lennie

holding the cab while Billy or I ran in to see if the place was open. We finally succeeded at a Chinese (I think) place in midtown. We ate and, of course, drank until it was nearly light. A bit of a blur, but it was a great time and Lennie was full of stories about Buddy Rich, Maynard, and others. The cab finally dropped me at the hotel as the sun was about to rise.

What has really impressed me every time I have dealt with Lennie is that he has such respect for the musicians—a respect that was evident from the first time I spoke to him on the phone. He makes you instantly comfortable, encourages you to relax and have a good time, and clearly cares about the players. He and Armand seemed to head up the artist relations at Zildjian in a way that let you know you are part of a family, not just on a list of artists in a file cabinet.

Lennie remains one of my favorite personalities, and I will always be thankful to him for recommending the 20-inch K Custom Ride he sent me in 1987.

—*Dave Tull*

Lennie with LA percussionist Billy Hulting

I remember very vividly the first time I met Lennie and Jim. They were down on their hands and knees barking at a waitress.

—*Ray Brinker*

It seems that an individual, named Alan Abel, contacted Zildjian West sometime in 2001, stating that he had a long career in the music business and sought an endorsement with Zildjian. Why he contacted Zildjian West is not known, but he spoke first, I believe, to Jair, Alex Acuña's son, who was working at the time in artist relations out of that office. Upon speaking with Abel, Jair contacted Norwell, where Lennie nearly fell out of his chair. Alan Abel, the great percussionist, PAS Hall of Fame member, and legendary teacher from the Philadelphia Orchestra (he thought), was calling to express interest in moving to Zildjian from Sabian. (Alan Abel was one of Sabian's first, and most respected, endorsers.) This was obviously a coup of coups, and it was time to roll out the red carpet. After getting permission from the front office, Lennie contacted Abel and made arrangements for him to travel from New York to Norwell. As I recall, a deposit was sent to Abel, and he, in turn, provided Zildjian with bio information, including detailed background on his musical life: a jazz drummer, a member of the Ohio State Marching Band, 1947 winner of the NARD Snare Drumming Championship (Charlie Wilcoxon dedicated a solo to him), and a regular participant in the Macy's Thanksgiving Day Parade. An impressive vitae, but no mention of anything related to the Philadelphia Orchestra!

None of this seemed to matter in the state of euphoria that was created at Zildjian at Lennie's announcement. He began the process of welcoming the heralded star, a gregarious, tall, and somewhat overweight fellow. Lennie arranged for a private car from Logan Airport, hotel, dinner, a private session in the cymbal room with Lennie, Leon, and others, and—a check. The trial session began very simply, with Abel being offered a pair of the finest cymbals to try. He declined and asked Leon to play the cymbals for him. Although Leon thought this a little strange, he struck the first pair.

Phil Collins

"Those sound great. Wrap them up," Abel said. Finally, Abel played some of the newly designed hand cymbals. A few clanging crashes later, Leon thought, surprised, that anybody could have a bad day. Abel went on to say that a 16-inch pair would be great for playing the Macy's parade.

Later, after spending a day at Zildjian filled with greeting the staff, and a wonderful dinner with Lennie and the crew, Abel was dropped off at his hotel. Arrangements had been made for the private car to pick him up in the morning for his return to the airport. The following morning, the driver contacted Zildjian to say that Abel had not shown for his pick-up, and the hotel had stated that he was not there or perhaps had checked out earlier.

This seemed strange to Lennie, but not alarming. However, he began to call some of the other Zildjian orchestral artists, describing the funny guy who had humored the plant. To his horror, the reaction was the same—"That's not the Alan Abel I know!" Watching his life with Zildjian flashing before his eyes, Lennie took his time before breaking the news to the head office, where, fortunately, they were good-natured about it, and it checked out to just be a case of mistaken identity.

There is a postscript to this story. A few months later, John Whitman from Yamaha called me and asked what I knew about Alan Abel. I replied, "Which Alan Abel?" Silence.

—*Bob Breithaupt*

I shall never forget the nose and how he so beautifully wore it with distinction.

—*Jim Sewrey*

This story took place at a Mid-West Band Clinic. We had all been hanging out at the bar, and I split to go to bed. Of course, everyone gave me shit, but I was bushed and had a big day coming up. I got to the room, got undressed, and went to bed. About a half-hour later, there was a knock on the door. When I opened it, there was a great-looking chick standing there. I said thanks but no thanks and sent her away. Well, every half-hour for the next two hours, I had four more. By now I was really getting mad, assuming the guys were giving my room number just to keep me awake because I wouldn't hang. When I told the last one to go away, she said, "Okay, but Lennie said to tell you to invite me in because this is the last one he's paying for."

—*Sandy Feldstein*

It was back in 1977 and Maynard Ferguson was featured in concert at a summer NAMM convention in Atlanta, Georgia, and the concert was sponsored by the Zildjian, Slingerland, and LeBlanc/Holton companies. The concert was a big success, and I was lucky enough to be invited to dinner afterward

Steve Gadd, Lennie, Rob Wallis

Director Ed Sorrentino (top left) and the South Shore Conservatory of Music Percussion Ensemble

with Maynard and the head honchos of those important musical companies. As usual, the dinner was held on the top floor of a swank hotel, in the Omni Center, and included champagne, wine, and delicious food. After dinner, we all retired to the floor where there was a nightclub. Someone in our party had heard that a "hip band was playing there."

The band was hip, and they were playing. Maynard, Armand, Lennie, Jim, Lloyd McCausland, myself, and perhaps six others or so all found our way to a large table and immediately began to order bottles of champagne. As you might imagine, the mood at the table was festive and potentially rambunctious. Well, it became quite rambunctious and also contagious. While I was busy sitting in with the funk band, Maynard was inviting a young lady from another table to leave her date and dance on our table. Maynard was very persuasive—so she did come over, drank some champagne, started to dance on the table, as well as started to take off some of her clothes (or so I was told, because I missed most of the action since I was jamming with the band and the table was behind me in the back of the club). As things looked like they might get out of hand, Lennie went over to the bouncer, or manager, and some money exchanged hands. So, between that and the continued flow of champagne, we had carte blanch to raise hell and have fun, resulting in a most memorable evening.

Fast-forward a few years and we were all back in Atlanta for another summer NAMM show. One night after dinner, Lennie, Jim, Lloyd, a few drummers, and I wanted to go someplace to hang for a while. We start talking about that club where the gal danced on the table for Maynard, the hip band that I had sat in with, and so on. Everyone in the party wanted to find this place and check it out, and by some miracle we found it. It was the same place, a band was playing, and everything. So we got a table, only this time it was in front of the band, and any shenanigans we tried to get into, or noise we made, drew the ire of the lead singer. We were only drinking some beer and carousing a bit—and the band took itself way too seriously as far as we were concerned.

Anyway, we were busy trying to re-create the madhouse of yesteryear when the lead singer addressed our table with: "Say, are you fellows with the music convention?" We were delighted that he recognized us, and we all shouted back: "Yeah, man! Woo hoo! Hey! Yeah! The band sounds cool! Right on, fellas! Jump back, baby!" And then he gestured for quiet and pronounced, "Then just remember! It's people like us who keep people like you in business!" (Telling that story now, years later, I think he had a point.) Lennie immediately stood up, offed his glass as if gesturing a salute, but shouted, "Hey, pal, Fuck you!" and turned to our table and said, "C'mon, let's get outta here. There's nothing happening in this joint." And he led the way out of the club.

Tom Brechtlein, Lennie

Finally, as I recall, Lennie ended up falling asleep in his suit in my hotel room on one of the beds. I remember he did that a few times.

God bless Lennie, who always had time for us drummers—young and old alike. He was my first real contact in the music business, and I still treasure his letters to me when I started out, at the age of 18, playing drums in the Stan Kenton Orchestra.

—Peter Erskine

Lennie, Bill Morgan, and I went to see Toots Thielmans at the Regatta Bar in Boston, and Adam Nussbaum was the drummer. We were having a great time, and after a few cocktails, Lennie looked over at me and said, "Hey, Marco, I'm going to the bathroom." So I told him I'd go with him. The bathroom was outside the club down a hall. The club was located in a mall, and I did what I had to do and told Lennie I would wait for him in the hall. A few minutes later, Lennie came out of the bathroom. He had forgotten to pull up his pants and his salami was hanging out. I said in Italian, "Lennie, pick up your pants." We started laughing and laughed all the way back to the club. When we walked in, still laughing, it was really quiet and everyone was looking at us because we were laughing so hard.

We waited for the show to end, said hello to Adam, and had some more cocktails. It was getting really late and I had to be at Zildjian in the morning to pick out a set of cymbals. Bill was driving, Lennie was in the front seat, I was in the back seat, and Lennie said, "Let's go and get something to eat." It was four in the morning, and Bill said, "Lennie, we got to go home because Marco has to be at the plant at nine to pick his cymbals. Lennie shouted, "Food!" So while Bill was driving along, Lennie saw a food place on the side of the road, reached over, and pulled the wheel in the direction of the food place. The car swerved and we almost ended up in a ditch. But thanks to Bill, the car was saved and we ended up getting something to eat after that. It was a great night.

—Marco Soccoli

Obviously, Lennie is a one-of-a-kind character with a great sense of humor and a great heart. I was honored to have him at my wedding. In 1994, at the Modern Drummer Festival, Lennie pulled his "handicap" stunt. My wife Debbie was driving and I was in the passenger seat. Lennie and Johnny DeChristopher were in the back. Lennie said, "Debbie, please park in the handicap parking." I got out of the car and assisted Lennie out. He said, "You know, Debbie, I know you are a nurse and, you know, I have this handicap," as he limped and dragged himself to the other side of the car. "It's my leg. It really bothers me." I looked down, and then Debbie looked down and gasped. There *it* was: the ankle replica of "The Nose" hanging outside his pants cuff. Lennie yelled, laughing, "Hey, check out my handicap!" A classic Lennie story.

—John "J.R." Robinson

Lennie! An icon of the music industry whose stories will live forever. Jump back, baby!

—John H. Beck

In the late '70s, Premier Drums, Latin Percussion, and Zildjian put on a four-day summer workshop called PLZ at Farleigh Dickinson University in Madison, New Jersey. Lennie, Jim Coffin, Jim Petersczak, Glenn Weber, and I were there. Jim C. was the head of Premier at that time; I was a Premier sales rep. Jim P. was a Premier educational consultant, and Glenn had a teaching studio in West Orange, New Jersey, and was the coordinator for the workshop. Counting participants, artists, and clinicians, 70 people were in attendance. As you would assume, the workshop balanced between serious work and a lotta laughs and pranks. At the conclusion of PLZ, I wanted to give each of the sponsors their day in the sun, and as part of the ceremony, Lennie was asked to come forward to receive and give acknowledgments as well as receive thank-you's from the audience.

Previously, Lennie had agreed to personally award a 20-inch ride cymbal as the Zildjian door prize. However, he didn't know we had taken an old, cheap imported piece-of-junk cymbal that we had hammered every conceivable way and soldered on tire nuts and other metal material. *Ugly* was the operative word. Lennie very seriously thanked the students, teachers, and sponsors and then proudly announced the name of the student who was about to receive the "wonderful new Zildjian cymbal." At that point, we came down the aisle carrying the ugly clunker, which when struck sounded like a tire iron. The crowd roared, and Lennie, in his inimitable style, laughed and muttered, "That was really funny, man. Jump back, baby."

We also pulled a gag on Jim C. He was sitting behind a set of Premier drums doing a demonstration, and just as he was finishing up, Lennie, Jim P., Glenn, and I walked down the aisles of the auditorium and proceeded to take away the cymbals and stands and the floor tom. We took them up the aisle and then went back. Two of us picked up the bass drum and the rack toms while the other two picked up the hi-hat and the snare, leaving Jim with just the drum stool and his sticks. He pretended to keep playing, all the time laughing like crazy. It brought the house down.

—Bud DiFluri

I met Lennie in 1972 when I joined Woody Herman's band. Lennie came to the gig and afterward asked if I needed anything. I asked for and got a 22-inch Pang with a lot of rivets, which I used happily for the rest of that gig and for my years with Mangione. I realize this story is not special, except that it could be told by hundreds of other drummers as well. Lennie has helped so many of us over the years and has been so supportive of our efforts—to the extent that it's hard not to think about him when we are pulling out the "pies" every night. When we think about our cymbals, we usually think about Lennie.

—Joe LaBarbera

What a mix of talents Lennie had to work with, and the question is: How did he stay Lennie while remaining open to the changing musical styles and business? To me, he was probably laughing a little all the time. He would sometimes do such undignified things. Yet there was a clear and unique dignity about his values. One-of-a-kind. There is a curious viewpoint about him: so many of those players trusted him. Armand did. Lennie seemed to have an uncanny sense of what was good. I wonder: Could he have liked every drummer he worked with? Respected every band they played in? Enjoyed every musical style he came in contact with? For years, like almost no other person in the drum world, Lennie was the guy you needed to know. Every artist needed him to understand what they did and what they needed. And everyone, some of the best players in the world, needed Lennie—to be Lennie. Did he know this? Was that why he was so constant in the insanity?

—Steven W. Ross

My story is about the nice side of Lennie, or should I say the good side of Lennie. He has always been a good guy. It was after a NAMM show, and I was having dinner with Jim Coffin, Lennie, and Lloyd McCausland—the JEWOPs. Jim introduced me to Lennie, who had had a few drinks before dinner, and the first words out of his mouth were: "Tommy, the pies you are playing on right now aren't worth shit. When you're ready, call me up and I'll take care of you." That was in 1982, and in 1985 I decided to take him up on his offer. Since that first meeting, I hadn't spoken with him. I called him up and said, "Hey, Lennie, this is Tom Brechtlein. We spoke in '82, and I was wondering if your offer is still good?" He said, "Tommy, how are you? Can I call you back in five minutes?" I said okay and hung up. Five minutes later he called me back. He said, "Tommy, what's your jacket size?" He hooked me up with the West Coast Zildjian rep and got me a company jacket and some cymbals. That's Lennie, a man true to his word! (Jim, so are you.)

—Tom Brechtlein

Although nothing in particular stands out, I just remember and know, that *any* hang with Lennie has always been, and always will be, an *event*— usually having to do with food and drink, tons of jokes being passed about, stories from the past, and lots of laughs.

—Dave Weckl

Sometime in the early '80s, Lennie asked me to do a clinic at PASIC. I don't exactly remember where or when it was—maybe it was in Arizona. The point of this is: I was scared shitless. That's probably why I have trouble remembering the details. I had done only one master class before, which had about 20 people in attendance and I was frightened to do that. But this was a full-on clinic in front of a few hundred serious drummers. At that time, there weren't many drumset clinics at PASIC—it was mainly focused on classical percussion. I was to be the first rock drummer to do a PASIC clinic. I had been playing with Journey since 1978, so I was comfortable playing in front of crowds, but not talking to an audience. Actually, I had never spoken to an audience at that point—I was always safely hiding behind the drums.

I had known Lennie since the early '70s, when I was touring with the Lin Biviano Big Band, a band made up of Buddy Rich and Maynard Ferguson alumni. I had been playing Zildjian cymbals for a long time, but in the early '80s I was a new endorser. Lennie wanted me to make a presentation, which I was honored that he asked me, but I didn't really know what to do.

Lennie helped me with every step in preparing for the clinic, and we spent the day and every hour together before the clinic. I was a nervous wreck, but he was very comforting and supportive. We talked and talked about how the clinic would go, what I could talk about, what I could play, and so forth. I think he even literally held my hand for a while to calm me down. When I finally did the clinic, I looked out and saw Arnie Lang in the audience; one of my teachers—the great Alan Dawson; and a few hundred other drummers. Lennie sat by the stage the whole time, encouraging me and giving me looks that let me know I was doing okay. I eventually calmed down enough to play and have some things to say.

After that, I was still nervous while doing clinics, but I would think back to the support Lennie gave me during that first clinic and it would help calm me. Lennie is obviously one of the most fun people in the world to spend time with, but he is also a very soulful and caring man with a lot of knowledge and experience. It was that side of Lennie that came out during that time. The fact that he asked me to do a PASIC clinic meant a lot to me, and I didn't want to let him down. That was how I started doing clinics, and now clinics have become a big part of my musical life. I look forward to them and enjoy getting onstage, talking and playing for other drummers. But that has been a long process, starting back in the early '80s, with the help and encouragement of my friend Lennie DiMuzio.

—*Steve Smith*

This is a little story about Lennie. There are many stories about him, most of which can't be printed. But this story occurred when I wanted to go to a Zildjian Day that was going to be held in Chicago. Zildjian had started these Zildjian Days—the first one was in L.A., the second in Chicago, and the third in Boston during the first year they presented them. At any rate, it was a day when Zildjian would bring a lot of great drummers to perform, sort of like a huge clinic, a new thing that had never been done before. I had just finished a year's tour with John Mellencamp—John Cougar at that time. We were the new band with the number-one record and the number-one single. So I had just gotten off tour and wanted to go to Zildjian Day. I gave Lennie a call, I think it was on a Tuesday, and the Zildjian Day was scheduled for Sunday. I asked Lennie if I could buy a ticket and come up there, since I was living in Bloomington, Indiana, about four and a half hours from Chicago. Following is a summary of the many phone calls between Lennie and me:

"Hey, this is Lennie. You don't have to buy a ticket, and we will get you a hotel room or you can sleep in the Zildjian suite."

On Wednesday: "Hey, Kenny, baby, it's Lennie."

I said, "Hey, is everything cool?"

He said, "Oh, yeah, everything is cool. Well, you know, Tommy Aldridge's wife is having twins any day now and he isn't going to make Zildjian Day, so we have to get a replacement."

I said, "Wow, well who are you going to get?"

He replied, "Well, we kinda thought since this was the Midwest, you'd be a good replacement."

My response: "What? Are you kidding me? I'm going to replace Tommy Aldridge?"

I was blown away—just off a tour, preparing for a wedding, and not in a mindset to do such a thing. You have to realize that the other guys on the bill were Steve Gadd, Ralph MacDonald, Steve Smith, Larrie Londin, Bernard Purdie, and Alejo Poveda—and I was going to be there in place of Tommy. It wasn't enough that they were going to put me up in their suite—I just wasn't used to such treatment—and now I was going to perform. Even though Lennie had given me a Zildjian endorsement the year before, this was mind-blowing.

The next few days were hectic. I went down to John Cougar's rehearsal place and pulled out my Tama tour kit and started working on a program. Since I had only two days and an evening to prepare for this event, I narrowed down my program to five major points—beat, time, groove, creativity, and less is more. I packed up the kit in my little Honda Accord and drove to Evanston, a suburb of Chicago. I got to the venue and set up my drums. Man, I was nervous. I asked a guy where to set up my drums. He asks my name and then said, "Well, you are the first guy, so you set up dead center." I got set up and in walks Steve Smith, who was on tour with Journey. He set up his drums right in front of my kit and said, "Let's play." We started jamming and played for three hours. I'm telling you, in five minutes I played every lick I knew. That three-hour workout made me lose all of my fear for the next day's performance.

Sunday, Zildjian Day, the cameras and the local TV were there, and because I was the first guy, I would get most of the footage. Larry Londin was eating a big sandwich and said, "Dude, I'm going to be standing up here in the balcony. If you get nervous, just look at me. You're going to do fine." Then I was about to go on. The curtain went up, the audience was screaming, and there was no Tommy Aldridge double bass drum kit. They were all yelling, "We want Tommy."

Lennie said, "You'll be fine, Kenny. Don't worry." I said, "They want Tommy."

He replied, "No, no, you'll be fine," and walked out onstage and said, "Ladies and gentlemen, thank you very much for coming to our second Zildjian Day. As you can see, Tommy Aldridge is not going to make it. His wife is having twins, and we have a new young drummer from the Midwest who is going to take his place, and I want you to give him a warm welcome—Kenny Aronoff."

I walked out, Lennie greeted me, put his arm around me, and stayed right there with me to make sure I was okay. I'm telling you, man, the crowd was like—well, not everybody was cheering; there were people booing because they wanted Tommy.

Lennie made me feel so at home and so comfortable, and that's what I want to stress in my message. He really cared and had so much compassion, sensitivity, and love. I was the new guy, and he gave me confidence to do a great job. There are still people who come up today and mention, "Man, I was just a little kid and I saw you do that. You were so cool and great." Some of those drummers have become famous, like Gary Novak, who was in the audience with his dad. The whole point of this story is that Lennie is a very caring and loving guy. He really knows how to have a good time and makes you have a good time with him. Lennie is the kind of guy you want to have in your life every day.

—Kenny Aronoff

Lennie has always had a soothing voice and a style that encouraged drummers to call him on a regular basis, so they can go to confession and get his support. A trait that is uniquely his. Love, peace, and support are what Lennie D. has for each and every drummer he meets. No matter what age or style of player—even if they play the competition's product—they have his respect and support.

I would be remiss if I didn't add the following: Lennie is not a Lone Ranger. Lennie, Jim Coffin, and Lloyd McCausland, the JEWOPs, define the industry's support for percussion education and clinics—not only as a way to sell products but also to teach teach kids how to play better. They are absolutely the most influential and ultimately the most important people in the percussion movement.

—Jim Petersczak

More of Lennie's Drummer Friends

Debbie Peterson and the Bangles

Sue Hadjopoulos, freelance artist

Roxy Petrucci of Vixen

Sherrie Maricle, leader of the Diva Jazz Orchestra

Chapter 42

It's Not Over Yet, Baby

Sabian Press Release, August 2003

In August 2003 Lenny DiMuzio, the legendary percussion industry figure, joined SABIAN INC. as a Consultant to SABIAN's worldwide Artist Relations program and Sales and Marketing Team. With over 40 years of experience, DiMuzio has been influential in shaping the careers of many of today's leading drummers and percussionists, and is acknowledged within the industry as the originator of "Artist Relations."

Commented SABIAN General Manager, Dan Barker: "Lenny DiMuzio is the man who effectively put 'relations' into the term artist relations. He is a uniquely qualified individual whose personality, talent, and dedication have not only made him one of the percussion industry's favorite people, but one of its most influential. With roles ranging from artist relations, director of education, manager of sales, to personally selecting cymbals for the greats, Lenny has done it all. Lenny's personal dedication to expanding the world of percussion and his shaping of the careers of many of today's leading players has made him an industry icon."

A drummer from a very young age, DiMuzio performed as a distinguished member of the U.S. Army Band before continuing formal studies at the New England Conservatory of Music and Schillinger House (now the Berklee College of Music). Private studies with such greats as Charles Alden and Alan Dawson ensured his status as a prominent drummer and orchestral percussionist, as well as a highly valued industry insider. Along the way, he enjoyed numerous achievements, including serving on the Board of Directors with the Percussive Arts Society and as a member of organizations such as IAJE, NBA, MENC, NAMM, NRD, DCI, TBA, American Symphony Orchestra, TMEA, and Midwest Band.

Said DiMuzio: "I enjoy music and people, and I welcome this opportunity to work with SABIAN, whose enthusiasm and dedication I have admired for years. It's wonderful to be part of a team who really does care about players as people. SABIAN really is "the gathering place for drummers."

Concluded Barker: "Lenny DiMuzio is a true global ambassador for the art of percussion. He's a tremendous talent and personality, and we're very pleased to have him."

"After retiring from the Avedis Zildjian Company in January of 2003, I realized, after six months, that taking my pail and shovel to the beach was not exactly what I wanted to do for the rest of my life. I had happily spent my entire adult life in the mainstream of the drumming world and hanging with the cats and, after four or five months I missed it terribly. (Plus I was only 72 years old and just getting started.) I was feeling good, but not happy just laying back and chilling out. I realized I needed some action again.

"In the summer of 2003 I got a call to join Sabian as a consultant. When the call came I said, 'jump back baby, let the good times roll.' I realized that this would give me the opportunity to be back in the mainstream of the percussion world and do the same things I had done all my life: work with the leading products and all the great drummers of today's percussion world and industry. So I am back clangin', hangin', and bangin'.

"For the end of the book, I wanted to acknowledge and show some of my family members, plus a compilation of photos of many drummers, industry figures, and others who are all my close friends.

"This new period of my life could start an entire new book of its own, but we must bring this book to a close. Unfortunately I present all of these great friends without the full story they deserve, but I know you will enjoy this nonetheless, because they are all groovy people and some of the hottest drummers of today."

Lennie DiMuzio Jr., commander American Legion post, Duxbury, MA

Thèrése DiMuzio performing with the Tommy Dorsey band

"Lovely" Lucy DiMuzio sitting in for kicks

Lennie's granddaughter Nicole drumming into the fourth generation of DiMuzio drummers

Lennie's son-in-law, Darin Colucci, voted Boston Magazine's best super lawyer 2005, 2006

Lennie with brother Eddie in concert as The Swedish Buskievonda Brothers comedy act

Lennie's daughter Cecilia Colucci with her band Stardust, rated one of "Boston's Best Bands"

Lennie's granddaughter Jillian

Lennie as Santa Claus with his great-grandchildren Taylor and Josh (2007)

Tony Tedesco, Cecilia Colucci, Fred Taylor (club owner), John Pizzarelli, Thèrése DiMuzio, Sculler's Jazz Club, Boston (2005)

Cecelia with Lou Rawls

John Blackwell, Paul Cellucci, Andy Zildjian, Lennie, Horacio Hernandez

UNLV percussionist Greg, Lennie, Dean Gronmeier (chairman, UNLV Percussion Dept.)

Chicago-based drummer Mike Arturi

Dave Mattacks, east coast Jazz artist

Industry veteran Bill Morgan and Lennie

Lennie with Vinnie Colaiuta

Cathy Rich with her son Nick and Lennie at a NAMM show

Lennie with Will Calhoun of Living Colour

Lennie with country music vocalist/guitarist Glenn Stewart and drummer Mike Rorick

Remo Belli in the Remo company's 50th anniversary photo

Thèrése DiMuzio, Vic Firth

Lennie, Dennis Chambers, Thèrése DiMuzio

Brooke Ludwig Crowden and husband Bill

Los Angeles drummer Howard Kurham, Lennie, Louis Bellson (NAMM 2007)

Bernard Purdie and Lennie

Lennie, Melba Sparks, Marvin Sparks

Paul Cellucci, Dave Garibaldi, Lennie

Lennie, Thèrése DiMuzio, and Rick Medru, director of Duxbury Schools Music Dept., along with some student band members. Standing to the far right is Lennie's granddaughter Nicole, one of the percussionists in the program.

LA jazz artist Jay Burrid, Lennie, Jay's wife

Ralph Pace Jr. and father Ralph Sr., the well-known drummer, teacher, and author

Efrain Toro (1970)

New York Jazz Master Grady Tate

Dave Black

Tony Verderosa and Dennis DiBlasio

Terreon Gully, New York freelance artist

Javol Bell, Bernard Purdie, John Lamkin

Ralph Peterson

Chad Smith, Lennie

Derico Watson of Victor Wooten's band

Lennie and Nashville drummer Terry Lee Bolton

Danny Gottlieb and Kirsten Shiner McGuire

Lennie, Billy of Jack's Drum Shop, and Horacio Hernandez in Boston, MA

Simon Phillips and Lennie sharing a laugh at a PASIC Show

Vinnie Colaiuta and Hilary Jones

Marvin Sparks, Andy Zildjian, Lennie

Chester Thompson, Lloyd McCausland, Jim Coffin, Lennie

New York jazz artist John Riley

Lenny with Steve Arnold at the NAMM Show (2005)

Boston drummer Jerome Dupree

Lennie, Bill Morgan, Billy Mason, Paul Cellucci, Joe Healy

Crane School of Music percussion dept. chair Jim Petersczak with Lennie during a 2006 clinic presentation

Andy Zildjian and Billy Mason

Vater Percussion president Alan Vater with Lennie backstage at a Red Hot Chili Peppers concert

Lennie with Barry Greenspan of Drummer's World in New York City

Jose Corsello and Lennie

Sabian Vault Tour clinic outside a drum shop: Sabian cymbal maker demonstrating the creation of a hand-hammered custom cymbal

Former Zildjian artist relations representative Jim McGathey

Lennie and Adam Nussbaum

Andy Zildjian, Zoro

Steve Smith, Charlie Persip, Ben Riley, Eddie Locke, Billy Hart, and Adam Nussbaum during the filming of their Brush Masters DVD (2007)

Lennie's clinic presentation at Dale's Drum Shop, Harrisburg, PA (2004)

Gary Johnson from the Artie Shaw Band

Joe Samuelian, former Sabian customer service rep., and Lane Davy, current executive director of Sabian's new Gon Bop Percussion division.

Lennie and Boston's finest guitarist, Don Alessi (2005)

The Sabian Vault Team: L-R: David Williams, Mark Love, Andrew Bull, Lorenzo Wright, Jason Lozier, Kevin Lasky

Don Alessi's trio (1970)
Don, Lou Lamonica, Lou Magnano

Ed Uribe at the 1986 Montreal Jazz Festival

Armand Zildjian, Sandy Feldstein, and Lennie with Roy Burns at the drums (circa 1975)

Max Roach and Lennie during one of Max's visits to the Zildjian factory to select some cymbals

Alan Dawson, world renowned jazz drummer and educator

Members of the Bolshoi Ballet percussion section with Lennie and Boston Pops percussionist Richard Flanagan (far right)

Billy Kilson, freelance jazz, funk and R&B artist

Neil Peart behind his new custom DW drum set at the Mohegan Sun during the 2010 Rush U.S. tour

Lennie then and now. A lifetime with the drums. (Top) Lennie selecting cymbals for Buddy Rich during his early years at Zildjian. (Bottom) Lennie behind the drum today (2010)

Sabian founder Bob Zildjian addresses the press yesterday as the company announced plans for its 25th anniversary as well as its new Legacy line of cymbals.

Sabian Celebrates 25th, Launches Legacy Cymbals

Sabian kicked off its 25th anniversary yesterday at the show with birthday cake and a major announcement.

The Canada-based cymbal maker launched its new line of HHX Legacy cymbals, which were created in conjunction with Dave Weckl to embrace some of the darker tones and timbres the master drummer looks for in his music.

Weckl and Sabian spent four years developing, designing and, finally, producing the HHX Legacy line.

"We make these cymbals not because we can," said Sabian's Billy Zildjian. "We make them for drummers and percussionists. Because, overall, sound matters."

Founded in 1981, Sabian has grown from a small family-owned manufacturing concern into one of the drum industry's best-selling brands sold in some 120 nations around the world.

The company's dedication to old-world cymbal-making while using new technologies and alloys has resulted in a wide variety of honors and awards for such products as the AAX, HHX, XS20 and Vault cymbal lines.

Sabian is betting that Legacy will be the next award winner in that group.

"Legacy will be appealing to many drummers," said Mark Love, master cymbal specialist at Sabian. "It's still an exciting sound."

INFO **Sabian (sabian.com)**

Press release announcing the 25th anniversary of the Sabian Company along with news about a new Legacy cymbal line.

Chapter 43

A Tribute to Bob Zildjian

"Over my many years at Zildjian I performed a number of different duties, but ultimately focused on two key areas. In the first I spent a lot of time working closely with Armand Zildjian selecting and matching cymbals, developing new products, and as director of the artist relations department. In the second, and as I got more involved in sales and marketing, and the education and orchestral departments, I became involved with Bob Zildjian and his international department.

Bob was and, of course, is, a very interesting and brilliant man. He speaks several languages, he's a great creative writer, and an engaging speaker. Bob always said, "It doesn't matter what your education is, your genius or talent, in the end nothing outweighs hard work and determination."

In his years with Zildjian Bob was constantly traveling around the world handling all the company's foreign affairs, sales, and the international artist relations programs. He gave many presentations and performed many clinics, and he introduced me to some of the top classical percussionists and orchestral cymbal players in the world.

Bob was also a lover of big band jazz. He played the upright bass in college and in his hometown local band, and was a very good friend of the great band leaders Stan Kenton and Woody Herman.

As I worked with Bob I also got to know and began working with many of his close and special associates. These included James Blades, the author and percussionist from England who authored the encyclopedic reference work *Percussion Instruments and Their History*, which is really a must-read for serious players; John Noonan, a renowned teacher and percussionist from the University of Indiana who wrote the first cymbal chart on how to play cymbals for the Zildjian company; Sam Denov, the great cymbalist from the Chicago Symphony Orchestra who also wrote a book called *The Art of Playing the Cymbals*; and the late great cymbalist Harold (Tommy) Thompson who spent his illustrious career with the Boston Symphony Orchestra.

Bob has been a lifelong cymbal maker and in 1981 he founded the Sabian Cymbal Company. As director of Sabian he has received numerous accolades and awards. The industry media, as well as many artists, have said that Bob grew Sabian to become the most innovative cymbal company.

Bob continues to expand Sabian's popularity throughout the world. He is also a large contributor to the music community through his products, scholarships, and donations.

Bob Zildjian has had an extraordinary career throughout his entire life in the music and cymbal business. He recently celebrated his 25th anniversary at the helm of one of the world's finest cymbal companies. In the following pages I am honored to show Bob in some of my favorite photographs of him throughout the years."

Robert "Bob" Zildjian with Kenny Clarke in London, 1968

Lennie, Kenny Clare, and Bob Zildjian (circa 1975)

Sam Ulano, Bob Zildjian, Papa Jo Jones (circa 1975)

Lennie, Bob Zildjian, two show models, Sam Ulano, Al Wolf, John Pagnotti

Lennie, Jane Ippolito, Bob Zildjian, Sam Ulano

Margaret Zildjian (Bob's wife), Stuart Pope, Mrs. Pope, Bob Zildjian

Sabian's first trade show (1983)
Standing L-R: Willard Way, Bob Zildjian, Roy Edmunds, Peter Sayers
Front L-R: Bill Zildjian, Nort Hargrove

Vice president of manufacturing Nort Hargrove with Bob Zildjian (2003)

Robert "Bob" Zildjian in his office at Zildjian. 1970

Bob Zildjian doing the honors at the 2006 25th anniversary tree planting at the current Sabian factory in Meductic, Canada

Chapter 44

Finally, the Finale

To bring *Tales* to an end was a difficult task. With so many memories lingering, stories still to tell, and so many drummers' names and pictures not yet included, we're not ready for the end, but the rest will have to come in the next book.

Lennie talks about friendship a lot, and his line is "We became good friends." As I got closer to this finale, I began to realize this book is not just about drummers, musicians, and people involved with the manufacturing, marketing, and selling of percussion instruments, but it is also about friendships—lifetime friendships. The drumming fraternity is a very close one, bonded not only by music but also by lugging equipment, broken drumsticks, worn-out heads, cracked cymbals, late for a gigs, early for a gig, no gas, boring gigs, exciting gigs, can't find the damn drum key, dropped my brushes on the floor and they rolled under the floor tom, despicable leaders, noisy club dates, no sleep, no food, and on and on. When drummers get together, there is so much to talk about, so many laughs, stories, and most of all, some great bullshit. Can you imagine going to a flute convention? What do they have to talk about? A hunk of metal—"You know, just last week one of my pads fell out." Now there's something to talk about. Yeah, right.

To quote the song: "The Party's Over," so we must close this book. It could have gone on and on, because Lennie always seems to remember something or someone at the last minute. As I kept telling him, "I want to finish this thing while we're still both alive to see it published." As I mentioned in the intro about the trials and tribulations of being an artist relations person, I hope you have realized as you read this book that the job is not only about fun and games. There must be a belief in the product and the people who use the product. Also, there must be honesty, no stories to further the sale of the product. Reread those stories in Chapter 41 of how Lennie was always there for the drummers and saw to their needs. The craziness and off-the-wall antics were safety valves to let off the stress involved with the never-ending daily challenges. It isn't always easy.

This has been quite a trip, but an interesting one. And, as I said, it was a fun learning experience for both of us. The JEWOPS are still going strong. We get to hang with each other at the various conventions and keep the stories alive. That's the most important thing. Oh yes, Lennie and I still refuse to go along with any of McCausland's outrageous get-rich schemes. When Lloyd retired from the Remo Company, they had a very nice party for him. Lennie and I got to roast him a little, but the audience was much different from Lennie's roast, so we had to be a little careful and he got off easy. We're still involved in the business, with Lennie being active in artist relations and traveling and performing master classes for the Sabian Cymbal Company. Lloyd is consulting for REMO. I'm writing and editing for PAS as well as working for NAMM. We continue to stay in touch with our many musician friends, who, for some strange reason, are mostly drummers.

Tales From the Cymbal Bag is completed, and you can unfasten your seat belt. We hope you have enjoyed this inside look at the incredible life that Lennie shared with the world's greatest drummers and percussionists.

Lennie says, "In closing, Jim, I just want to leave a few words of encouragement to my young drummer friends. I hope that this book will inspire all the young players out there in their pursuit of happiness, and desire to make a living in the drum world or music business. Take it from a guy who has been involved all of his life with drummers and music lovers. I can honestly say that some of the happiest moments in my life have either been hanging out with drummers, listening to them play, checking out their new music, or sitting down behind a drumset knocking time with a band. If you really love to play and that's what you really want to do, go for it, and make sure you do it well. Forget about getting rich and making a fortune that may or may not come. If you're lucky and hook up with a hot band, okay, but if not you can still make a good living being part of something good, either teaching or working in the music industry.

"Looking back at all the great drummers I have worked with over the years, I realize they all had certain things in common that made them who they are: confidence, determination, and a belief in themselves and in what they were doing. They also had the passion and were very positive people, and most important, had tremendous respect for one another. I will always remember Louie Bellson telling a bunch of students to always try to play with better musicians than yourself—that's one way you can judge and feel yourself getting better and develop more confidence. So be patient, friends. There is no secret to being successful—it's all about hard work and sacrifice."

To finish with the most famous words from the man himself: "Jump way back, baby! Over and out. Good luck, go in peace, and not in pieces."

Lennie D.

Chapter 45

Suggested Reading

My grateful acknowledgment goes out to the following prolific authors and artists who I have listed below. They have given me so much inspiration and friendship over the years. I highly recommend their materials for selective reading, especially for the serious drummer, but also for the not so serious drummer, and really for anyone who just loves drums, percussion, and drumming. (Listed alphabetically by author.)

Beck, John H. *Encyclopedia of Percussion*. Garland Publishing Inc., New York & London, 1995.

Blades, James. *Percussion Instruments and Their History*. Faber and Faber Limited, London, 1975.

Cook, Rob. *The Ludwig Book — A Business History and Dating Guide Book*. Rebeats Press, 2003.

Epstein, Frank. *Cymbalisms — A Complete Guide for the Orchestral Cymbal Player.* Hall Leonard, 2007.

Hart, Mickey & Lieberman, Fredric. *Planet Drum, A Celebration of Percussion and Rhythm.* HarperCollins Publisher, New York, 1991.

Hart, Mickey & Stevens, Jay. *Drumming at The Edge of Magic. A Journey into the Spirit of Percussion.* HarperCollins Publisher, New York, 1990.

Klauber, Bruce H. *World of Gene Krupa: That Legendary Drummin' Man.* Pathfinder Publishing, California, 1990.

Korall, Burt. *Drummin' Men.* Schirmer Books, New York, 1990.

Meriwether, Doug, Jr. *We Don't Play Requests: A Musical Biography/ Discography of Buddy Rich.* Creative Communications Corporation, Maryland, 1984.

Peart, Neil. *Roadshow: Landscape With Drums: A Concert Tour by Motorcycle.* Rounder Books, 2007

Peart, Neil. *Traveling Music: Playing Back the Soundtrack to My Life and Times.* ECW Press, 2004

Peart, Neil. *Ghost Rider: Travels on the Healing Road.* ECW Press, 2002.

Peart, Neil. *The Masked Rider: Cycling in West Africa.* Pottersfield Press, 1999

Pinksterboer, Hugo. *The Cymbal Book.* Hal Leonard, 1993.

Spagnardi, Ronald. *The Great Jazz Drummers.* Modern Drummer Publications, New Jersey, 1992.

Torme, Mel. *Traps The Drum Wonder, The Life of Buddy Rich.* Oxford University Press Inc., New York, 1991.

Uribe, Ed. *The Essence of Afro-Cuban Percussion and Drum Set.* Warner Bros. Publications, Miami, FL, 1996.

Uribe, Ed. *The Essence of Brazilian Percussion and Drum Set.* Warner Bros. Publications, Miami, FL, 1993.

Not just a master of the cymbals and drums, but a damn good banjo and spoon player as well. (Playing at a New Year's Eve party 2000)

Some 60 years after starting his career, Lennie is still clangin', hangin', and bangin' with the best drummers in the world. Here is Lennie with rock drumming icon and dear friend Neil Peart, backstage at the Mohegan Sun Casino in CT at a recent Rush concert in July 2010.